IN CHRIST ALONE
366 DAILY REFLECTIONS

ROBERT GRIFFITH

Copyright © 2024 Grace and Truth Publishing

All rights reserved. No part of this book may be reproduced, stored in a retrieval system, or transmitted in any form, without the written permission of Grace and Truth Publishing.

GRACE AND TRUTH PUBLISHING
PO Box 338, Gunnedah NSW 2380 Australia
www.graceandtruthpublishing.com.au

All Bible quotes are from the New International Version (NIV) expect where otherwise stated.

NEW INTERNATIONAL VERSION (NIV), Copyright 1973, 1978 and 1984 by international Bible Society. Used by permission of Zondervan Publishing House. All rights reserved.

Other version quotes are from:

AMPLIFIED BIBLE (AMP), Copyright © 1954, 1958, 1962, 1964, 1965, 1987 by The Lockman Foundation. Used by permission.

ENGLISH STANDARD VERSION (ESV), Copyright © 2001 by Crossway Bibles, a division of Good News Publishers. Used by permission. All rights reserved.

NEW AMERICAN STANDARD BIBLE (NASB), Copyright © 1960, 1962, 1963, 1968, 1971, 1972, 1973, 1975, 1977, by The Lockman Foundation. Used by permission.

NEW KING JAMES VERSION (NKJV), Copyright © 1979, 1980, 1982, by Thomas Nelson Inc. Used by permission. All rights reserved.

THE MESSAGE (MSG), by Eugene Peterson, Copyright © 1993, 1994, 1995, 1996, and 2000. Used by permission of NavPress Publishing Group. All rights reserved.

REVISED STANDARD VERSION (RSV), Copyright © 1973, by Thomas Nelson Inc.

Used by permission. All rights reserved.

Quotes in square brackets are the author's comment.

ISBN 978-0-6486439-2-0

JANUARY 1

The New Day Dawns

It was early January 1997. My family and I were on holidays. That was a rare treat for us. As usual I rose well before the sun did and I recall sitting at the dining room table watching the fog slowly burn away across the grassy paddocks as the first light of day pierced the darkness of the night.

I was in a reflective mood as I often was in January as I looked back and forward, seeking the Lord's guidance for the road ahead. I picked up my pen and began to write and what transpired was a song which soon became very special to me at various points in my spiritual journey Let me share the words God gave me that day in the hope that they might resonate with you as you begin this new chapter.

The New Day Dawns

The sun begins to rise, a new day dawns
the morning dew is sparkling on the ground
the darkness of the night, is quickly put to flight
as golden beams of light shine all around

*As the new day dawns, I leave the past behind
all the disappointments and the pain
the joys I will cherish, from the tears I will grow
as by faith I journey on in Jesus' name*

A sense of expectation fills the air
my heart responds as birds begin to sing
just like the potter's clay, we are given each new day
a precious gift to mould and shape for Him

Your mercies are new every morning
Your grace will supply all my needs
yesterday has gone – Lord, help me now press on
to run the race that You prepared for Me

© 1997 Robert Griffith

JANUARY 2

God's Work – God's Way

I read a lot of Francis Schaeffer's books early in my Christian pilgrimage. Whilst I don't agree with him in everything, there is no doubt his contribution to Christian thought and practice was substantial and ahead of its time in many ways. There is this one statement Schaeffer made in his lectures and books many times which has remained with me.

"The Lord's work must be done the Lord's way."

If you're in a hurry, you can make it work your way. It may have a pure motive and all the marks of spirituality, but it won't be the Lord's way. This is a lesson we don't seem to learn easily. That is probably because at the heart of our fallen, broken human nature lies a stubborn independence.

John Pollock, in his splendid book *The Apostle*, states this:

"The irony was not lost on him that the mighty Paul, who had originally approached Damascus with all the panoply of the high priest's representative, should make his last exit in a fish basket, helped by the very people he had come to hurt."

That about says it all, doesn't it?

Just to set the record straight, you and I are neither the *"masters of our fate"* nor the *"captains of our souls."* We are meant to be wholly and continually dependent on the mercy of God if we want to do the Lord's work the Lord's way. The great Apostle Paul had to learn that. So must we.

So, my question is: Are you learning that? If not, today may be a good day to start. If you are into New Year's resolutions, then perhaps *"Doing the Lord's work the Lord's way"* would be a great one to put at the top of your list for this next year.

JANUARY 3

The Paradox of our Time

We have taller buildings, but shorter tempers; we have wider freeways, but narrower viewpoints; we spend more, but have less; we buy more, but enjoy less. We have bigger houses and smaller families; more conveniences, but less time; we have more degrees, but less common sense; more knowledge, but less judgement; more experts, but more problems; more medicine, but less wellness. We spend too recklessly; laugh too little; get angry too quickly; stay up too late; get up too tired; watch TV too much and pray too seldom.

We have multiplied our possessions but reduced our values. We talk too much; love too seldom and lie too often. We've learned how to make a living, but not a life; we've added years to life, not life to years. We've conquered outer space, but not inner space; We've done larger things, but not better things; We've cleaned up the air, but polluted the soul; We've split the atom, but not our prejudice; We write more, but learn less; plan more, but accomplish less.

We've learned how to rush, but not how to wait; We have higher incomes; but lower morals; more food, but less appeasement; more acquaintances, but fewer friends; more effort, but less success. We build more computers to hold more information, to produce more copies, but we have less communication. We're long on quantity, but short on quality.

These are the times of world peace, but domestic warfare, more leisure and less fun, more kinds of food, but less nutrition. These are days of two incomes, but more divorce; fancier houses, but broken homes. There is much in the show window and nothing in the stockroom.

Of course, none of the above is inevitable – it is simply the result of the choices we make each day. So let's make better choices!

JANUARY 4

Taking the Calvary Road

Our central job is not to solve the world's problems. Our job is to draw our entire life from Christ and manifest that life to others. Nothing could be simpler or more challenging. Such a life requires us to die to self. It is easier and more gratifying to assume a morally superior stance and feel good about doing our Christian duty and condemn sin in others.

Perhaps this explains why many Christians spend more time fighting against certain sinners in the political arena than they do sacrificing for sinners. But Jesus calls us and empowers us to follow His example by taking the more difficult, but less obvious, much slower, and more painful road - the Calvary Road. It is the road of self-sacrificial love.

When love is placed above all those kingdom-of-this-world concerns (Col. 3:14; 1 Peter 4:8), the options placed before us in this broken world dwindle in significance. What if the energy and resources Christians use to preserve and tweak religion was spent feeding the hungry, housing the homeless, befriending the drug addict and visiting the prisoner?

What if our focus was on sacrificing our resources to help inner-city schools and safe houses for battered women? What if our concern was to bridge the ungodly racial gap in our country by developing friendships and collaborating in more endeavours with people whose ethnicity is different than our own? What if instead of trying to defend our religious rights, Christians concerned themselves with siding with others whose rights are routinely trampled?

Living in the kingdom of God always requires that we bleed for others. It may not immediately adjust people's behaviour, but this is not what it seeks to accomplish. Rather, it is meant to transform people's hearts and thereby transforms society.

JANUARY 5

Growing a Healthy Church

One of the most common conclusions from the thousands of Church Growth studies done over the past 50 years is as simple as it is profound and that is: *healthy Churches grow easily*. This premise is so simple that Church leaders have been overlooking it for years as they search for more complicated principles and strategies – all the time neglecting or ignoring the most important aspect of real Church growth and that is the *health* of the Church, which is rooted in the maturity, the character and the spirituality of its members. As researchers have woken up to this radical but simple truth, a lot of recent research has focused on Church health.

One researcher, Christian Schwarz, studied many hundreds of Churches of various denominations in over 100 countries and his discovery was fascinating. He found that every healthy, growing Church had eight essential characteristics:

- Passionate Spirituality
- Inspiring Worship
- Loving Relationships
- Holistic Small Groups
- Relational Evangelism
- Empowering Leadership
- Functional Structures
- Gift-Oriented Ministry

An underlying premise of growing healthy Churches is that as obstacles to growth are removed, the Church will grow naturally as God intended.

If we want a healthy, growing Church, we need to ensure that the obstacles to good health are continually removed so that the life which God has placed within each of us can emerge. Developing the eight characteristics above will go a long way to ensuring the Church remains healthy and fruitful.

JANUARY 6

God's Will or my Will?

Most of us in the Church seem pretty good at telling people the will of God for their lives. But what about following God's will in our own lives? Truth be told, it's a lot easier to preach it to others than to put it into practice for ourselves. These words from the apostle Paul's come to mind:

Romans 2:18–23 *"[If you] know His will and approve the things that are essential, being instructed out of the Law, and are confident that you yourself are a guide to the blind, a light to those who are in darkness, a corrector of the foolish, a teacher of the immature, having in the Law the embodiment of knowledge and of the truth, you, therefore, who teach another, do you not teach yourself? You who preach that one shall not steal, do you steal? You who say that one should not commit adultery, do you commit adultery? You who abhor idols, do you rob temples? You who boast in the Law, through your breaking the Law, do you dishonour God?"*

Let me ask you a penetrating question, are you really willing to do God's will ...

... more than pleasing people
... more than staying comfortable and safe
... more than completing your education
... more than building a new sanctuary
... more than getting published
... more than getting your house paid for
... more than anything else

You want to do the will of God? I do, and I believe that you do too. Well, let's make this priority the driving force of our life and ministry as we move further into this new year, relying fully on His Spirit as we surrender to the will of God each and every day.

JANUARY 7

That Still Small Voice

Do you ever have those unidentified inner promptings? I'm talking about when the Spirit of God urges your spirit in a very specific direction. I'm talking about that still small voice. The book of Jude offers a wonderful example of the powerful prompting of the Holy Spirit:

Jude 3 *"Beloved, while I was making every effort to write you about our common salvation, I felt the necessity to write to you appealing that you contend earnestly for the faith which was once for all handed down to the saints."*

Jude started to write a letter about salvation, about the finished work of Christ on the cross. That was his original plan ... until the Holy Spirit prompted him to do otherwise. *"I felt the necessity to do so,"* Jude admits.

That was nothing less than an inner prompting from the Spirit of God. God will often prompt us to follow a certain direction. No audible voice. No image of Jesus standing by the foot of your bed. Nothing mystical or magical. But as you are moving along, trusting Him, staying sensitive to that all-important prompting of God through His Holy Spirit that still small voice will come to you.

Proverbs 16:9; 20:24 *"The mind of man plans his way, But the LORD directs his steps ... Man's steps are ordained by the LORD, How then can man understand his way?"*

I love that! When all is said and done, you'll say, *"Honestly, this direction didn't come from me. It must have been from God."*

Talk about mysterious! The longer I live the Christian life, the less I know about why He leads as He does - but one thing I know for sure – God always leads.

JANUARY 8

The Power of One

It is easy to underestimate the significance of one person. With so many people, most of whom seem so much more capable, more gifted, more prosperous, more important than us, who are we to think our contribution amounts to much?

"I'm just one person, I cannot make much of a difference."

Aren't you glad Henry Ford didn't think like that? Or Martin Luther King, Jr.? Walt Disney? Or the great reformer Martin Luther? Winston Churchill? Irving Berlin? Abraham Lincoln? Charles Wesley? Dwight L. Moody? Corrie ten Boom?

"But it's a different world today. Back then, there was room for an individual to emerge and stand out in a crowd, but not now!"

Wrong. God has always celebrated individual involvement, and He still does.

How many did it take to help the victim who got mugged on the Jericho Road? **One**

How many were chosen by God to confront Pharaoh and lead the Exodus? **One**

How many sheep got lost and became the object of concern to the shepherd? **One**

How many were needed to confront adulterous David and bring him to his knees in full repentance? **One**

How many prophets were called to stand before wicked King Ahab and predict a drought? **One**

How many did the Lord use to get the attention of the land of Israel and prepare the way for Messiah? **One**

Never underestimate the power of one! That one might just be you someday!

JANUARY 9

Let Go!

Can you remember when life was joyful? Even funny? When did everything get so serious? When did a well-exercised sense of humour get sacrificed on the altar of adulthood? Who says becoming a 'responsible person' means a long face and an all-serious attitude towards life? Sadly, I've met many Christians who don't seem to be embracing the abundant life Jesus died to give them. A lot of adults I know are *so* serious.

My calling as a Pastor is among the most serious of all. As a minister of the gospel and pastor of a Church, I have had to deal with life at its worst many times. The needs are enormous, endless, and heart-wrenching. It's easy to become grim. I know of no greater need in the Church than the need for joy - inexplicable, glorious, contagious joy. The secret of abundant living is the same as the secret of joy: both revolve around the centrality of Christ.

To you, my fellow pilgrim, I say, *"Let go!"* Let go of your habit of always looking at the negative. Let go of your need to fix everybody else's problems. Let go of your drive to compete or compare. Let go of the needless inhibitions that keep you from celebrating life. Quit being so protective, so predictable, so in control, so proper.

When Christ becomes our central focus, our very reason for existence, then contentment will replace your anxiety, fear and insecurities. Many think that happiness is something that happens to them rather than something they pursue. Joy comes to those who determine to pursue it in spite of their everyday circumstances. Our mind is like a bank awaiting our deposits. If we regularly deposit positive, encouraging, and uplifting thoughts, we will withdraw the same. And the interest paid will be joy and abundant life. So, decide today to let go and embrace all that God has for you!

JANUARY 10

Stand Strong and Stay Faithful

Tucked away in Hebrews 11 is a two-word biography worth our attention. *"he endured"* (11:27). The NIV translation reads, *"he persevered,"* the Amplified Version says, *"he held staunchly to his purpose."* Moffatt renders it, *"he never flinched."* The *"he"* is Moses, the one who hung tough, who was committed to God's desires for his life, and who decided not to surrender to rising odds. He had staying power. He was faithful. He possessed the discipline of stickability. There aren't many qualities we need more than this one.

Moses endured despite the contempt of Pharaoh, who was the mightiest monarch of that era. Moses stayed at the task that God gave him despite the stubbornness of the Hebrews who were grumbling, complaining and rebelling. Nothing they said or did caused Moses to retreat. Misunderstood, maligned and misrepresented, Moses never flinched.

So, what's the lesson we can learn from his example? Stand firm when conspirators and critics seem to prosper. Stay faithful when the wicked appear to be winning. Endure in times of crisis in Church, in your finances, in your family, in your workplace. Stand firm even when no one would notice if you compromised. Stand firm, stay faithful, and endure!

I have no idea where this finds you. For all I know, you are stronger than ever, determined not to shrink back, pressing on with a full tank of resolve. That's great. Or maybe your moral purity and ethical integrity are wearing thin. Perhaps you've begun to listen too closely to your critics or you need the approval of others too much. Maybe you led with decisiveness in the past, but today you're feeling yourself weakening. Maybe you've started shrugging off your better judgment. Don't go there; it's just not worth it! Remember Moses' example: stand strong and stay faithful.

JANUARY 11

The Church is Messy

The Church is messy, isn't it? When I look around, I see that we're often unsafe for the hurting, unkind to those who don't see the world the way we do, and unlike Jesus in how we relate to people. We often tack our nationalism, patriotism, racism, favouritism, classism, or our preferred political-economic model such as socialism or capitalism onto our faith and find ways for the Bible to support our views.

We often overpromise and underdeliver on solutions for human needs like connection, significance, and belonging. At times we even confuse materialistic prosperity with divine blessing while ignoring the poor or marginalized. We become dogmatic about all the secondary, non-essential issues and we splinter, split, and scatter. We institutionalize what should be organic and over-spiritualize what should come naturally.

Jesus had this radical dream that the Church could touch and change and affect communities for good; be a voice for both moral conviction and empathy and compassion. Jesus invites us to come and to see what He is all about, what He stood for, whom He died for, and what He's doing in the world today as the living King of a new kind of kingdom. He invites us to die to ourselves, to lay down our selfish ambition and all our traditional understanding of power structures as we adopt a whole new way of thinking and a whole new way of life.

I can't give up on the Church because, as messy as it is, the Church His idea. Jesus died for the Church, was raised for the Church, and commissioned the Church to be the light in the darkness and love to the lost until He comes back to fix it all.

Are you ready to get messy? You'll never know how greatly God wants to use you in this world until you're willing to move toward the mess – not run from it.

JANUARY 12

Transformation

Real faith uses information for the purpose of transformation. The Bible was not given merely for our information, but for our transformation. The purpose of the Bible is to produce real, lasting, tangible change in your life. It's meant to change the condition of your soul and your heart and your Spirit, so that you live differently than you did before. That's what James meant in his letter when he wrote, *"Faith by itself, if not accompanied by action, is dead."* In other words, real faith *does* something. It changes me in some way.

I can remember the time when I first embraced the salvation Jesus gifted me. In that moment, there was a lot going on. I needed to believe the fact that Jesus Christ was the son of God. I needed to believe that He had died for my sins. I needed to believe that He had risen from the dead, but I also needed to *act* on those beliefs and allow Him to transform my life.

The way that we do that is by stepping out in faith, by resting in Him. Not just believing that He's there, but saying, *"I take my life and I put it into Your hands. I'm going to be different because I am now following You. My faith is going to be a faith in action. It's going to be faith that works."*

Real faith is not just collecting information. A lot of us grew up in an atmosphere where we thought the most spiritually mature people were the ones who knew the Bible the best. Hopefully we're coming to understand that's simply not the case. Satan knows the Bible better than anyone – he arguably has the most 'information' about God. But that certainly does not produce a mature faith in God in him!

The most spiritually mature people that I know are not the people who know the most information - they are the ones who have experienced the most transformation. Real faith always uses information for the purpose of transformation.

JANUARY 13

Expectations

Expectations are relationship-killers. A wife expects her new husband to be Prince Charming of her dreams. A boss expects the new secretary to read his mind. A congregation expects the new pastor to reverse the declining attendance, preach inspiring sermons, and attend every social occasion. A pastor expects the members to support him, keep down dissension, and respond to every challenge he throws their way. I expect everyone who reads this to be challenged and inspired.

In Luke 6:32-36, after exhorting us to love our enemies and do good to those who do us wrong, Jesus cautions us to expect nothing from the people to whom we minister.

It's just like the carnal world, He says, to do things to others then sit back, expecting a proper response. *"But love your enemies, do good to them, and lend to them, without expecting to get anything back."*

Everyone who ministers in the Church or through the Church would save themselves so much grief if they just let go of their expectations. If the people respond, fine; if not, that is their choice. Do your job and go on to the next task, with eyes firmly fixed on Jesus.

Luke 7:1-10 tells of the Roman centurion who intercedes with Jesus for his ailing servant, then sends a delegation to ask Him not even to bother coming to the house. *"I do not consider myself worthy,"* he said, then added, *"But say the word, and my servant will be healed."* This man has focused everything on Jesus. That's the point. We never go wrong in looking to Jesus as our Shepherd, Saviour, salvation and strength!

The bottom line is this: regarding your expectations of all those people around you, *give them up!* Regarding your expectations of Jesus, *lift them up!* It really is that simple.

JANUARY 14

Faith and Doubt

Many Christians today assume that faith is the antithesis of doubt. In this view, a person's faith is thought to be strong to the extent that they don't question their beliefs or struggle with God in whom they believe. As widespread as this view is, I believe it is unbiblical and profoundly unhelpful. My experience as a pastor and teacher has taught me that when people assume faith and doubt are not compatible, they invariably try to avoid the latter. Those who are afflicted with this unfortunate model of faith find it hard, if not impossible, to honestly acknowledge, let alone feel the full force of the merits of any perspectives that may challenge their beliefs.

To challenge this tendency, consider the name God gave his covenant people, 'Israel.' According to the Genesis narrative, this name goes back to a rather bizarre event that took place at a turning point in Jacob's life. This forefather of the nation of Israel apparently found himself wrestling with the Lord, in the form of a man, for an entire night (Genesis 32: 24-32). Oddly enough, we are told that the Lord *"could not overpower him"* and that Jacob would not let the man go until he *"blessed"* him (v.25). It was because of this tenacity that God renamed him 'Israel' (Yisra'el), which, according to this narrative, signifies one *who struggles with God* (v.28). It was for this reason that God's people were called *Israelites* - people who tenaciously wrestle with God.

The scriptures are filled with examples of Jacob-like wrestling matches with God. While expressing doubts and challenging God may be antithetical to the modern, popular notion of faith, it is fully compatible with the biblical understanding. The essence of 'faith' in the biblical tradition is not blind, unthinking submission or even an unwavering psychological certainty. Faith is fundamentally a covenantal concept that expresses our willingness to trust God, in spite of our doubts.

JANUARY 15

What Do You Long For?

Augustine once prayed, *"You have made us for yourself, and our hearts are restless till they find their rest in you."* We all have an unquenchable yearning in our hearts, a yearning for nothing less than to share in God's own eternally full life. This is why our deepest desires will never be permanently satisfied by anything in this world. The life of God is nothing other than the perfect love that eternally unites the Father, Son, and Holy Spirit, and this Triune God spoke creation into being with the ultimate goal of inviting humans to share in this life.

The great Puritan theologian and pastor Jonathan Edwards painted a portrait of the Trinity in which the love and joy of the three divine persons was so full and intense, it simply could not be contained. God's fullness thus yearned to be expressed and replicated by sharing it with others. So, this fullness overflowed as God brought forth creation and that mirrored His triune beauty. The pinnacle of this creation is created beings whose yearning for God mirrors His yearning for them. Whereas God's yearning comes out of His fullness, our yearning comes out of our emptiness.

It's a beautiful arrangement. The God of overflowing love longs to pour His love into others, so He created beings that long for His love to be poured into them. It wasn't God's intention for us to ever go a moment without this longing being satisfied. Living without the fullness of God's love is a reality we have brought upon ourselves through rebellion, and it is unnatural to us.

God's ultimate goal in creation is nothing less than for the very same perfect love that the Father has for His own Son to be given to us and to be placed within us. God's plan is to envelop everyone who is willing, into the threefold loving eternal dance of the Father, Son, and Holy Spirit.

JANUARY 16

Faith is Not Magic!

Many Christians today treat faith like magic. While the content of what Christians believe is obviously different from the pagan practitioners of magic, the way they believe and the motive they have for believing, may be very similar. Magic is generally understood to involve people engaging in special behaviours that empower them to gain favour with, or to influence the spiritual realm in order to get it to work to their advantage.

For instance, when praying for someone who is sick, it is often assumed that if we engage in a certain behaviour - namely, making ourselves sufficiently certain that the person will be healed - then we could influence the spiritual realm and God would act in a way that would benefit that person. While this might on the surface appear very similar to how a person with a biblical understanding of faith might pray, the assumption about what is going on is much closer to magic.

Another example is seen in the common view of salvation. The prevailing view is that for a person to be 'saved,' they must believe those doctrines that are 'essential to salvation.' And for most Christians, to 'believe' means that a person has become sufficiently certain that a doctrine is true. If they believe the right things then they are in.

One of the key differences between 'magic' and biblical faith is that magic is about engaging in behaviours that benefit the practitioner, while biblical faith is always about cultivating a covenantal relationship with God that is built on mutual trust.

Faith is about trusting in the beautiful character of Christ, about being transformed from the inside out by the power of His unending love, and about learning how to live in the power of the Spirit as you increasingly reflect His love and His will *"on earth as it is in heaven."*

JANUARY 17

In Christ

With the coming of Jesus Christ, the Father, Son, and Spirit made a way for us to be incorporated into the triune fellowship. We are placed in Christ through the power of the Spirit. This doesn't just change how God views us and relates to us. It changes who we really are. We actually are *in Christ*, and through the Spirit, Christ really is in us! Much harm has been done by teachers who stress how our union with Christ changes how God sees us without emphasizing how this union really changes us at our core. God doesn't just view us with *'Jesus spectacles,'* as some have said. God re-creates us in Christ, through the Holy Spirit. We are *"created in Christ Jesus for good works"* (Eph 2:10). *"If anyone is in Christ,"* Paul says we are *"a new creation."* (2 Cor 5:17).

When God says that we are righteous, holy, and blameless in Christ, we are in fact righteous, holy, and blameless! Take some time to read Romans 6:1-12. This is the point that Paul makes there. Paul makes it clear that our union with Christ isn't a fictitious thing - it is very real. We really do participate in Christ's crucifixion, burial and resurrection.

Our thinking about ourselves should line up with the truth of who we really are. Our new identity must give rise to new ways of thinking, which in turn gives rise to our new way of behaving. Paul does not ask us to behave a certain way in order to become something we are not. Rather, he asks us to remember who we already are in Christ and live accordingly.

The life believers live is no longer a life of their own efforts; in Christ, this old life is dead and buried. Being incorporated into Christ, the life we live is the life that Christ Himself lives, and this life is eternally toward God. Just as we participate in the love and life Christ receives from the Father, so we also participate in the love and life Christ lives to the Father.

JANUARY 18

Confidence

I love reading The Psalms. So many of them fill my mind with ideas and images about who God is and what He does and why. God is the One enthroned in heaven, Most High, maker of all, majestic, righteous ruler & judge, our rock, our refuge, our strength, the One Who sees, and that's just the beginning!

As for His actions, in the first few Psalms alone, we see God surrounding the righteous with His favour like a shield. He watches over them and leads them. He blesses all who take refuge in Him. He listens to their prayers and answers them. He delivers, gives relief, disciplines them, and judges evil. He fills hearts with joy and peace and brings prosperity.

God is the King of kings, Who made the world, owns the world, rules the world and sustains the world. So, what does all this mean for us? God chooses to be involved in the details of our lives. He is worthy of our confidence and trust.

David, who wrote many of the Psalms we have today, had such a deep and abiding confidence in God. I'm convicted by it, in the area of belief. I don't usually struggle with doubting God. But sometimes I struggle with doubting me. Deep down, that's an issue of confidence in God - that He is who He says He is, that He does what He says He'll do, and especially, that He does it for me.

At some point in life, even the most self-confident among us will experience their confidence being shaken. We are human, and in this state, we are dependent on God, whether we admit that or not.

It doesn't matter how much confidence you were born with or how much you develop through the various circumstances of your life. What matters most is that our hope and trust is always in God.

JANUARY 19

'Nearer My God to Thee'

Dr. Robert Bateman gently helped his sister-in-law into the lifeboat. *"Don't be nervous, Annie. This will test our faith. I must stay and help the others. If we never meet again on this earth, we will meet again in heaven."* He dropped his handkerchief to the woman as the boat descended toward the dark, icy water below. *"Put that around your throat, Annie. You'll catch cold."*

Dr. Bateman then gathered about fifty men at the stern of the ship and told them to prepare for death. Earlier that day, he had conducted the only religious service on the ship, a service that ended with his favourite hymn, *Nearer My God to Thee*.

Bateman founded the Central City Mission in Jacksonville, Florida, a spiritual lighthouse in a city regularly full of drunken sailors. He had been called 'the man who distributes more human sunshine than any other in Jacksonville.'

Bateman went to England to study Christian social work and he was returning to the USA to put into practice what he had learned. However, late on the night of April 14, 1912, Bateman's ship struck an iceberg. Bateman led the men with him on the stern of the ship in the Lord's Prayer. As the band played *Nearer My God to Thee* with courage and conviction, the great and mighty Titanic slid under the ocean – where it remains to this day.

Nearer, my God, to thee, nearer to thee!
E'en though it be a cross that raiseth me,
still all my song shall be, nearer, my God, to thee;
nearer, my God, to thee, nearer to thee!

Though like the wanderer, the sun gone down,
darkness be over me, my rest a stone;
yet in my dreams I'd be nearer, my God, to thee;
nearer, my God, to thee, nearer to thee!

JANUARY 20

Love Wins in the End

Love sees a wrong and rights it. Love walks into a heart to open it. Love loves when it doesn't feel like loving. Love climbs over walls that block its path.

Love crushes the obstacles surrounding it. Love sets down swords to bring bouquets of flowers. Love beats out pain over time, to touch the most callous heart. Love continues to try. Love always waits. Love heals. Love brings life.

Love never fails. Love seeks truth. Love fights for itself. Love doesn't count the cost. Love doesn't add up the damages. Love doesn't dwell in the days of old but sees the dreams of new. Love doesn't lose its endurance. Love doesn't move away from always-there, glimmer-of-light hope.

Love doesn't part from passionate perseverance. Love doesn't see eye-constricting anger, but ever-flowing grace. Love doesn't forgive once, but a thousand times. Love doesn't always feel happy but finds smiles through prayer. Love doesn't always have answers but seeks God's solutions. Love lets the originators of the word make it come alive.

When our arms fall down and our back falls back, Father God, the Son and the Holy Spirit step up. They teach us the real meaning of love. Then we see how love wins even when it feels like it is losing. Love isn't easy and Jesus proves that.

Love sometimes means being nailed and beaten by those we love. Love still remains. Love still works out. Love knows the alternative to love is hate and hate is the quick funnel to all pain, agony and despair. Love presses on. Love continues to die to self and live to Christ. Love brings life.

Love wins in the end.

JANUARY 21

Surrender

"It's not about you." I have lost count of the number of times those four words have hit me with a palpable force ... and the times my pride wanted to take over and convince me that the statement was a lie. But deep down, I know it was the truth.

The circumstances were all very different, but the heart issue was always the same, as once again, I needed to come to terms with the truth that my life, my ministry, my very purpose in being here is ultimately not about me; it's not about my needs; it's not about my ideas and plans and dreams and hopes; it's not about my wounds or my betrayal. At the end of the day; in the final analysis, when the rubber hits the road – it's all about Jesus and His mission.

When this truth offends my mind and captures my heart again, something inside of me unlocks. I realize that my focus has been inward, but true freedom comes when we fix our eyes on Jesus. When I turned away from God, my focus was on myself. When I strove to behave and be the model disciple, perfect Pastor and the best husband and father I could be, my focus was always on myself. Suddenly, instead of focusing on me, I centred my thoughts on the One Who gave me life.

Our sacrifices will never replace what God desires from us the most: a surrendered heart. With a surrendered heart, I see that God is sovereign even in the midst of uncertainty, turmoil and heartbreak. Because we live in a broken world, I see suffering is inevitable but also a means of growth.

As I focus upward and outward instead of inward, that bitter root dissolves; what was once resentment turns into gratitude; my glass is not half empty or even half full anymore but overflowing – because God has given me all that I need to live the best version of myself, every day of my life. Amen!

JANUARY 22

Joy comes in the morning!

Your pain, your emotions and your story are not for nothing. Behind all the painful circumstances of life, God always has glory waiting to be unveiled; He has power waiting to be revealed; He has encouragement awaiting your soul; He stands ready to show you how to see His glory – hidden in your present-day circumstances.

Psalm 30:5 *"So take hope. For in the moment is pain, but joy comes in the morning."*

The story of a blind man paints an incredible picture for us. He was actually born both blind and poor. We can only imagine his struggles, his loneliness, his embarrassment and his feelings of hopelessness. We may ask, "how could this happen to him? Blind and poor? What hope did he have for work? How demotivated must he have felt?"

Mark 9:23 *"Yet, with Christ, all things are possible for those who believe."*

Jesus often rescued others to reveal His glory.

John 9:6 *"Jesus spit on the ground, made some mud with the saliva, and put it on the man's eyes."*

After the mud was applied to the blind man's eyes, Jesus told him to go and wash his face. He did – and the blind man could see! Just imagine his joy when his blurry eyes gave way to the glory held within the eyes of Christ.

When we look at this story, we see Jesus was faithful to heal. But the blind man played a very important role too. He had to take a moment, to step out of his suffering; to step out of the place of despair and to get up and walk to the water. He had to obey Jesus, then joy most certainly came his way!

JANUARY 23

Rise and Shine!

Isaiah 60:1-3 *"Arise, shine, for your light has come, and the glory of the Lord rises upon you. See, darkness covers the earth and thick darkness is over the peoples, but the Lord rises upon you and his glory appears over you. Nations will come to your light, and kings to the brightness of your dawn."*

What a great promise! That's God's promise to us each and every day. I remember the voice of my mother every morning all through my childhood, *"Rise and shine …!"* Well this passage is God's call to us every new day and depending on where we are in our journey any given day, *"Rise and shine"* can mean a lot of different things.

It's time to step out; come out of hiding; let your true colours shine; be who God made you to be; it's time to be fearless; to be courageous; to be passionate; it's time to take a risk; to move from your calm, safe ground to unsteady, risky and rocky terrain – that terrain where you feel vulnerable, a place where you know, by yourself, you can't stand on your own.

Why is it time? Because too much is on the line not to - and the idea of not taking that adventurous step means living in mediocrity. It's so worth it. You only have one life; one chance to pour out love; one chance to give all you have - to be all in, no holds barred; to share grace; to encourage in truth; to live without fear; to give with faith; to help those in need. This is your chance. Life is not a dress rehearsal – this is it.

Are you sick of living trapped, beholden to this world? At the end of the day, when all is said and done, you will never, ever regret living all out – full of love – for God. You won't do this perfectly, by any means, but that is the point. That is why we need Christ, and when we rely on Him, we find peace, we find safety, despite the unsafe, rocky terrain beneath our feet.

JANUARY 24

When God Closes a Door

You were praying. Others were praying for you too. God seemed to be opening a door and ushering you through it, but just as quickly as the door opened, God seemed to close it. Disappointed, maybe shocked and even embarrassed, you felt like you had failed.

I am sure you have been there before. I have. But eventually I look back at Jesus – the ultimate reject. The ultimate failure in the eyes of the world. He was mocked and scorned. Jesus, like us, had a partially unanswered prayer. He said, *"Father, if you are willing, please take this cup of suffering away from me. Yet I want your will to be done, not mine."* (Luke 22:42).

Jesus though, despite His pain, was looking for godly gain. Above His need for deliverance, He embraced perseverance. He endured humiliation for the plan of God – a plan to save us. Jesus didn't take the opportunity to exert His godly power and avoid the cross. He was faithful. He trusted. He waited. He served others on the cross – even through His pain. He wasn't knocking down any doors.

He knew the Father's plan and purpose. We can trust this plan too – because it is from Him. We don't need to fear at all. He has directed our steps all the way; He has given us His words and His inspiration; He has helped us to encourage those around us and to change other people's lives. He has given us excitement and passion.

We must remember there is a plan greater than our own; for a purpose bigger than our own; at a time better than our own. Our ways are not His ways.

Isaiah 55:8 *"My thoughts are nothing like your thoughts," says the Lord. "And my ways are far beyond anything you could imagine."*

JANUARY 25

It's all About Jesus

We are the only Jesus this world will ever see and they don't care much about our spiritual gifts; our power ministry; our theological knowledge; our anointed worship; our spiritual discernment; our biblical leadership structure and all the other wonderful things which seem to draw our focus.

Those things are all important and they have been used by God and will be in the future but they are for us, the Church. But what about them - the ones who are yet to bask in God's glory? What about those outside the Church who have no choice but to look at you and me and make a judgement about God based on what they see in our character and our life. Our unbelieving families and friends will do the same.

They don't care how gifted we are or how prominent we are in ministry; they don't care how long we've been a Christian; they don't care about our training; they don't care that we got a word from the Lord for someone last Sunday; they don't care about anything that happens inside the Church; they don't care that we gather together and worship a God of power, if that same God has not changed us so radically that they see it with their own eyes and hear it with their own ears and are gripped by the reality of who we now are in Christ.

Do you know what you're unbelieving workmates and family and friends are saying to you? Do you know what your own children who are yet to embrace Christ are saying to you? Whether you know it or not, whether they even know it or not, effectively they are crying out:

"Show me God in your life. Live it. Prove to me that this stuff is real as it transforms you. Don't tell me about God. Don't witness with empty words and prayers. **Show me the living Jesus** *- in the way you live. Then, maybe, maybe I might see the truth in what you say."*

JANUARY 26

Brokenness

We value human strength and earthly perfection. We admire people for 'being strong' when they're mourning a loss. We are proud of friends for 'standing tall' in the face of adversity. We put images of our most talented athletes on the covers of magazines. Weakness is looked down upon as unnatural and subpar in our culture. It's not something to be exalted, but to be rejected. Only the strong survive. However, in God's way of doing things this could not be further from the truth.

There is an ancient Japanese form of art called *Kintsugi*. It involves joining together broken pottery pieces with gold or another precious metal. Kintsugi means 'golden patchwork,' which is what this art is all about. The artist takes the broken pieces of pottery - such as cups, bowls, or plates - and puts them together again to form the original items. Rather than hiding the flaws of the pottery, the artist highlights the cracks by sealing them with gold. Brokenness is not hidden but showcased for all to see. The reason why Kintsugi is found in museums throughout Japan is because the 'broken' art is given more value and revered as more beautiful than a cup or bowl that is unbroken.

God's ways are like Kintsugi. God has chosen to use broken people to do extraordinary things. He has planned to use pain and suffering for our good and His glory in ways beyond our wildest imagination. In God's plan, weakness is attractive. Kintsugi reminds me of these words from the Apostle Paul:

2 Corinthians 4:7-10 *"But we have this treasure in jars of clay, to show that the surpassing power belongs to God and not to us. We are afflicted in every way, but not crushed; perplexed, but not driven to despair; persecuted, but not forsaken; struck down, but not destroyed; always carrying in the body the death of Jesus, so that the life of Jesus may also be manifested in our bodies."*

JANUARY 27

God is still in control

We are outside the garden now; we have eaten of the tree; there is no going back. We know too much to return to its innocence and safety. The world is scary, accidental, and random, but the more we attempt to control the chaos, the more we fear what remains outside our control.

Sadly, at one level the world of Genesis beyond chapter 3 confirms our fears. Outside the garden, the human race faces a world of violence and pain; the soil is hard, the thorns are sharp, and from the moment Cain killed Abel, jealousy and envy have marked nearly every human story. Sarah envies Hagar, Jacob envies Esau, Laban envies Jacob, and Rachel envies Leah.

In the midst of unanticipated outcomes, failed attempts to make things better by our weak understanding, and that ongoing presence of sickness and sadness - no matter what we do - despite our best efforts - we truly do not know how it is going to be. It is hard to admit, but we are actors in a play who know only a small piece of the script, and we long for a director who knows what is next. As C. S. Lewis writes:

"We do not know the play. We do not even know whether we are in Act I or Act V. We do not know who are the major and who are the minor characters. The Author knows. That it has a meaning, we may be sure, but we cannot see it. When it is over, we may be told. We are led to expect that the Author will have something to say to each of us on the part that each of us has played. It is playing it well that matters."

After the garden, one might suppose God would leave us to our own devices; after all, if this is what humanity wanted, we got precisely what we reached for. But God does not stop caring. God has never abandoned us and He is still in control.

JANUARY 28

Waiting on the Lord

To wait on the Lord means to place your hope in Him - to trust that God is the One Who can deliver you. Your entire confidence rests on Him. We wait on Him because He's God and we're not.

Waiting is difficult because our whole cultural mindset tells us that we're not doing anything when we are waiting. And that's the whole point. We're not doing anything, but God is. Waiting is one of the greatest applications of the Christian faith. We are putting our trust in God, placing our hope in Him, and expressing confidence that He is in control. Waiting puts us in an uncomfortable place where we are not in control of our lives. This is active patience at work and a season when God can shape and define us.

However, waiting is not easy. The uncertainty of what may or may not happen can be haunting. It can occupy too much space in our thinking. I've had it affect my sleep and assault my mind with the first thoughts of the day. Waiting can be hard because of the fear of the unknown. Our inability to do anything but wait is a powerless feeling. We want to know what's going on. We want to know, *"What's the point of this? Why is this happening? Why is my life not as I want?"*

Rather than resisting this season, waiting is an opportunity for life-changing lessons. If you are in a position of waiting, then you need to let go the control of your life and say, *"God, I don't know what you're doing or why, but I'm going to trust You because You are God and I'm not."*

God desires to teach us many lessons, and those lessons often come slowly - after we have stopped trying on our own, at the point we are broken and ready for Him to lead us. In the midst of suffering and uncertainty, always remember that waiting on the Lord is never a waste of time.

JANUARY 29

Integrity

There is a very famous floating hotel and museum in Long Beach, California - the Queen Mary. When this magnificent vessel was first launched in 1936, it was the largest ship to cross any ocean. It served through four decades and even in the second world war. There are many wonderful stories about this magnificent vessel.

One of those stories is not very grand at all - it concerns what happened during its conversion process from a sailing vessel into a museum. As you can imagine, everything had to be restored, repaired, re-painted and made ready for the millions of people who would enter this grand floating mansion.

One of the tasks was to remove her massive smokestacks to be stripped down and repainted. The three huge structures had been the most stunning feature of this magnificent vessel. Slowly they were lowered onto the dock by crane. As the workmen began applying paint stripper to remove the external layers, each of the three smokestacks disintegrated.

What had once been 4-inch steel plate had become wafer-thin. The steel, in fact, had rusted completely away. All that remained were thirty coats of paint that had been applied over the years. There was nothing left but an appearance, an outward shell. Simply put, they had no integrity. There was no substance beneath the painted surface.

Integrity is defined as *"the state of being whole and undivided."* Applied to the huge metal smokestacks on the Queen Mary, it means there should have been substance, strength and reality beneath the paintwork. If applied to our lives it means who we project ourselves to be on the outside, must come from the real substance of our life on the inside. We practice what we preach. We walk the talk. Who we are when nobody is looking is our true condition. That's integrity.

JANUARY 30

What are You Doing, Lord?

Proverbs 29:18 *"Where there is no vision, the people perish."* (KJV)

The word 'vision' has been given all kinds of meanings in the modern world and most of them have nothing to do with this verse. But when the NIV Bible was written, the translators tried to be more accurate to the original meaning of the text and this verse became:

Proverbs 29:18 *"Where there is no revelation, the people cast off restraint."* (NIV)

What the King James Version translated 'vision' the NIV translates 'revelation.' You see, vision can (and most often does) come from us. But revelation always comes from God. Now this is not just an issue about how a verse is translated. This verse, when properly understood, becomes a clear explanation for nearly all of the Church's highs and lows over our entire history.

When the day-by-day revelation of God is not continually being sought, discerned and applied, then we 'cast off restraint.' We go our own way - tragically thinking it's God's way because we opened our 'vision' meeting in prayer! When Eugene Petersen wrote *The Message,* a contemporary Bible translation, he unpacked this truth even more and made it abundantly clear what this verse really means for us today:

Proverbs 29:18 *"If people can't see what God is doing, they stumble all over themselves; But when they attend to what He reveals, they are most blessed."* (The Message)

That verse is why for years now I have encouraged people to ask two questions every morning as they begin each new day. *"What are You doing, Lord?"* and *"How can I be part of it?"* Why don't you try it and see where God leads you?

JANUARY 31

The Outrageous Love of God

God created us in love - for love. Our primary purpose in life is to have a loving relationship with God and then, in turn, with those around us. God's sovereign love is not just His choosing of us; it's not just His affection for us; it is also His power within us. His love impacts us and does something to us, in us and through us. It affects our being. You cannot be truly impacted by the love of God and remain the same.

Religion is very concerned about what you should be and many churches are passionate to tell you what you could be, but God simply comes to you in love, just as you are.

However, when that amazing truth, God's amazing grace, really sinks in and God's unconditional love impacts you deep down in your soul, then a transformation will begin and it continues and intensifies day by day.

The more you drink in the unconditional love and grace of God; the more you embrace the empowering presence of God, then the more you become all that you could be and all that you should be! This is the gospel! This is the good news!

Now that we have been chosen and loved by God and this love has affected us in life-changing ways, this is where we are to stay at all times - rooted and established or grounded in that love. We don't move on from that reality. We don't grow out of our need for God's love. We don't 'mature' to a place in our relationship with God where we don't need His empowering presence and love every moment of every day.

We need to always be rooted and grounded in what God has done for us and it's out of the reality of God's outrageous love that we can then minister and do things for God and with God in the world around us.

February 1

Acceptance and Change

We humans are complex creatures. There's a lot to sort out before we understand ourselves or others. However, when we drill down through all our differences and idiosyncrasies, we are all the same when it comes to what we really need. I believe there are two things which every human being wants and needs more than anything else: *acceptance* and *change*.

We all want to be accepted as we are, don't we? Those people in our lives who have truly loved us, the ones from whom we really have felt genuine love, will be the ones who accept us as we truly are. They know all our shortcomings and yet love us anyway. We don't want to have to follow someone's rules or fulfil someone's expectations in order to be accepted.

That acceptance we long for; that unconditional, no-need-to-jump-through-any-religious-hoops acceptance we crave and need is given to us in the Gospel! We are 100% accepted by God regardless of anything we do or don't do! Only the gospel, only the good news of God, in Christ can meet one of the most basic and important human needs: acceptance.

But you also know that we humans are a paradox. Whilst we desperately need to be accepted as we are and not be expected to change in order to earn God's love or the love of His people, deep down we actually want to change. We want to grow. We want to mature but we don't want to be forced to in order to earn the acceptance of others or of God.

Enter again: the life-changing good news – the Gospel in Christ! God accepts us totally as we are, but He loves us too much to leave us there! God's love is not static. It is dynamic. It impacts us. It changes us. It leads us to repentance and faith. It gives us life as God intended us to have – abundant life! This is what God is all about and this is what the Church should be all about: acceptance and change.

February 2

God Comes to Us in Love

When God comes to us, He always comes to us in love.

This is so important for us to grasp. However, I would suggest there are millions of sincere believers in the Church today who have not yet fully embraced this truth. They may affirm God's love in their minds, but in practice, many Christians still feel accused or judged and like they don't measure up before God. We can read all the Bible verses which proclaim our salvation and our freedom in Christ; we can sing the victory songs on Sunday; we can preach and proclaim God's forgiveness, grace, mercy and love, but we can still live like it's all about our performance. So where does that come from?

Well, in the first instance, it comes from our failure to hear or accept the true gospel of God's saving grace, but in the spiritual realm the Bible tells us that all accusation against God's much-loved, children comes from 'the accuser' - Satan. If you ever feel accused in your spiritual walk, it is never God who accuses you. It is always the lies of the accuser and your tortured conscience which prevent God's love and grace from being fully effective in your life. But that accuser has no authority in God's kingdom and the law of God against which he accuses us has already been fulfilled completely by Christ, and we now stand in Christ. Satan still accuses, but we simply need to ignore those accusations because Jesus has overcome the accuser once and for all.

Jesus fulfilled the law of God and gave that fulfilment to us as a free gift. We stand in Christ: in His perfect life; in His atoning death; His powerful resurrection; His victory over sin and death and Satan - once and for all. That's our reality.

We are in Christ and this all comes to us in love: *"This is love: not that we loved God, but that he loved us and sent his Son as an atoning sacrifice for our sins."* (1 John 4:10)

February 3

This is Love

Ephesians 1:3-14 is one of the most amazing passages of Scripture have been given. If you haven't read it recently, I encourage you to do so soon. In light of the amazing truth in that passage, allow me to make the following statement which I would encourage you to remember always:

In the kingdom of God, the quality of my life depends firstly not on what I do for God or for others, but on what God has already done for me, and continues to do for me, in me and through me.

So, what has God done for you? According to that Ephesians passage: everything! Everything you could ever imagine, plus some! Welcome to the Good News! Welcome to the Gospel! This is why our life in Christ is anything but religion!

At the heart of religion, you will find a list of things you have to do in order to honour and please God. At the heart of the Christian faith, you will find Christ, Who has already done everything that religion expects you to do.

Jesus has already done everything that God requires and He has given that to you as a free gift, once and for all by His grace! Jesus Christ did what no human had ever done before. He fully obeyed the perfect law of God. He scored all 'A's on his heavenly report card as a man and then He did the most outrageous thing: He paid the price for our inability to obey the law of God – He suffered and died on our behalf.

He then conquered sin, death and Satan as He rose from the dead and became the first man in history to enter heaven as He ascended to the right hand of God the Father. That's when Jesus approached the throne of God and handed His perfect report card to the Father which now has your name and my name on it, and He declared, *"Father, it is finished."*

February 4

The Fruit is Within Us

Have you ever walked through an orchard when the fruit is forming on the trees? When the trees are young, they are just trees, with wonderful leaves and a beautiful shape and they certainly look great in rows across a whole orchard. But they are just time-consuming, expensive ornaments which take up space - until the day arrives when the fruit starts to form. What a miracle that is and when you are there, standing in the middle of that orchard watching that abundant, succulent fruit appear before your eyes, what you can hear? If you go right up close to one of those trees - what you can hear? Absolutely nothing!

Isn't that a miracle? There's no grunting, no groaning and no straining on the part of the tree. The fruit just forms. If the tree is well fed and watered, the fruit will always form and it will be rich and succulent. If the tree is healthy, it doesn't have to exert any effort to produce the fruit – it forms automatically because that is the God-ordained purpose for that tree.

Just as a healthy, well fed and watered tree in an orchard will always produce rich, succulent fruit, so too will a healthy, well fed and watered disciple of Christ always produce rich fruit in their life and within the life of the Church. Trees don't have to 'do more or try harder' or beat themselves each day into submission to bear fruit. Trees just need to be still and know that the fruit is within them – just as their Creator intended. If they are healthy, the fruit will always appear, in season – it's guaranteed.

The source of our food is Christ in us. It is the gift of God's Son, our Saviour and His indwelling presence within us, which is the source of all life, all effectiveness, all power, all gifts and all fruit in the Kingdom of Heaven. We don't need to imitate Jesus - just need to surrender to Him each day.

February 5

What Has Jesus Done?

Do you remember the WWJD movement in the 1990's? It began in America and spread throughout the world. Young people in particular wore these WWJD bracelets everywhere. WWJD stands for 'What would Jesus do?' and the intention was that the constant reminder of this question in our daily lives was supposed to help us ponder what Jesus would do in any particular situation. This then prompted us to go and do likewise. Well, hundreds of millions of WWJD bracelets later, the Church is weaker and less effective than ever. So, what went wrong? Did we just lack the courage and commitment to act, once we worked out what Jesus would do if He were here? Or were we asking the wrong question completely and was that entire movement theologically flawed from the very beginning?

Think about this for a moment. Asking, 'What would Jesus do if He were here?' suggests that Jesus isn't already here and it suggests that Jesus has not already done everything.

In the Kingdom of Heaven, where we live and move and have our being in Christ, through Christ and for Christ, the reality is that every single situation you and I will face has already been dealt with by Jesus! Every challenge we face in our lives has already been overcome by Christ and in Christ. Every problem which presents itself today or tomorrow in our lives has already been solved by Christ and in Christ and He is present now and active in our lives through His Spirit to bring the fruit of His finished work into our journey.

We are not called to imitate Jesus; we are called to surrender to Jesus. Maybe it's time we started a whole new movement and manufactured some new bracelets with the acronym WHJD: *What Has Jesus Done?* The answer to that question will always be: *absolutely everything!*

February 6

Bigger vs. Better

Most Pastors want bigger Churches. Church members? Not so much. Sure, a lot of people go to big Churches. That's what makes them big, after all. And the majority of them are strong, healthy Churches doing great ministry. But if you ask the average member why they attend, *"because it's big"* is not the answer. And non-attenders? Quite frankly, the default is to distrust any Church they deem as 'too big.'

When people go to a Church, or when unchurched people think about going to Church (if they ever do), they're not looking for a bigger experience, they're looking for a better experience. That better experience can happen in any Church. Small, big or mega; denominational or non-denominational, traditional or contemporary.

What people really want from the Church are those things the New Testament tells us the Church is supposed to be about. People want to attend and serve at a Church where they can experience being loved by the God who made them. They want to know why they exist and to be called into something greater than themselves.

They want to connect with others who are asking the same questions and looking for the same answers. They want to participate in doing good for others, with others. They want to be in a community of people they trust so much that when they fail to live up to their ideals, someone will call them on it without getting legalistic or judgmental about it.

The most powerful evangelistic tool in the world is not a new program, a special service, a booklet or a flashy presentation. It's a community who live what they believe; worshipping Jesus, loving each other and caring for their community. In other words, a healthy Church just as God intended.

February 7

Church Attendance Woes

Why are fewer people going to Church? And what can we do about it? This may be the main topic of conversation among Pastors today. I read social media posts every day containing sarcastic takes on how sad it is that people can get up early for a sale at KMart or sit on freezing seats for a sporting event, but they can't get up for Church on Sunday. There are so many things wrong with that kind of thinking.

Shoppers and sports fans don't choose to go to the store or to a game instead of going to Church on Sunday. Firstly, those acts are not mutually exclusive, but more importantly, most people who don't attend Church services are not making a conscious choice against it.

Choosing requires awareness and that awareness exists for fewer and fewer people every day. They haven't rejected the idea of going to Church. It simply isn't on their list of options. They're not lazy, they're apathetic. Until we understand this, we will never reach this generation for Christ.

If we keep complaining about people not attending Church services, we will continue to miss actual opportunities to meet them where they are. Guilting people into Church attendance won't work. Offering them a better Sunday morning 'show' won't work. Getting people to attend Church is not the same as getting them to commit to Jesus.

Church attendance is not, and never has been the issue. Jesus did not say *"I have come that they may get out of bed early on their day off to sing songs together and listen to a sermon."* Gathering with fellow believers matters, if they are believers to begin with. But what if they're not? The lack of Sunday morning Church attendance is not an issue then. What's happening in their heart is what will determine what happens on Sunday!

February 8

What's Wrong with the Church Today?

"The church today is compromised!"

"The modern Church is about entertainment!"

"The contemporary Church is more about personalities than it is about Jesus!"

"Today's preachers just say what people want to hear!"

I don't disagree that there's a whole lot of mess going on. But one of the fastest ways to get me to stop listening is to complain about *"the church today."*

Why? Because it betrays a lack of understanding about our history. Yes, the Church today may be compromised, shallow, legalistic, petty and unforgiving. But no more than it's been in every chapter of its existence - including the over-idealized Church of your childhood and even the first century Church.

The Church has never been without compromise, without shallow, toxic people, self-serving preachers, you name it. If the Church had been perfect in the first century, we wouldn't have several of the New Testament books.

The Galatians abandoned grace for old-school legalism. The Ephesians quickly lost their first love. The Laodiceans were lukewarm. And the Corinthians? Oh dear, where do I begin? Yet God used that faithful, imperfect, striving, in-need-of-radical-forgiveness Church to literally turn the world upside-down. That gives me hope. Yes, the Church has problems. It always has and until we're fully in heaven, it always will.

God has continued to use imperfect people and Churches, because that's all there is to work with. That means God can use me ... and the Church I serve ... and you ... and the Church you serve. That may be one of the reasons Jesus gave us that promise, *"I will build my church."* Because He knew we'd always be a work in progress.

February 9

Are You Serious?

Are you serious about following Jesus and really embracing His mission? The Apostle Paul gave us some of the most profound words ever written and one of those statements is found in his first letter to the Corinthians.

1 Corinthians 13:1-3 *"If I speak in the tongues of men and of angels, but have not love, I am only a resounding gong or a clanging cymbal. If I have the gift of prophecy and can fathom all mysteries and all knowledge, and if I have a faith that can move mountains, but have not love, I am nothing. If I give all I possess to the poor and surrender my body to the flames, but have not love, I gain nothing."*

Let me paraphrase those words:

"If I have God-ordained and empowered spiritual gifts operating in my life and yet possess some fundamental character flaws – I am a spiritual child, drinking spiritual milk! If can hear the voice of God and translate it into powerful prophetic words through preaching or prophetic utterances but continue to hide habitual sin, resentment or bitterness in my heart - then I am a spiritual child, drinking spiritual milk!

If I have allowed God to lay the essential foundation of grace in my understanding of Him but have not allowed Him to transform the foundations of my personal life and character – I am a spiritual child, drinking spiritual milk!

If I have an overwhelming spiritual burden for the lost and a passion and frustration for the Church to reach them in evangelism but are still carrying personal baggage in my character – I am a spiritual child, drinking spiritual milk! If I can pray eloquently and exalt the Lord and intercede for His people and yet speak to or about my wife like she is a hired hand or worse – I am a spiritual child, drinking spiritual milk!"

That's the real meaning of this often sanitised 'love chapter.'

February 10

Already Burned

A young boy grew up on a large wheat farm and he was out in the field with his grandfather one summer just before harvest. They were talking about the threat of fire which was always there at that time of year. The boy's grandfather told him to always carry a box of matches with him when he was out in the fields.

He explained that if a fire started, and he couldn't escape, he should start another fire around him, let it burn a little, and then stand right in the centre of the burnt patch. Why? It's simple. He said, *"Fire cannot pass where fire has already been."*

When we believe into Jesus Christ – completely emerging our whole lives into Jesus by faith – we believe into the only place in the universe where the fire of God's judgement has already passed.

Let's make no mistake about it, the Bible tells us that there is a terrible judgement coming upon the earth. The holiness and purity of God will one day burn against all unholiness and impurity. Our God is an all-consuming fire. The good news is that in Jesus Christ, you have already been burned – the fire of God has consumed all that is not holy.

2 Corinthians 5:21 *"God made him who had no sin to be sin for us, so that in him we might become the righteousness of God."*

The fire of God's judgement has passed through Jesus, and we stand in Him. By placing us in Christ, through faith in Him, we are credited with His performance and then we have been made righteous in Him. Justification sets us free from the burden of failing to please God. It sets us free to be ourselves. The power of sin is broken. This is the gospel. This is the truth. Praise God for His love and grace!

February 11

Pressing On

What drives you? What is it that you are really passionate about in your life? What really pushes your buttons and gets you going? Some people are passionate about sports. Other people are passionate about the latest fashion. Some people are passionate about music.

Every person is interested in some things more than others and that's normal. But more important than that, what do your passions move you toward? Where do your passions lead you? Do your passions drive you toward becoming the person you want to be and the person God wants you to be?

The apostle Paul had one goal in life. His goal was Christ. Everything else in his life revolved around reaching that goal. Is Christ your goal? If He is, then we can learn from Paul the qualities he had that we need, the daily choices he made which we need to make also.

Philippians 3:10-14 *"I want to know Christ and the power of his resurrection and the fellowship of sharing in his sufferings, becoming like him in his death, and so, somehow, to attain to the resurrection from the dead. Not that I have already obtained all this, or have already been made perfect, but I press on to take hold of that for which Christ Jesus took hold of me.*

Brothers and sisters, I do not consider myself yet to have taken hold of it. But one thing I do: Forgetting what is behind and straining toward what is ahead, I press on toward the goal to win the prize for which God has called me heavenward in Christ Jesus."

There are three qualities that we see from that passage that we need to emulate, with God's help. Like Paul, we must have an unconditional dedication to Christ, an unquenchable desire to know Christ personally and intimately, and an unstoppable determination to follow Christ completely.

February 12

God Hates Religion!

The English word 'religion' is etymologically derived from the Latin word *religo,* meaning to 'bind up.' Religion binds people up in rules and regulations or in ritualistic patterns of devotion. Christianity, on the other hand, sets us powerfully free and should never be defined as a religion. In contrast to religion, Christianity is the dynamic spiritual life of the risen Lord Jesus indwelling our spirit and transforming our life.

Sadly, mankind has attempted to force Christianity into the mould and forms of religion for centuries. That is evident by all the steeples and sanctuaries and ecclesiastical programs that dot the landscape of societies across the world. It is the propensity of fallen mankind to take that which comes from the invisible God and attempt to make it visible, tangible and controllable. That produces man-made religion!

Religion is essentially idolatry. Religion is our feeble attempt to establish and maintain a relationship with God through every means possible other than that which He ordained, provides and empowers.

Jesus and Jesus alone *is* the gospel. Jesus and Jesus alone *is* our salvation. Whenever we add anything to Jesus and His finished work on the cross, we have removed ourselves from the power of the gospel and seek once again to save ourselves by our self-righteousness. That's religion!

We seek to relate to God through our performance and our behaviour. That really is the essence of religious behaviour. It despises God's grace. Religion is an ugly distortion of what God intends for us. We fully experience the freedom we have in Christ when we look to Him alone, not just for our salvation, but for our ongoing walk in the Christian life, depending on Him in all things all the time.

February 13

The Most Important Question

There was one dialogue between Jesus and His disciples which is, in my opinion, one of the most important passages in the whole Bible and the exchange between Jesus and the Apostle Peter at the end is foundational in our understanding of what Christianity is all about.

Matthew 16:13-16 *"Now when Jesus came into the district of Caesarea Philippi, He was asking His disciples, "Who do people say that the Son of Man is?" And they said, "Some say John the Baptist; and others, Elijah; but still others, Jeremiah, or one of the prophets." He said to them, "But who do you say that I am?" Simon Peter answered, "You are the Christ, the Son of the living God."*

All of Jesus' teaching, miracles and ministry up to this point in time had been intentionally leading to this one question, *"Who do you say that I am?"* Everything hinges on this question for them, for us and for every human being who ever lived. According to the Bible, everything in your life and everything in eternity is determined by how you answer this question. So, who do you say Jesus is? Embodied in this question is the absolute scandal of Christianity. This sets the Christian faith apart from everything else.

There's something we really need to understand about the Bible. In fact, there's something we need to understand about reality and truth. In our culture today, we are being told that reality or truth is anything you believe it to be at the time. But that's just post-modernist nonsense. Truth and reality are defined as that which most certainly is.

The question is not, *"Who is Jesus to you?"* or *"Who do you want Jesus to be?"* or *"Who do you make Him out to be according to your personal convenience?"* The question is, *"Who is Jesus in reality?"* The Bible provides the answer, but do you agree with it?

February 14

Your Kingdom Come!

In the model prayer Jesus gave us, He encouraged us to pray and declare, *"Your kingdom come, your will be done on earth as it is in heaven."* But what does it look like when that prayer is answered? What does it mean to live in the kingdom of heaven whilst still being a citizen of this broken, fallen earthly kingdom?

What kind of lifestyle do we live once we are fully devoted to Jesus Christ? Heaven functions very differently to earth, so what it is like to live in what the New Testament calls the kingdom of God or the kingdom of heaven?

These are important questions because learning how that kingdom functions is one of the primary mandates given to believers. Heaven is supposed to be a present tense reality, a kingdom that is discernible, measurable, understandable and able to be experienced. The kingdom of heaven is meant to have an impact on how we view reality and how our values are established. The more we personally experience the practical expression of the kingdom of heaven and the more we learn how to build and organise our lives around the central values of that kingdom, then the more we will become transformational within this earthly kingdom.

This prayer represents the heartbeat of Jesus for our lives. This is His heart's desire for each of us – that we will radically impact the world around us as we live out His mission on earth – a mission which can be summed up in the words: *"Your kingdom come, Your will be done on earth, as it is in heaven."*

When Jesus told us to pray this, it wasn't just a pipe dream or a plan to keep us spiritually minded and occupied until He comes back. This was our strategic military assignment in the war against God's enemy and the ruler of this broken world.

February 15

Fruitful in Christ

Matthew 13:23 *"But he who received seed on the good ground is he who hears the word and understands it, who indeed bears fruit and produces: some a hundredfold, some sixty, some thirty."*

The concept of bearing fruit is used often in Scripture. In the Gospels, Jesus told the story of a Sower who went out to sow seed. The seed fell on various types of ground. Some of the ground was rocky and hard. Other ground was receptive, but weeds choked out the seed. But there was a portion of ground that was neither rocky nor weedy, and in that soil the seed took root. Jesus said that this was a picture of the different people who hear the gospel. Those who are true believers will bring forth fruit (Luke 8:15).

What is bearing fruit? Essentially, it is becoming like Jesus. Spiritual fruit will show itself in our lives as a change in our character and behaviour. As we spend time with Jesus and get to know Him better, His thoughts become our thoughts; His purpose, our purpose; we will become like Jesus.

What does spiritual fruit look like? The Bible gives us an excellent description of a life characterized by the fruit of the Spirit. Let's read this in The Message translation:

Galatians 5:22-23 *"But what happens when we live God's way? He brings gifts into our lives, much the same way that fruit appears in an orchard - things like affection for others, exuberance about life, serenity. We develop a willingness to stick with things, a sense of compassion in the heart, and a conviction that a basic holiness permeates things and people. We find ourselves involved in loyal commitments, not needing to force our way in life, able to marshal and direct our energies wisely."*

Is that what others see in your life?

February 16

I Have a Dream

I have a dream. I think it's as bold as Martin Luther King's dream in 1964. I have a dream that very soon the people of God across our nation will finally get to the point where we are sick and tired of letting the enemy have his way.

I dream that we will all see the truth together and affirm that we are here representing another world, we are representing God Himself, and the Governor of that world, Jesus Christ, is here, present with us through His Holy Spirit.

In my dream, God's people decide to finally connect their heart to His; they decide to live aware of Him and all that He is; the words that He breathes; until we think what He thinks; we want what He wants; dream what He dreams. Then finally that abiding presence becomes the primary influence in our conscious and unconscious mind.

In my dream I see two or three people in prayer here and another two or three there and still more in the workplace, in hospitals, in every corner or our communities – hundreds and thousands of people manifesting the simplicity and the power of *ecclesia* – God, in the midst of His gathered people.

Simply put, my dream is to dream what God dreams. My passion is to think what God thinks. My focus is to do what God is doing and speak only the words God gives me to speak. My dream is that every disciple of Christ will soon burn with this unquenchable fire which is only found deep in the heart and presence of God Himself.

I dream that very soon this will not be the dream of just a few disciples of Jesus – but the heartbeat and the very purpose of all of the disciples of Jesus. In my dream, the Church awakens from its slumber and embraces the mission of Christ firmly, as the Kingdom of heaven invades the kingdom of this world!

February 17

Loving God

1 John 4:19 *"We love because he first loved us."*

With just those seven words, John encapsulates one of the most important and foundational truths in the Christian faith and if we are serious about being fully equipped as Jesus' disciples, this truth must dominate our understanding of the gospel, our worldview and our purpose in the Church. We love because He first loved us. That means I can only love God in the measure I receive love from God.

Receiving the love of God gives me a capacity for love I did not have before. I was designed to be a lover of God. I was designed to love God with everything that I am – every part of my being. The Bible says I am to love God with all my heart, all my soul, all my mind and all my strength. Everything about my spirit man is geared up to love God completely.

Perhaps you've heard someone being described as being, *'so heavily minded, they're of no earthly use.'* That's a really stupid thing to say. It's also a contradiction because the only way you can be of any earthly good is to be heavenly minded. If I am not heavenly minded, I am missing the whole point of life. I am called to love God with all my heart, soul, mind and strength. There's an emotional capacity to love that must find expression in my relationship with God. I never stop to grade myself – I just keep going forward. I'm just loving with all my heart and soul – but also my mind. The intellect is actually at its finest when it considers God. *"The fool says in his heart, there is no God."* (Psalm 14:1)

We are designed for love and first and foremost that is love for God. We were hard-wired to love God – that's our design. However, the culture around us is trying really hard to erase the whole concept of design. Don't let that happen!

February 18

The Divine Romance

True discipleship is a divine romance; it's a sacred dance; it's a journey of surrender; it's a daily journey to the cross of Jesus Christ. It's all about us embracing the most privileged opportunity we have been given which is to die to ourselves and trust God for our resurrection and reward. He says, *"Humble yourself under My mighty hand and I will exalt you in due time."* In simple terms that means that nothing is held closer to my heart than God Himself

When you drill down through all the waffle, all the legalistic requirements and the confusing theological language about discipleship that is bouncing around out there, you will find one simple reality: *relationship*. It's all about our relationship with God. The source of all those wonderful qualities of a good disciple which we are exhorted by well-meaning preachers to achieve through hard work and discipline, is our relationship with God.

Our greatest need is God Himself. Our greatest desire should be God Himself. Our moment-by-moment responsibility is to die to ourselves and intentionally live for God. We are not called to seek the rewards and blessings of God, we are called to seek God Himself, in His essence. We are not called to produce fruit, we are called to abide in the vine and the fruit will come naturally in the context of relationship.

It's wonderful to worship God as our Creator, Redeemer and deliverer, but His greatest desire and our greatest need is to draw near to Him and enter the 'holy of holies' of His heart – that place where we know we are His friends and even more than that, we are His sons and daughters – He is our Father.

Jeremiah 29:14 *"You will seek me and find me when you seek me with all your heart. I will be found by you," declares the Lord.*

February 19

Hearing God

It's funny how so many scientists and medical experts are amazed at how well we human beings are designed and yet they don't believe in the Designer. The fact is we have been wonderfully and intricately designed for many things, one of which is this: we are designed to hear from God. It's in our nature as born-again believers to have faith, but it's in our nature as human beings to hear from God.

Many times, in my ministry I have heard a brother or sister say, *"I am in a very dry season right now; I'm just not hearing from the Lord very well. I can sense His presence at times but I can't hear His voice."* We tend to reduce God to our human level. We know that a human being can be right in front of us but not say anything because their presence is not the same as their voice. But when God is present in Christ – He is the Word of God. When the Word shows up, so does His voice. **If God is present – God is speaking and God is always present.**

So, there is a huge difference between God not speaking and us not hearing. The end result looks exactly the same – we don't hear from God – but the problem is always on our end.

For example, at this very moment, wherever you are, there are literally thousands of voices bombarding you. Multiple television stations are transmitting their signal; many more radio stations; short wave signals from around the world are also occupying the same space as you. There are police, fire and ambulance signals and countless mobile phone signals. They are all there, all the time. There's only one reason you cannot hear them – you are not tuned in. You have not made a conscious decision to connect and to listen.

That's how it is with God. He is always speaking - collectively to the Church and specifically to each of His children. We just need to choose to connect and listen to His voice.

February 20

Unbelief

Unbelief is the mother and father of all sins. Every other sin that we feel bad about is our futile attempt to earn the things that God has already freely given us. God said to Adam and Eve: *"I give you everything in abundance. It is all good."* Then the serpent said, *"God is withholding something from you. If you really want to live, then in addition to all that God has given you, you need to take this forbidden fruit."* Taking the fruit was not Adam and Eve's first sin. Not believing what God had told them was their first sin. Unbelief was the first sin and the cause of almost every other sin!

Ephesians 1:5-6 *"In love he predestined us to be adopted as his sons and daughters through Jesus Christ, in accordance with his pleasure and will – to the praise of his glorious grace, which he has freely given us in the One he loves."*

There is no more that we need. We just have to believe what we are told and step out and act on it. We have ALL we need for life in Jesus Christ; ALL we need for godliness; ALL we need for happiness; ALL we need for an authentic life; ALL we need for our Church to become the Church which Jesus promised to build. If we have good, rich, open, receptive soil; if we accept that we already have everything in Christ, then we will begin to experience what the Word promises to us.

Our problems arise from one primary sin: unbelief. When we finally believe that we are unconditionally loved, accepted and made holy before God and empowered by His free grace as given to us in Christ, then we will no longer be intimidated. We may identify sins in our lives which need to be dealt with, but the sin of unbelief lies at the foundation of all those sins. When we decide to truly believe all that God has said, done and promised, then everything else in our lives will fall into place. That's a promise!

February 21

Bloom Where You are Planted

How would you describe your current level of contentment? When you look at your life now, how would you describe the feelings you have toward it? Look at the various component parts of your life. So many things are involved – where you work, where you live, who you're married to or not, how much money you have, how much education you have, how much you weigh, how many opportunities you have, and on and on it goes. If you were to go through each item and rate your level of satisfaction or dissatisfaction in each area, where do you think you would be?

All of us may have some level of dissatisfaction about many things. But the two questions I would like to ask are these: *Where does that come from?* and *where does it lead?* Why are you so dissatisfied? Stupid question perhaps. You're dissatisfied because you're not happy with life. Have you considered that you may be unhappy because your perspective has been altered? Maybe you have been programmed to be unhappy.

Our whole society promotes dissatisfaction with life. In some ways, it is built into the economic system of capitalism. Goods and services are marketed through advertising – and the goal of advertising is to create a felt need for the product. They want to convince you that you need this new thing – and to do that they need to convince you that you are not satisfied with what you have now. If you could only get the new, the improved, the bigger and better whatever – then the quality of your life would take a giant step forward.

So, what's the solution? It's simple. God wants you to bloom where you are planted. He will use your current situation for your good and for His glory. God wants us to work with the hand we have been dealt and trust Him to make whatever changes He thinks we need!

February 22

Be Still

I want you to imagine you are sitting in Carnegie Hall or the Sydney Opera House, waiting for a concert to commence, featuring a major Symphony Orchestra. However, before magnificence, you must experience chaos. The sound of the musicians tuning their instruments is really odd. Screeching strings echo; strange blasts come from the wind section. It is chaotic and unpleasant and you may be wondering how all that noise could actually become something beautiful.

Finally, the conductor emerges from stage left. The audience erupts in applause as he takes his position on his platform. He calmly raises his arms over his noisy orchestra. There it is ... the most important time of the whole evening and essential to everything else which follows: *silence*. The time for tuning their instruments is over. The discordant noise is no longer. The entire orchestra is still.

The conductor stands motionless, waiting for the complete attention of every musician, each of whom now forgets about their experience, the tuning of their instrument, the people around them. All they are focused on is the conductor and as he holds his arms up there – they remain focused and that essential silence continues. Finally, the conductor's arms move and the magnificent, soul-stirring music begins.

Why is it so hard for us in the 21st century western Church to be still and focus only on the Conductor? Like an orchestra tuning their instruments, contemporary western Christianity seems to be producing a lot chaotic and unpleasant noise in the name of God and the Church.

Rather than adding to the noise, perhaps it is time for us to finally be silent, to be still, and to wait in quiet anticipation for God to begin a new work in us and through us. Just some food for thought you may like to ponder.

February 23

Shake it off and step up!

One day, a farmer's donkey fell down into a well. The animal cried piteously for hours as the farmer tried to figure out what to do. Finally, he decided the animal was old, and the well needed to be covered up anyway. It just wasn't worth it to retrieve the donkey. A sad but necessary decision under the circumstances.

So, the farmer invited a number of his neighbours to come over and help him. They all grabbed a shovel and began to shovel dirt into the well. At first, when the donkey realized what was happening, he cried horribly. Then, to everyone's amazement, he went very quiet.

A few shovel-loads later, the farmer looked down the well. He was astonished at what he saw. With each shovel of dirt that hit his back, the donkey was doing something amazing. He would shake it off and take a step up onto the dirt pile!

As the farmer's neighbours continued to shovel dirt on top of the animal, he would shake it off and take a step up. Pretty soon, everyone was amazed as the donkey stepped up over the edge of the well and happily trotted off – with a look of relief on his dirt-covered face! The moral of this story is as simple as it is profound.

Life is going to shovel dirt on you, all kinds of dirt. Of that, I am sure. Some of it might be self-inflicted because of poor choices you have made, but most of it will just come from a broken world where we are surrounded by people and situations which throw dirt in our face every day.

The trick to getting out of the well is to **shake it off and step up.** Each of our troubles is a stepping stone. We can get out of the deepest wells just by not stopping and never giving up. Just shake it off and step up!

February 24

Be the Church – or Step Aside!

Why does the Church exist? It's not to get people together for meetings; or to keep our theology pure; defend our traditions; to look cool and appealing to the unchurched. But it's so easy to fall into one or more of those traps if we are not constantly reminding ourselves why we actually exist.

As defined clearly by Jesus in both the Great Commandment and the Great Commission, the Church exists to love God and share His love with others. We're not about denominations or creeds or meetings – although all of those have had and will continue to have a place. We are about relationships. It is our calling and our mandate to introduce people to Jesus, connect those people with each other, then prepare them to help others meet Jesus too.

Through the command to *make disciples,* Jesus created a self-perpetuating system to keep the Church alive, vibrant and adaptable. For over 2,000 years now the Church Jesus started and promised to build Himself has been the most relentlessly growing, most adaptable, most life-changing, most liberating organism in the history of the entire world.

Despite all the cries of alarm and concern, the Church Jesus is building is not in trouble. It's not dying. Its best days are not behind us. The Church is alive and well, with far greater days ahead than any we may have seen come and go so far. But the formats we're currently using are flawed.

I think we really need to rediscover and re-commit ourselves to truly *being* the Church Jesus called us to be. Or, while we're off chasing other ideas, someone else will offer a knock-off version that feels better than what we are doing. So, the challenge to us all is to *be the Church* or move aside and make room for those who will.

February 25

The Gospel in 90 Seconds

In the beginning there was light and life and love. There was the Father loving His Son in the joy of the Holy Spirit and everything has come from light and life and love. And out of this has come a world that is destined to share in light and life and love.

But we know that the world is not like that. We look around and we see darkness and death and disconnection. Where has that come from? Well, we've turned from the light, and when you turn from the light, where else do you go but to darkness.

And when you turn from love, where else do you go but disconnection? And when you turn from life, where else do you go but death? So, this is the kind of world we live in.

But what does love do? When love sees the beloved in trouble, love says, "Your pit will be my pit, your plight will be my plight, your debt will be my debt, your darkness will be my darkness, your death with be my death."

So, who is Jesus? Jesus is love come down. The Son of the Father comes and becomes our brother, to be with us in the darkness. To take that darkness on Himself on the cross. To take that disconnection on Himself. Even to take that death that we all deserve for turning from God. He took that on Himself – on the cross – plunged it down, into the hell that it deserves. And He rose up again, to light and life and love.

Then He says, "You in the darkness, do you want My light? You in death, do you want My life? You in disconnection, do you want My love?" And if we simply say "yes" to Jesus, then we get Jesus in our life. We get His Father as our Father, we get His Spirit as our Spirit, we get His future as our future. It's all for free and it's forever. So, do you want Jesus?

Source: *Glen Scrivener*

February 26

Pressing the Reset Button

I've always been drawn to the book of Acts. Apart from some of Paul's wonderful theological reflection in his letters, the book of Acts would have to be my most read part of the Scriptures. Our roots, our origin and our purpose as a Church are all there in this wonderful, confronting narrative.

In that narrative, we learn that this miracle which we call 'the Church' began as a loosely structured, dynamic community of called-out brothers and sisters who were led daily by the Holy Spirit to fulfil the mission of Jesus Christ. That Church then moved to Greece and became a philosophy. It moved to Italy and became an institution. It moved to Europe and became a culture. It then moved to America and became a business. We have been struggling to break free from those mission-killing yokes ever since!

Until the book of Acts becomes a commentary on today's Church, we are just dancing in the dark pretending we are making a difference. Now all of that only happened because those first disciples did as they were told by Jesus and we read what that was in the opening few verses in the book of Acts. Just before Jesus left them, this is what He said: *"Do not leave Jerusalem, but wait for the gift my Father promised, which you have heard me speak about. For John baptized with water, but in a few days, you will be baptized with the Holy Spirit."*

I wonder at times what would happen if we were ever brave enough to press the reset button on our Church. The best way to fix a mobile phone or computer that's not working is switch it off completely, then wait – with nothing happening – no activity, no work, no struggling, no frustration – just wait … and then switch on the power again, To our amazement – everything works again – the way it was designed to work. Perhaps that's what we need to do with the Church?

February 27

The Next Great Move of God

How will we know when the next great move of God is happening? I believe we will know when it is felt outside the Church as well as inside. All my life I've heard preachers talk about a coming worldwide revival - but it hasn't happened. There have been pockets of excitement. From the Jesus Movement of the 1970s to local spiritual outbreaks today. Along with controversy over their genuineness and questions about their effectiveness, the one thing they all have in common is that the average person has no idea they occurred. Because of that, I never thought I'd be the one to say this … but I think something may be happening now.

There's a God thing nagging at the back of my brain and challenging my heart. I can feel it rising on the fringes of the Church right now - and also outside the Church. It's popping up in the frustrations of sincere believers who are fed up; in the longing of seekers who don't like what they are not finding; and deep in the souls of believers who keep looking, working and praying for more, for better - for Jesus.

I'm tempted to give it a name, but I won't, because it won't fit any buzzwords. It's not *renewal, revival* or *reformation*. It's not *emergent, emerging* or *relevant*. And it will probably look more *pre-modern* than *modern* or *postmodern*. It will actually make us scramble for new labels but they will all fall short.

It's not about worship styles or different denominations. It's extra-denominational, multiethnic and cross-generational. It's holiness without legalism, grace without compromise, and peace that really does pass all understanding. It will meet people where they are, but it won't leave them there. It's coming *to* the Church - not *for* the Church, because Jesus wants to do something new through us, not just among us. Get ready, keep your eyes and your heart open. It's coming.

February 28

Heal our Nation, Lord

2 Chronicles 7:14 *"If my people, who are called by my name, will humble themselves and pray and seek my face and turn from their wicked ways, then I will hear from heaven, and I will forgive their sin and will heal their land."*

It doesn't matter how many scholars, linguistic experts and theologians you gather together to pull this verse apart; the end result is the same. Our God issued His people with a challenge many years ago which remains today. In issuing that challenge, God also gave us a glorious promise – but it's a promise which depends on our action for its fulfilment. It's one those "if, then" scenarios. God has promised to heal our land if we will humble ourselves, pray, seek His face and turn from sin. In other words, if the people of God live in a way which honours Him, then God will move and heal our land.

Why does God issue this conditional promise? God could just move in power and heal our nation and all nations any time He likes, He doesn't need us. So why involve us? Why even suggest that our obedience will in some way move the hand of God? The reason is as simple as it is confronting. God has always wanted to fulfil His plan and purpose in and through His people – His much-loved children. God doesn't just want the world to acknowledge Him – He wants the world to see Him in action in and through His people, which in our case is the Church which Jesus birthed and promised to build.

It is great to pray that God will heal our nation and we should never stop praying that. However, we also need to pray that we, the people of God, will hear the cries of God's lost children and rise up and take a stand and speak the truth. God promised to draw people to Himself, but we are the ones He commissioned to make disciples of those whom He draws.

February 29

God's Potential Principle

Everything in life was created with potential and possesses God's potential principle. In every acorn there's an oak tree; in every dream a Disneyland; in every child a great man or woman of God. Tragedy strikes when a tree dies in the seed, a dream dies in the mind, or a man or woman never dares to become who God created them to be. For millions of people in the world, visions die unseen, songs die unsung, plans die before they're executed and futures die buried in the past.

The Bible tells a story about talents and potential in Matthew 25:14-30. The talents in Christ's parable are symbols of the vast store of abilities our Creator has planted within each of us. In the story, the master of the estate entrusts some of his wealth to three of his servants. The first man invests his talent and doubles the wealth his master had entrusted to his care. The second servant does likewise. Their master is extremely pleased with both of their performances.

Finally, the master asks the third servant, *"What have you done with your talent?"* The servant answered, *"I was afraid to misuse the talent, so I carefully hid it and took no risks. Here it is! I am giving you back exactly what you gave me."*

The master was extremely upset and said that this servant was lazy and wicked. *"How dare you not develop the potential I entrusted to you and take full advantage of the possibilities you were provided. Someone take away what was given to him and throw this useless scoundrel out into the street!"*

We must learn to embrace, develop and effectively use the potential God has placed within each one of us. Failure can become our enemy if we accept it as fatal. Success can equally become our adversary if we simply settle for what we have already accomplished.

March 1

God's Job – Our Job

As I looked over my bookshelves recently, I noticed how many 'Church Growth' books I have bought and read over the last four decades in ministry. I reflected on the number of conferences I have invested time and money in during that period in pursuit of the same goal: Church growth. Then I tried to imagine all the time, energy and resources that have gone into Church growth in the last generation across the whole world. It was a sobering time of reflection which brought more questions than answers.

Is it naïve to wonder what the world and the Church would look like today if all that effort and all those resources had been invested exclusively in Church *health* instead of Church *growth?* Is it possible that if the Church had prioritized health, not as a means to growth, but as an end in itself, we would be in a greater position to represent Jesus to the world?

We are told that one of the reasons so many Churches remain small is a lack of faith. I wonder if the reverse could be true. Might our obsession with bigger Churches be rooted in a lack of faith? Perhaps we are afraid God might not do His job (building His Church) if we simply stayed faithful to doing our job (making disciples). Is it possible that the plethora of Church growth books and conferences in the last forty years has been our attempt to help God out – or do God's job?

I'm not against big Churches. I'm not against Church growth. I have Pastored congregations as small as ten and as large as five hundred. All were a blessing. But I'm just wondering out loud if all our Church growth strategies have diluted – or at least diverted our limited resources away from what should be our main priority: making disciples who produce healthy Churches, no matter what size they may be. Maybe … maybe not … but I think the question at least needs to be considered.

March 2

Only One Mission

If we truly want to stop 'going to church' and start 'being the Church' then we need to accept that the majority of what we have experienced as 'church' throughout our lives is man-made and part of an organization, an institution we have built and it did not come from God or the New Testament! But somewhere, buried under all those structures, programs, regulations, activities and buildings is the Church which Jesus promised to build and God has called me to devote my life to finding that true Church and re-connecting God's people to its heart, which is the mission of Christ.

To do that we need to get back the New Testament – as we once again, *"devote ourselves to the Apostles teaching, to fellowship to the breaking of bread and to prayer .."* (Acts 2:42) and re-capture the vision and the purpose of the Church Jesus birthed and promised to build. What is the purpose of that Church? Put simply, we are here to advance the Kingdom of God, by His grace and for His glory. The Kingdom of God is the rule and reign of Jesus Christ – as it has always been in heaven, so shall it increasingly be on earth.

The Church doesn't have a mission – Jesus has a mission and His mission has a Church. The mission of Christ is the only mission the Church ever had as Jesus commissioned us to make disciples and teach them everything He has taught us.

We must get back to the core purpose of the Church which is to join Jesus in His mission. We need to get back to the place where it's all about Jesus and His Kingdom; where it's all about the gospel – the good news of Who Jesus is and what He has done and promised to do; where it's all about bringing heaven to earth which is what Jesus did when He was here and what He has commissioned us to continue doing.

March 3

The Key to a Great Life

Every morning in Africa, a gazelle wakes up, knowing it must run faster than the fastest lion or it will die today. Every morning a lion wakes up, knowing it must outrun the slowest gazelle or it will starve today. It doesn't matter whether you are a lion or a gazelle; when the sun comes up, you had better be running! In the Christian life, it's not enough to simply wake up. We are called to run, to become more like Christ.

The Apostle Paul possessed the unusual ability to soar into spiritual heights one minute and then descend immediately into the valley of the intensely practical. In Philippians 3, Paul stressed the necessity of a personal experience with Jesus as a prerequisite to obtaining a right-standing with God. His daily fellowship with the Lord gave him the recourse, strength and power to live each day triumphantly.

Paul immediately assured his friends at Philippi that he knew that he had not yet completely arrived concerning Christian growth. But he also assured them, that he was striving each day to reach the goal Christ had for him. The Lord had a great purpose in mind for Paul. Paul was now seeking to reach God's goal for his life.

The Lord also has a purpose in mind for you and this involves several steps. Consider the three keys Paul gives us in this chapter that will enable us to have a great life in the Lord.

1. *Forget the past*
2. *Embrace the future*
3. *Keep your eyes on the goal*

Take some time to read Philippians chapter 3 and allow the Spirit of God to refocus you in your spiritual journey though Paul's challenging words.

March 4

Meeting God

A young boy wanted to meet God. He knew it was a long trip to where God lived, so he packed his suitcase with Tim Tams and a six-pack of apple juice and he started his journey. When he had gone about three blocks, he met an old man. He was sitting in the park just staring at some pigeons. The boy sat down next to him and opened his suitcase. He was about to take a drink from his apple juice when he noticed that the old man looked hungry, so he offered him a Tim Tam. The man gratefully accepted and smiled. His smile was so pleasant that the boy wanted to see it again, so he offered him an apple juice. Again, he smiled. The boy was delighted!

They sat there all afternoon eating and smiling, but they never said a word. As it grew dark, the boy realized how tired he was and he got up to leave, but before he had gone more than a few steps, he turned around, ran back to the old man, and gave him a hug. The man gave him his biggest smile ever.

When the boy opened the door to his house a short time later, his mother was surprised by the look of joy on his face. She asked him, *"What did you do today that made you so happy?"* He replied, *"I had lunch with God."* But before his mother could respond, he added, *"You know what? He's got the most beautiful smile I've ever seen!"*

Meanwhile, the old man, also radiant with joy, returned to his home. His son was stunned by the look of peace on his face and he asked, *"Dad, what did you do today that made you so happy?"* He replied, *"I ate Tim Tams in the park with God."* Then he added, *"You know, he's much younger than I expected."*

Too often we underestimate the power of a smile, a kind word, a listening ear, an honest compliment, or the smallest act of caring.

March 5

Encountering the Eternal

Sometimes life seems unreal. All of us have had days where we felt like we were in a fog. We may have felt like we were actually dreaming. At those times nothing seems real. How do we know what's real anyway? How do we know that this is not all a dream? People have been asking these questions for years.

Everyone wants to believe that they know what is real, but sometimes we doubt our own perception of reality. This is compounded by the fact that we live in an age of doubt. Scepticism, speculation and so many differing opinions all characterize our age. We live in a time where it's hard to know what to believe. It's hard to know what is true, what is real.

This is nothing new. In every age there have been the sceptics, doubters, speculators, philosophers and debaters of opinions. Perhaps today we have refined it a bit with the television talk show and social media where totally ignorant people can share their preposterous opinions and where gullible viewers and readers believe them!

Many people live their entire lives without thinking very much about unseen realities. Some are more concerned with the material world than the spiritual world, and when they do begin to think about the spiritual realm, they are often easily duped by those who seek to lead them into darkness, not light. Because most people have no knowledge and experience of the true eternal God, they are easy prey for many of the new age gurus who are ready and waiting to help them – help them out of their money, that is!

We need to know what is real. We need a personal encounter with the eternal - a personal experience of the life of God with us and within us. That's what Jesus came to give us.

March 6

Evangelism Myth Busted

For too long there has been a myth disseminated in the Church which says that evangelism is a particular ministry for which some are gifted and called and others are not. The trouble with that view is it cannot be found anywhere in the New Testament!

Of course, there are individuals with a specific gifting who have a more focused ministry in evangelism and we might even call such people 'evangelists.' However, the work of evangelism belongs to every disciple of Jesus Christ.

Evangelism is not a separate ministry. Evangelism is not a task to be ticked off on a list. Evangelism, when it is fully understood, is far more organic than that and it should permeate our lifestyle and be at the core of our life and calling as disciples of Christ.

Let me put it this way: evangelism is not the cause of something, evangelism is actually the fruit of something else.

Just think about that statement for a minute. Evangelism isn't something we do to achieve something else. Evangelism is what happens as a result of something else which happens. Evangelism is the natural outflow of a healthy Church.

The clearest example we have of this can been found at the very beginning of the Church as we know it. In the closing verses of Acts chapter 2 we have that wonderful snapshot of the Church in action and the fruit of that action. Read it again today.

Simply put, when we are doing what we have been called to do; when we are being who we are called to be – then Jesus does what He promised to do – He builds His Church!

March 7

Life is Not a Movie!

I enjoy a good movie. But I have to remind myself that so much of what I see on the screen is not what it seems. Much of it is an illusion. Hollywood is the land of illusion. If we believe everything we see in a movie, then we will believe …

> The ventilation system of any building provides a perfect hiding place.

> Men show no pain while taking the most ferocious beating but will wince with pain when a woman tries to clean their wounds.

> Cars that crash will almost always burst into flames.

> It is always possible to park directly outside any building you want to visit.

> Any lock can be picked by a credit card or a paper clip in seconds – unless the building is on fire and a child is trapped inside.

> It doesn't matter if you are heavily outnumbered in a fight involving martial arts; your enemies will always wait patiently to attack you one by one by dancing around you in a threatening manner until you have disposed of all their colleagues.

Sadly, those are not the only ways that movies twist reality. If we are not careful, many movies will subtly pressure us to believe that life is not a sacred and precious gift; that marriage is a consumer item rather than a life-long commitment; that the end always justifies the means – no matter how immoral and corrupt those means. If we are not careful, Hollywood will transform our worldview and the dividing line between reality and fantasy will blur and the choices we make will reflect an imagined world, not a real one. Beware!

March 8

Did God Really Say That?

That is the question Satan asked Adam and Eve just before they stepped over the line and plunged humanity into sin. Satan continues to ask that question every day and especially to those within the Church. One of Satan's primary tasks is to lead us away from the truth which God has spoken over time. A very long time ago, God incarnate, Jesus Christ, spoke this truth: *"I am the way, and the truth, and the life. No one comes to the Father except through me."* (John 14:6)

The Truth is always confrontational and the truth about Jesus Christ is the most confronting of all. His exclusive claims are offensive to the humanist mindset which dominates this modern age of 'inclusion.' However, if there was any way to God other than through Christ, then Christ didn't need to come and the entire Christian message is foolishness. If the life, death and resurrection of Jesus is not the only means by which we enter God's Kingdom, then why did He come?

You may already embrace Jesus' exclusive claim to be the way, the truth, the life and the only means by which we can be reconciled to God. You may have grown up listening to preaching like that. If that's what you still believe then I congratulate you and pray that God will strengthen your faith in that foundational truth and protect you from the tsunami of false teaching which is being unleashed on the Church every day. I wonder if you know that we have preachers in Churches across this land who do not believe Jesus is the only way to God. They do not believe that the exclusive claim of Jesus in John 14:6 is what Jesus 'really' said.

The Truth Jesus brought was and still is counter-cultural and in stark contrast to the wisdom of the world. Don't let that intimidate you. It still is the only truth that will set you free!

March 9

Pick the Fruit and Burn the Rest

A ministry colleague of mine, Dr Ken Blue, told me a story about his grandfather's farm in the USA where Ken used to spend holidays when he was a child. In the paddock next to the house there was this huge pear tree which Ken used to climb and sit at the top for hours. He felt like he could see forever from up there. It was his special place.

Many years later, after Ken was married with his own children and living a long way from the farm, his grandfather called him with some bad news. A huge storm had hit the farm and the magnificent old pear tree had been uprooted. He knew how special that tree was to Ken and so he asked him if he wanted to see it one last time before it was removed.

Ken drove out to the farm, reflecting on the way about the special times he had in that tree. As soon as he arrived, Ken and his grandfather walked over to the next paddock and they both just stood there in silence next to this majestic old tree, which was totally uprooted and lying on the ground.

Ken finally said, through tears, *"So what do we do now grandfather?"* The wise old man put his arm on Ken's shoulder and said, *"Son, we pick the fruit and burn the rest."* That one statement remained with Ken the rest of his life and became a powerful principle for living.

As we face each new chapter in our lives and reflect on the journey which brought us to that point, we need to be able to 'pick the fruit' – that is, learn from the past; grow from our mistakes; cherish the memories; be thankful for the good times; but then we need to 'burn the rest' – all of those disappointments, failures and things we wish had happened differently. We have to move forward into the 'new day' God has prepared for us and not stand there beside a dead tree longing for a day which has passed.

March 10

The Ten Most Important Words of Jesus

Depending on your translation, you will find there are just under 800,000 words in the Bible. If you remove all the duplications across the Gospels, a little over 1,000 of those words were spoken by Jesus. So, to select only ten of those words and declare them to be the 'most important' is a bold move. However, I am confident in my selection.

The first five words appear in the dialogue between Jesus and Peter which we can read in Matthew 16, just after Peter rightly declares Jesus to be the Messiah. The second five words appear in what we call 'The Great Commission' at the very end of Matthew's gospel.

Matthew 16:16-18 *"Simon Peter answered, "You are the Messiah, the Son of the living God." Jesus replied, "Blessed are you, Simon son of Jonah, for this was not revealed to you by flesh and blood, but by my Father in heaven. And I tell you that you are Peter, and on this rock* **I will build my Church***, and the gates of Hades will not overcome it."*

Matthew 28:18-20 *"Then Jesus came to them and said, "All authority in heaven and on earth has been given to me.* **Go therefore and make disciples** *of all nations, baptizing them in the name of the Father and of the Son and of the Holy Spirit, and teaching them to obey everything I have commanded you .."*

If we put these two statements together, we see the simplicity of the mission of Christ and our part in it: *"I will build my Church, go therefore and make disciples."* When Jesus builds His Church, He does so by using disciples just like you and me. Through imperfect people like us, God works to create His perfect and beautiful Bride, the Church. What a wonderful, yet mysterious partnership we share with God. May we have the courage today to do our job and trust God to do His.

March 11

Making Music

On Saturday November 18, 1995, world-renowned violinist Itzhak Perlman came on stage to give a concert at the Lincoln Centre in New York City. If you have ever been to a Perlman concert, you know that just getting onto the stage is no small achievement for him. He was stricken with polio as a child, and so he has braces on both legs and walks with the aid of two crutches. To see him walk across the stage, painfully and slowly, is an awesome sight. Then he sits down, slowly, puts his crutches on the floor, undoes the clasps on his legs, tucks one foot back and extends the other foot forward. Then he bends down and picks up the violin, puts it under his chin, nods to the conductor and proceeds to play.

As always, on this occasion, the audience held their breath as they waited for the master to play. Just as he finished the first few bars, one of the strings on his violin broke. You could hear it snap – it went off like gunfire across the room. There was no mistaking what that sound meant. Everyone knew what he now must do. He would have to go through the painful process of leaving the stage to get a new string or a backup violin. But he didn't. Instead, the master waited a moment, closed his eyes and then signalled to the conductor. The orchestra began and Perlman played with passion, power and such purity as people had never heard before.

It is impossible to play a symphonic work with just three strings but that night Itzhak Perlman refused to accept that. You could see him modulating, changing, re-composing the piece in his head. When he finished, there was an awesome silence in the room, before everyone rose and cheered. When interviewed later about what happened, Perlman said, *"Sometimes it's the artist's task to find out how much music you can still make with what you have left."* What a wonderful life lesson for each of us.

March 12

Relationship, not Religion

Unfortunately, the word *religion* has been used in a positive or descriptive sense all throughout history to describe the Christian faith. People still refer to that which you and I believe in and live as *'The Christian Religion.'* But when you look up the definitions of religion in secular dictionaries you will not find any mention of the word *relationship*. That is interesting because even a quick browse through the Bible will reveal to the most unenlightened, sin-impaired mind that the Christian faith is <u>all</u> about *relationship!*

From Genesis to Revelation we have the story of God creating us to be in relationship with Himself and with each other. The Bible is about relationships and where they went wrong and what God did to fix that and what we are meant to do (and not do) to participate in His global campaign to re-establish close, intimate, eternal relationships with all His lost children.

I am not talking in some abstract philosophical sense here. That is what religion does. I am talking about our personal relationship with God – our face-to-face intimate communion. That concept is foreign to religion, and yet that is what the Bible is all about! That's what the Great Commission is about. That's what the Golden Rule is about. That's what the Ten Commandments are about. That's what every teaching and instruction from Jesus and Paul and all the Biblical writers – it's all about: *relationship*. None of it is about religion.

Religion is our feeble attempt to establish and maintain a relationship with God through every means possible other than that which He ordained, provides and empowers. What Jesus secured for us through His life, death and resurrection is a new relationship with God. That's what the Christian faith is all about and that's the good news the Church should be bringing to the world every day!

March 13

Jesus + Nothing

You may have grown up in the Church or you may have come to faith later in life. Either way, you heard the message of forgiveness of sin, the love and acceptance of God, eternal life in a new relationship with Him, and your heart was pierced by the Holy Spirit as you responded to what God had already done for you. You knew without any doubt that God was real and powerful. He was your gracious, loving heavenly Father. You were filled with joy and everyone around you knew it.

Then maybe you were taught that if you want to go on from there – if you want to be a 'first-class' Christian and really see the blessings of God, then you needed to add disciplines to your life and soon these disciplines became standards or rules by which you judged yourself and others. You were told that Jesus is the only way to the Father, but then you need to do your bit. That is a lie from hell, and we desperately need to expose that lie with the gospel: 'Jesus + nothing!'

Let me make it clear – if you hear 'Jesus plus something' you are not hearing an improvement on the gospel; or a new version of the gospel; you are not hearing a distortion of the gospel; you are hearing the absolute destruction of the gospel, along with its integrity and its power. When, by the revelation and power of God's Spirit, we have all those 'extras' removed as requirements, then the beauty, purity and power of the gospel will return to our hearts and lives.

This is what all those brothers and sisters who have walked away from the Church and God desperately need to hear: the true gospel. When it comes to our basic understanding of God and our relationship with Him, most of us don't need to hear something new, we just need to believe what we heard first.

Jesus + nothing is our salvation *and* our life!

March 14

No Spectators Beyond this Point

In the early Church everyone was a minister of the gospel and everyone was equipped to advance the kingdom of heaven by God's grace and for God's glory. There were no spectators – only team members. The New Testament only makes sense in the context of the early Church. Many of the exhortations we have in the New Testament only make sense when the Church looks like and functions like the Church Jesus birthed and the Spirit empowered. God's intention was that every disciple would be a spirit-filled, spirit-led, fully equipped minister of the gospel, exercising their gifts as God intended.

There were no spectators – only team members. There was no 'clergy' and 'laity' – only disciples operating within their calling and gifting. Yes, there were leaders and overseers, but they were never elevated above those whom they led. They led alongside their brothers and sisters. They didn't have any separated, elevated coaches, only player-coaches.

No doubt you have heard the old saying, 'Those who can – do and those who can't – teach.' It is a derogatory dig at those in leadership who often seem to separate themselves from the 'real people' on the ground and in the front line of the battle. In the New Testament Church, that was not the case because those who taught were also those in the front line of ministry, side by side with the ones they were called to nurture, teach, equip and encourage.

Every disciple of Jesus Christ was expected to grow up into Christ and be equipped with everything they needed to do God's will. Some of those gifts were leadership gifts, but there were many more gifts bestowed upon the people and they were all required to work in concert with each other. The further we drift from the New Testament model, the more impotent, irrelevant and ineffective the Church becomes.

March 15

God's Ways are not our Ways

We have all heard the saying, 'God works in mysterious ways.' In fact, many people believe that's actually a verse in the Bible. I can assure you that it's not – but there is a Scripture in Isaiah that does convey a similar thought.

Isaiah 55:8,9 *"For My thoughts are not your thoughts, nor are your ways My ways, says the Lord. For as the heavens are higher than the earth, so are My ways higher than your ways, and My thoughts than your thoughts."*

It may seem reasonable to us that God would open a certain door of opportunity for us, instead He may close the door. It seems reasonable to us that if God loves us and cares about our happiness that He would heal our sick loved one and give us more time with them; instead, He calls them home.

It seems reasonable to us that God would bring our time of trial or trouble to an end after we have asked Him to; and instead, He may allow that trial to go on and on. It seems reasonable to us that God would give us exactly what we asked for; and instead, He gives us something very different.

One of the greatest challenges to all of us in the Christian life is reaching a level of spiritual maturity where we completely trust God, regardless of His response or lack of response.

The reason why that may pose such a great challenge to us is because God doesn't always act as we expect Him to act and when God doesn't do things the way we think He ought to, some become disappointed or disillusioned with God; some get angry and bitter towards God; and some even lose their faith completely and give up on God.

We simply need to accept that God's ways are not our ways.

March 16

I Will Build My Church

Jesus said, *"I will build my Church."* (Matthew 16:18)
Jesus never said, *"I will build my social service agency."*
Jesus never said, *"I will build my para-church ministry."*
Jesus never said, *"I will build my university, college or school."*
Jesus said, *"I will build my Church."*

If you are passionate about the Church, then I want you to be encouraged today. I want you to know that you are involved in something extraordinarily important.

You and I and all of Jesus' disciples have been called to join Him in His Church-building mission. But we must never, ever, forget that it is HIS mission – from start to finish.

Mark 4:26-27 *"This is what the kingdom of God is like. A man scatters seed on the ground. Night and day, whether he sleeps or gets up, the seed sprouts and grows, though he does not know how."*

We don't know how to grow the kingdom of God. We don't know how to build the Church. I have been to many Church growth conferences over the years. I have read many Church growth books. I've lost count of the seminars and workshops I have attended on Church growth. The truth is, we don't know how to grow a Church.

The Bible says we cannot know this because that job belongs to Jesus, not us. It is mysterious, it is deep, it is awesome. You go to bed at night. You get up in the morning. You sow your seed. And it sprouts and you don't know not how. In fact, if anyone claims they do know how to plant a Church or grow a Church, it isn't the true Church they're growing.

This is, and always will be, a work of the Lord. It is a profound and supernatural mystery but it's also a promise.

March 17

His Name is John

John has wild hair, he wears a T-shirt with holes, torn jeans and he has no shoes. He is kind of esoteric and very, very bright. He became a Christian while attending university. Across the street from the campus is a well-dressed, very conservative Church congregation. They would really love to develop a ministry to the university students.

One day John decides to check out one of their services. He walks in with no shoes, torn jeans, his crumpled T-shirt and wild hair. The service has already started and so John starts down the aisle looking for a seat. The Church is completely packed, and he can't find a seat anywhere. By now people are looking uncomfortable, but no one says anything.

John gets closer and closer to the pulpit and when he realizes there are no seats, he just sits down on the carpet. (Although perfectly acceptable behaviour at a university fellowship, trust me, this had never happened in this Church before!) By now the people are really uptight and the tension is high.

About this time, the Pastor looks toward the back of the Church and sees a Church elder slowly making his way toward John. Now this elder is in his eighties, has silver-grey hair, a three-piece suit, tie and a pocket watch – a godly man, very elegant, very dignified, very courtly and he walks with a cane and so it takes a while to reach this young man.

When he arrives at the front of the Church, this elderly man drops his cane on the floor, and with great difficulty he lowers himself and sits next to John on the carpet so he's not alone.

Everyone chokes up with emotion. When the Pastor gains control, he says, *"What I am about to preach, you will never remember. What you have just seen, you will never forget."*

March 18

God, I Don't Understand

Have you ever uttered the words above? Have you ever faced a set of circumstances in your life which made no sense as you struggled to work out what God was doing? I'm sure you have uttered these words more than once.

Think about Abraham, the moon-worshipper living on Ur. He receives an amazing call from a God he knows nothing about, and he packs up everything and heads out to an unknown destination. Then this God promises this very old man and his wife a son. Sarah is barren and Abraham is 100 years old!

Then there is Moses. God ask him to lead God's people out of captivity and into the Promised Land. What should have been an 8-day journey takes 40 years and a whole generation dies before they make it into the land and Moses doesn't even get to be there.

David is anointed to be king as a very young man, but God does not open the door for him to begin his reign for many years. Worse than that, the current king is becoming more deranged by the day and tries multiple times to kill David.

Think about the disciples on that first Palm Sunday when hundreds of thousands of people line the road to worship the Christ. Within days, Jesus is betrayed, arrested, whipped, spat on, convicted on trumped up charges and then executed.

So where do you go when you just don't understand? I go to Philippians 4:7 where we are promised, *"… the peace of God, which transcends all understanding, will guard your hearts and your minds in Christ Jesus."*

If understanding is our focus, we will struggle through life. If we really want to experience the peace of God, then we need to give up the right to understand.

March 19

Follow Me

When Jesus calls me to follow Him as He heals or delivers people, it's a joy. When Jesus calls me to follow Him on Palm Sunday – surrounded by a million adoring supporters – it's unbelievable. When Jesus calls me to follow Him to Mary and Martha's village to see Lazarus rise from the dead, I am totally gobsmacked. When Jesus calls me to follow Him to the mountainside and hear Him deliver the most challenging and heart-gripping sermon I will ever hear – I am blessed.

But what about when Jesus calls me into His disappointment, His pain and His darkest hour? Will I follow Jesus there? Will I follow Jesus into my Garden of Gethsemane and watch my friends fall asleep and fail to keep watch for me? When Jesus calls me to sweat blood in anticipation of what is about to unfold for me, will I also be able to say, *"Not my will, but Yours be done?"* Am I prepared to follow Jesus there?

What about when Jesus calls me to face my accusers as they lie and make up charges so they can convict me and sentence me without due cause? Can I, like Jesus, keep my mouth closed and not defend myself?

Truly following Jesus is not selective. We don't get to choose the time, the place or the circumstances. Jesus calls us to follow Him absolutely everywhere! We too must face our Judas, our Peter, our mock trial, our unjust conviction, our Calvary – whatever they look like in our world. We will face these realities many, many times in our earthly life and this is all part of following Jesus.

We will never have to die the death of Jesus – His atoning sacrifice was unique. However, we should also know today more than ever, that when Jesus says, *"Take up your cross and follow me,"* He means that we must follow Him everywhere – yes, even, and especially to His place of greatest suffering.

March 20

Why we Worship

I remember in my early years as a Christian we had 'after Church' on Sunday night. We would go to someone's home who had a piano and we would just sing for an hour non-stop and worship God. Of course, supper always followed, but worship was what filled most of our time. I think it was those times which helped form in me the priority and joy of worshipping God.

Worship is where we can actually minister to God. He's not an egotist in need of our affirmations. We are the ones who really benefit from worship. It's important for us to recognise Who God is and when we see Him clearly, as He really is, we are changed in the process.

In fact, it can be said that we become like whatever we worship. People who worship money – become those who value material things. In fact, people who worship false gods of any description become just like those false gods.

The Bible says that God is looking for those who worship 'in Spirit and in truth.' The term 'in Spirit' identifies the nature of worship, it's a Holy Spirit-born activity. The Holy Spirit is really the One Who leads us to the Father and the Son to give them glory and honour.

But we are also called to worship 'in truth' and that means nothing is hidden. When we worship, we come to God in honesty; we come to God as an open book; we come with all that we are – our successes, our failures, the good, the bad, the ugly … and we lay it all before Him.

I have found through the years is if I pay attention to His worth and give Him honour – I change, I am transformed. We worship because God is worthy. But in that process, God transforms us more into the image of His Son.

March 21

Don't Take the Bait

Apparently, the Church is losing the culture wars. We must be, Facebook says so! Today it might be about genderless bathrooms; tomorrow it will be something else. Each issue is presented as 'The Most Important Issue of Our Time!' Until the next time, of course.

Many Christians – including leaders – get drawn into these endless debates with two primary responses: we complain, and we may even fight back. I would like to propose a third option: rise above it and don't take the bait! Quit complaining and being drawn into someone else's fight. When we do either of those things, we're operating in reactive mode. We're on the defence. We are letting others set the agenda. Following Jesus means following His lead always.

Have you noticed how Jesus never allowed others to pull Him into their debate? Not ever! His enemies tried to bait Him with an impossible question about taxation (Luke 20:20-26), instead of descending to their level He raised the conversation to His level. Debate over!

When His disciples saw a man born blind, they wanted Jesus to pick sides in a theological debate. Instead, He healed the blind man (John 9). Debate over!

Jesus was undeniable in His actions and His words. He was always 'on message' and never lost sight of His mission and purpose and never involved winning arguments – certainly not arguments about the moral issues of His day (and there were plenty!). He rose above all of that and focussed on His mission. He has called us to live the same way – always engaged with Jesus' agenda – nobody else's. Every minute you spend being drawn into the agenda of others is a minute you're not spending pursuing Christ's agenda.

March 22

Finding God in the Valley

Some of the most beautiful flowers in all of creation grow at the bottom of the darkest, most treacherous valleys. Very few people find them because we are all so focussed on climbing out of the valley and up to the mountains.

I have heard and preached this many times. But when you are the one at the bottom of the valley, trying to drag yourself through the mud and focus through the fog, sometimes you just want to slap the person who would suggest you look for flowers! But then it happens. You find one – usually where you least expect it, and when you are close to giving up.

This flower is so out of context to your current life and experience and yet there it is – unfolding right in front of you and nobody but you and God see it. It is just for you – just for that moment. You can ignore it, trample on it, despise it; or behold its beauty and know that God placed that flower there just for you and if you let it, that flower will change your life.

I have not had a lot of 'flower in the valley' moments in my life, but the ones I have experienced are memorable and have defined my life, my ministry and my view of God. Once I finally fall on my face in the mud, surrender to the fog and let God know that I have really had enough pain, betrayal, disappointment and heartache … then it happens: the flower blooms and everything changes – in an instant.

So let me encourage you, fellow valley-dweller. If you are not there now, you will be at some point and when you get there, don't be so focussed and so determined on getting out of the valley. Let the valley do its job.

When you learn to find God in the valley in a way you will never find Him anywhere else, your whole perspective on life changes.

March 23

An Inexhaustible Strength

Isaiah 40:30-31 *"Even youths grow tired and weary, and young men stumble and fall; but those who hope in the Lord will renew their strength. They will soar on wings like eagles; they will run and not grow weary, they will walk and not be faint."*

Sometimes I just get weary of it all. Sometimes I'm tired in body and in spirit. My strength is low, my determination is lower, I'm irritated with life, and fed up with everyone around me. At times like these, I'm ready to tell everybody where to get off and just go to bed.

Have you ever felt like that? Sadly, one of the plights of people, even redeemed people, is that our strength is exhaustible. We learn that we are not superhuman and we become weary.

While we must face the reality of weariness, there is hope from the Scriptures of a deeper reality in which we can tap into the inexhaustible strength of God. The above text from Isaiah reveals that although we all get weary, there is a source of strength for those who trust in and wait upon the Lord.

Do you need an inexhaustible source of strength for your life? Wouldn't it be fantastic to be able to draw upon an unlimited reserve of power to get you through the difficult times? That is precisely the promise contained in this text.

The prophet Isaiah points us towards two realities. One is really obvious: it is the reality that we all grow weary. The other reality is deeper. It's the reality that as we act in faith, trusting in and expectantly waiting on God, we will find that inexhaustible strength which can only come from Him.

That leaves us with one simple, but really important question: which reality are we willing to settle for?

March 24

One Act of Kindness

One stormy night many years ago, an elderly man and his wife entered the lobby of a small hotel in Philadelphia. Trying to get out of the rain, the couple approached the front desk hoping to get some shelter for the night. *"Could you possibly give us a room here?"* the husband asked. The clerk, a friendly man with a great smile, looked at the couple and explained that there were three conventions in town and they were booked out, but as he was working all night, he would be happy to let them stay in his room. The couple were thankful.

As he paid his bill the next day, the man said to the clerk, *"You are the kind of manager who should be the boss of the best hotel in the United States. Maybe someday I'll build one for you."*

Two years passed. The clerk had almost forgotten the incident when he received a letter from the old man. It recalled that stormy night and enclosed a round-trip ticket to New York, asking the young man to pay them a visit. The old man met him in New York and led him to a great new building there, a pale reddish stone, with turrets and watchtowers thrusting high into the sky.

"That," said the older man, *"is the hotel I have just built for you to manage."*

"You must be joking," the young man said.

"I can assure you I am not," said the older man, a sly smile playing around his mouth.

The man's name was William Waldorf-Aster; the magnificent structure was the original Waldorf-Astoria Hotel. The young clerk who became its first manager was George C. Boldt. This young clerk never foresaw the turn of events that would lead him to become the manager of one of the world's most glamorous hotels! It all began with one act of kindness.

March 25

One Thing I Seek

Psalm 27:4 *"One thing I ask of the LORD, this is what I seek: that I may dwell in the house of the LORD all the days of my life, to gaze upon the beauty of the LORD and to seek him in his temple."*

What is it that you seek? Are the things which you seek worth seeking? Some of the things we seek may not be what the Lord desires for us. Some things may even hurt us if we were to acquire them. We must therefore be careful to evaluate what we seek in light of the worthiness of that thing. We must also ask ourselves why we are seeking those things.

The road of life has many bumps and potholes. As we weave our way around the hairpin curves and over the steep hills, we find that some things which we thought were important no longer seem so important.

All of us struggle at times and have problems. Everywhere people are hurting and are in need, and what the world offers to meet those needs are only shallow substitutes of the real thing. It is the real thing which we should be seeking. That should be our priority in this day. We must seek that which will make life truly worth living.

King David was a man beset with the circumstances of life. He had enjoyed some measure of success in His life, yet that success was not without its problems. Not only did David have personal problems, but he also had people problems. On many occasions there were people who were set against him, seeking to take his life. David certainly knew what it was like to struggle with the serious issues of life.

However, David also knew what was important to seek. And in the Bible verse above, we see revealed for us life's most important priority. There is one thing above all others which we should seek. May that be your guide each day.

March 26

The Servant's Heart

Imagine if you will that your doctor has just told you that you have a month left to live. How would you live your final days? Think about that for a minute. Would you go bungee jumping or perhaps skydiving? Maybe you would go buy that beautiful new car that you have always wanted. Maybe you would take that long-awaited trip or Pacific Cruise.

We all have lots of dreams that have gone unfulfilled that we might try harder than ever to fulfil during those last few precious weeks. How many of us would gather together our closest companions and wash their filthy feet? Well, that's what we find Jesus doing in His final hours before His death. As John writes, *"Jesus knew that the Father had put all things under His power, and that He had come from God and was returning to God."* (John 13:3).

How odd that Jesus, knowing how little time He had left, would spend His few remaining moments, washing the disciples' feet – but that's what He did. Imagine the disciples' surprise when Jesus got up from the table, took off His outer garments, wrapped a towel around His waist and then, filling a basin with water, He bent low and did the unthinkable. He washed their feet. Jesus saw fit to teach the disciples a very important lesson that night before leaving them.

What is it that Christ is trying to teach us in this fascinating story in Scripture? I believe that Christ, through this amazing and confronting event, was trying to teach us the essence of true Christian love and show us a servant's heart in action.

When Jesus said He came to serve, and give His life as a ransom for many, this is a powerful snapshot of what that service looks like. The next snapshot was of Him dying on a cross in order to save us from an eternity without Him.

March 27

Trust in the Lord

Proverbs 3:5-6 *"Trust in the Lord with all your heart and lean not on your own understanding; in all your ways acknowledge him, and he will make your paths straight."*

Why trust in the Lord with all your heart? Because your heart is much bigger than your head. What you can fathom; what you can grasp; what you can see; what you can perceive; what you can connect to from the heart is so much more significant than what you can embrace with your mind. It's not that the mind is insignificant, the mind is important, but the Bible teaches some very profound things on the priority of the heart over the mind.

What happens with 'small-minded' people is they put the mind first. If the mind is first; if I understand everything that's going on in my Christian life; if I can fully explain where I'm at in life; if I understand everything that's happening, then I have actually reduced God to my size.

It's actually important that I have parts of my life which are buried in mystery. In our walk with God, mystery is as important as revelation.

In our quest to know God, to serve Him and to illustrate His kingdom purposes, we gain understanding. Things that I didn't understand several years ago, I now understand. That's how it's supposed to be. We are meant to increase in our understanding. But in our progression in the Kingdom, we have to always allow room for the stuff that we can't explain; the stuff we can't control in our life, so that we have a reason to trust God.

Our commitment should be to not let our understanding be the source of our strength. Rather let our strength always come from our heartfelt abandonment to the purposes of God.

March 28

Are You Stumbling or Seeing?

In Proverbs 29:18 we read a simple, yet profound truth, *"Where there is no vision, the people perish."* The word 'vision' has been given all kinds of meanings in the modern world and most of them have nothing to do with this verse.

But when the NIV Bible was written, the translators tried to be more accurate to the original meaning of the text and this verse became, *"Where there is no revelation, the people cast off restraint."* What the KJV translated 'vision', the NIV translates 'revelation.' You see, vision can (and most often does) come from us. But revelation comes from God. Now this is not just an issue about how a verse is translated. This verse, when properly understood, is an explanation for nearly all of the Church's highs and lows throughout our history.

The early Church exploded and grew at a phenomenal rate because they understood this verse. By contrast, the Church of today has been shrinking and losing its relevance and impact in the world because we have lost that simple truth.

When the day-by-day revelation of God is not continually being sought, discerned and applied, then we 'cast off restraint.' We go our own way – tragically thinking it's God's way because we opened our 'vision' meeting in prayer!

When Eugene Petersen wrote The Message, a contemporary translation of the Bible, he unpacked this verse even more and made it abundantly clear what Proverbs 29:18 really means for us today. I love this version:

"If people can't see what God is doing, they stumble all over themselves; But when they attend to what He reveals, they are most blessed."

Are you stumbling or seeing?

March 29

Receptive Soil

We sometimes think of the parable of the Sower as one of the ways Christ trained His disciples - and by extension, the Church - to be faithful evangelists. But is that the point of the parable? It doesn't describe any techniques or methods for sowing the seed of the gospel. In actual fact the parable isn't about the Sower at all; it's really about the soil.

Christ delivered this familiar parable to help prepare His disciples for the inevitability of people not responding to the gospel. The Lord was preparing them to face rejection in their future ministries. We need to learn the same lesson.

Here's the basic point of this parable. The result of the hearing of the gospel depends on the condition of the heart of the recipient, not the skill or method of the Sower. It is also not the attractiveness of the seed. It's all about the condition of the soil. So, what we are dealing with in this matter of evangelism is the character of those who hear.

I have known Christians all my life who have backed away from witnessing for Christ because they feel they are not effective because they don't see a lot of results. This parable is given to us to dispel that ridiculous notion, that the salvation of people around us is dependent on the skill of the Sower or on some manipulated capability in the seed. That's a lie. It's dependent on the condition of the soil.

When sowing the seed, you have to understand that it falls on unresponsive hearts, impulsive hearts, preoccupied hearts, or prepared, receptive hearts. We simply must be faithful to sow the seed and trust the Lord to oversee the results. Trust God to 'plough the field' and prepare people's hearts. If we are faithful to sow the seed, and trust God to do His job, then by His grace, the fruit will come.

March 30

Don't Share Your Faith

The postmodern culture in which we all live today really can't tolerate biblical evangelism. Their commitment to subjectivity and relativism cannot accommodate a faith that is exclusive, narrow, and declares non-negotiable truth. That shouldn't surprise us - Jesus told us to expect to be hated in the same way that He was hated (John 15:18).

The Scriptures also warns against appeasing (James 4:4) or embracing (Romans 12:2) the world's values. But we know that's easier said than done. We are called to separatism without monasticism; being in the world but not of the world. We can't live our lives and engage our mission field without coming into contact with our anti-Christian culture.

For most of us it's difficult to avoid immersing ourselves in the postmodern thinking of our friends, our families and colleagues. We see signs of this even in evangelism. The term *'share your faith'* is deeply embedded in the evangelical vernacular. Most of us use this term as a synonym for our evangelistic encounters. But those words reek of postmodern subjectivity! We don't share our faith, we announce it. It's not *our* faith, it is the *"faith that was once for all delivered to the saints."* (Jude 3). It is the Gospel of Christ.

I rejoice that the Christian gospel rests on objective historical facts that transcend my own experiences or validation: God's creation, man's fall and Christ's redemption.

The truth of the biblical Gospel crashes through all man-made barriers with God's own written testimony. It doesn't hinge on our personal skills or powers of persuasion. Paul reminds us that Gospel itself is *"the power of God for salvation to everyone who believes."* (Romans 1:16). So, don't share your faith, share Jesus Christ and Him alone!

March 31

Desiring Heaven

"He is no fool who gives what he cannot keep to gain that which he cannot lose."

Jim Elliot, the famous missionary, wrote those words in his journal on October 28, 1949. Just six years later they became a profound epitaph of his own life.

In 1952, Elliot traded the affluence of western civilization for the remote jungles of Ecuador. By 1956, he had been martyred at the hands of the very people he went to evangelize. Elliot probably didn't expect to die so young (28), but he knew the dangers were real. When most of his peers opted for safety and comfort, Jim Elliot chose to take the gospel where it had never been preached. Elliot owned an eternal perspective on life that all believers should embrace. As Jesus said:

Matthew 6:19–20 *"Do not store up for yourselves treasures on earth, where moth and rust destroy, and where thieves break in and steal. But store up for yourselves treasures in heaven."*

Yet for many Christians, there remains a huge chasm between believing Christ's words and living up to them. The promises on the pages of Scripture tend to take a back seat to the many tangible comforts of Western affluence that we experience every day, and it isn't easily overcome. Our lack of heavenly mindedness is a serious problem in the Church today.

Heaven is the true and ultimate home all Christians should long for. We should share the same passion as the Old Testament saints who *"desire a better country, that is, a heavenly one. Therefore, God is not ashamed to be called their God; for He has prepared a city for them"* (Hebrews 11:16). God's eternal rewards infinitely surpass anything this earth has to offer and outweigh every temporal hardship that we could possibly experience. We should desire heaven above all else.

April 1

The Pursuit of Happiness

Where does lasting happiness come from? Pleasure isn't the path to happiness. Possessions aren't the path to happiness. Isn't it ridiculous to spend your whole life trying to make yourself happy with things that are one day all going to end up in the garbage?

True happiness is never found in the cursed earth, and it's never ultimately and finally found in the evil system of this world. Why? Because physical things do not touch the soul. You cannot fill a spiritual need with something physical.

I'm talking here about contentment. I'm talking here about satisfaction. I'm talking here about what we tend to call happiness, inward happiness, a condition of bliss which is neither the result of external circumstances nor is it the result of some outside influence which is subject to change.

Jesus is committed to providing true happiness. For Jesus, the people who are truly happy are those with the right attitudes. It's not what you possess; rather it's poverty of spirit, mourning, gentleness, hunger and thirst for righteousness, mercy, purity and peace.

Such things produce happiness. It's attitudes that are Godlike attitudes that literally come to us by virtue of us sharing His divine nature.

Jesus taught that happiness starts from the inside and works its way out. And even where there is suffering and sorrow, happiness is not cancelled out - it is, in fact, generally aided and increased.

The kind of happiness which Jesus provides is not fleeting. It is grounded in the unchanging character of Christ Himself, and it's available to all who know Him and love Him.

April 2

Responsibility

In our quest for spiritual maturity, in our desire to grow up into Christ, I believe there are many obstacles to overcome and there are many significant issues to tackle. However, I firmly believe that there is one issue, one word in fact, which lies at the heart of Christian maturity; one foundation stone which is the key in building a strong faith and the key to our long-term effectiveness in the kingdom of God. That word is **responsibility.** This is the key to maturity.

You may say that Jesus is the foundation of a fruitful Christian life, but I want to be bold enough to suggest that Jesus is not the key to maturity. It is possible to have Jesus in your heart and be born again and still not be mature in Christ and still not be living a victorious, abundant Christian life. If you doubt that statement, just look around. There are thousands of defeated, depressed, self-absorbed, powerless Christians right across this nation and they are all saved – they all have Jesus in their hearts. They are defeated and beaten up because they have not taken responsibility for their life, regardless of how hard it is. They have not made the right choices.

If having Jesus in your life was the key to maturity, then we would all be instantly mature the moment we accepted His gift of salvation. That is clearly not the case. Responsibility is the key to maturity.

Remember the Garden of Eden? Just after the forbidden fruit was tasted, God asks Adam, *"What have you done?"* Adam immediately points to Eve and says, *"She made me do it."* When it was Eve's turn to explain, she blamed the serpent! Refusing to take responsibility for our actions is part of our fallen DNA.

The sign of immaturity is the failure to take responsibility for our choices and our life. Responsibility is not the most popular word today, but it may be the most important.

April 3

Embracing what we Already Have

A born-again believer is a new creation. But deception keeps people from accessing what Jesus has already accomplished. Let me put it this way: everything we will ever experience in this life, every breakthrough, every victory, everything we will experience throughout all eternity, has already been secured by Jesus and placed in an account for us. Part of the struggle we have is our ignorance over what He's already done and ignorance over what we already possess.

When we don't realize what we already have, we end up spending our prayer life praying for what God has already secured for us. When you pray for what you already have, you can't recognize the answer. Let me say that again. When you pray for what you already possess, you're already incapable of recognizing the answer to that prayer.

If I pray for what I already have, and I don't recognize it, then I don't have access to that joy from answered prayers. I now have to get my joy from the discipline of prayer. When you get your joy from the discipline of prayer, you begin to exalt form, above power and presence. Form above breakthrough. This is the birthplace of religion.

Our greatest challenge is to embrace what we already possess. This is what, *"Your kingdom come, your will be done on earth as it is in heaven"* really means. All healing; all salvation; all comfort; all righteousness, joy and peace have been secured for us already in Christ and that is our reality in the Kingdom of God. Our task is to progressively live in the reality of God's kingdom and by so doing we literally manifest that kingdom here for all to see.

So, let's stop asking God for what we already possess. Let's instead embrace what we already have and rejoice!

April 4

An Attitude of Gratitude

When the Apostle Paul wrote his first letter to the Church in Thessalonica, he exhorted them to, *"Rejoice always, pray continually, give thanks in all circumstances; for this is God's will for you in Christ Jesus."* (1 Thess. 5:16-18).

Giving thanks in all circumstances is not easy and yet God has been encouraging us to do just that since the beginning of our time on earth. From cover to cover in the Bible we find exhortations and encouragement to give thanks to the Lord, for He is good. But we humans have always wrestled with this challenge of being thankful when there's so much to complain about or be fearful of or resent and be negative about. We have a framed statement hanging in our house which I read every day:

> *It's not happy people who are thankful*
> *it's thankful people who are happy*

We know that statement is true, but at times it seems easier to want what we don't have, ignore what we do have and covet what our neighbour has! We tend to worship the past and fear the future. Such attitudes then cripple us in the present and rob us of the abundant life which God has given us in Christ.

We need to cultivate an attitude of gratitude. Life is so much better when your mindset, orientation, and entire demeanour and attitude is one of thanksgiving for what you have, where you are and who you are. If you focus on what you have, you'll always have more than you need. If you focus on what you don't have, you'll never have enough.

You are the only one who determines your attitude and if you choose every day to focus on what you are grateful for, your life will be transformed as feelings of anger, resentment, selfishness and negativity are overridden by gratitude.

April 5

Desiring God

I don't believe love is just doing the right thing. I don't believe love is just keeping commandments. I don't believe love is just being patient and kind and all those attributes we read in 1 Corinthians 13. That is what love looks like when it walks and talks. But that's not love. That is the fruit of love, the result of love, the evidence of love. I believe at the heart of love we always find a passion for God.

Do you desire God? Do you long for God? Yes, we all go through times when our hearts are dull. We go through times when we need encouragement. We all go through times when our eyes are distracted by things they should not be. But if someone looked at your life over the long haul, I wonder if they would say that your deepest passion is not for ministry, not for missions, not for evangelism, but for God Himself.

The sign of a genuine work of God in the heart is that you begin to hate the sin you once loved, and you begin to love the righteousness you once ignored. I am not asking if you agree with that or if you are challenged by that. I am asking is that a reality in your life? Are you continuing to grow in your hatred of sin and your love for righteousness? Are you being drawn deeper into the presence of God each day or not? It is not a question of doing the right thing or wanting to be moral or wanting to have a good life. The most important question is: *do you desire God?*

Your life is nothing; it has no value at all apart from Jesus Christ. Either you have Jesus and Jesus has you – or you are barren and lost. I'm not asking, 'Do you want a better life?' Or 'Do you want to go to heaven?' or 'Do you want to fix your marriage?' I have only one question: Do you desire God above everything else in your life?' When you can answer yes to that question, everything else will fall into place as God desires.

April 6

Confronting the Truth

Imagine that you spend your whole life building a house. It is a life project for you. You build it from the foundation up – every nail, every screw. You go for quality in everything you choose: fixtures, fittings, lights, curtains. Everything that is in this house is a reflection of you and your total commitment to excellence. This house is your pride and joy. It reflects your craftsmanship, your style and your values. It is the fruit of your labour over many years, as you have continued to make improvements, incorporating new ideas.

One day you meet a master builder. You have read about his work in magazines, so you invite him to come over and look at your house. You want to know if there is anything that he would do differently, change some fittings, move the deck, perhaps even open up a wall. What could he suggest that would make your house even better?

He comes in and he's very quiet. He looks around, shakes his head and says, *"This is a tear-down."* You are devastated! A tear-down? You've put your whole life into this house and he rights it off completely?

Well, that's exactly what's happening for Nicodemus in John chapter 3 when he is confronted with the Truth. Nicodemus is a highly successful man, a spiritual leader who is trusted and respected in the community. Jesus effectively says to him, *"You have come to me, thinking that I can add something that is missing in your successful life. I am telling you that your whole life 'tear down!' You need to be born again."*

Jesus didn't come to help us fix up the life we have built. Jesus came to give us a completely new life. Our old life is a 'tear down' and only then, can the new life which Jesus wants to give us, become a reality.

April 7

Church Health - Church Growth

I was talking to some fellow Pastors recently and sadly, the prevailing feeling was one of great discouragement as they reflected on the diminishing numbers of people who are committing to Church these days. Shrinking or inconsistent attendance can certainly short-circuit our plans, frustrate our expectations and reduce our ministry impact. It is also very discouraging. But it made me think that perhaps there's a problem with the way we look at this whole issue.

Then God reminded me of a truth which is foundational, but we often overlook it – to our peril: *It's not our job to get people to commit to the Church.* We are called to help people commit to Jesus. Committing to Jesus and committing to the Church, may be related, but they are certainly not the same thing.

As a Church leader, my emphasis has to be on helping people connect with Jesus and embrace His mission. The number of people attending services Church is only of value when it serves that cause. Gathering with other believers is a central aspect of spiritual growth, but we should never leave anyone with the impression that Church attendance is our primary focus or end goal. Following Jesus must be our end goal and the focus of all our Church activities.

Church growth is the natural outcome of a healthy Church and that health flows from our relationship with Jesus. At the end of Acts chapter 2 we have a snapshot of a healthy Church as they devoted themselves to worship, good teaching, the breaking of bread and prayer. It was the Lord Who added to their number daily those who were being saved.

It was the disciples' personal encounter with Jesus, through the Holy Spirit which produced a healthy Church and God will always bless a healthy Church with growth.

April 8

Why are we Here?

Hebrews 12:1-3 *"And let us run with perseverance the race marked out for us, fixing our eyes on Jesus, the pioneer and perfecter of faith. For the joy set before him he endured the cross, scorning its shame, and sat down at the right hand of the throne of God. Consider him who endured such opposition from sinners, so that you will not grow weary and lose heart."*

Jesus came to earth knowing that He would die in order to atone for the sin of all mankind. Prior to the creation of this universe, there was already a plan marked out for His life. He was aware that He would bear the weight of our guilt. He understood that He would suffer for our sins and receive the punishment which purchased our peace. His fate was to give His life in sacrifice for a people who, for the most part, would completely reject Him.

Jesus was motivated by the satisfaction of seeing us reconciled with God. Both in His words and in His deeds, His intent was clear. He laboured in the Garden of Gethsemane, but He made the decision to press on despite the impending suffering. His selfless commitment to God's plan kept Him concentrated on the outcome. The life of Jesus offers us many lessons.

You and I were born with a purpose. God planted the idea of eternity in our minds as soon as we arrived. He anticipated that we would require a constant source of motivation. We should be encouraged to keep going forward when we set aside our own thoughts and emotions and concentrate on the people God has asked us to reach for Him.

My prayer is that as you move forward and embrace your God-given mission, that the life of Jesus Christ manifest in you and give you comfort and hope.

April 9

For the Gospel's Sake

Mark 8:35 *"For whosoever shall desire to save his life shall lose it, but whosoever shall lose his life for my sake and for the gospel's shall save it."*

Luis was born in Vietnam, his father left the family when Luis was very young, and because his mother was unable to care for him, she took him to an orphanage, where he spent his younger years.

There was a missionary couple who used to come to the orphanage encouraging the children to believe in Jesus and they would be blessed. Luis wanted to be blessed and invited Jesus into his life. And then, he himself became a missionary.

Whatever he learned from the missionaries, he taught other children. He shared the gospel with whoever was prepared to listen. When he was older, during the Vietnam war, he was put in prison for sharing the gospel and spent over eleven years of his life locked away. He decided this was where God wanted him to share the Good News of God's love and forgiveness and so he told his fellow prisoners about Jesus. Over fifty prisoners came to Jesus through his ministry.

Luis now lives in North America and spends about 60% of a year traveling to un-evangelized areas of the world, many times living in squalid conditions, going from place to place setting up water filters to bring clean water and organising food, medical supplies as well as sharing the Jesus story on DVDs with thousands of villagers.

Jesus changed one life and that life has changed thousands of other lives. If everyone who embraced the salvation Jesus gives freely, then 'lost' their life for the gospel's sake like Luis, can you even image how the world might look today?

April 10

Faith

Hebrews 11:1 *"Faith is the assurance of things hoped for, the conviction of things unseen."*

Just read that verse again, slowly. In our 'enlightened' age it is a ridiculous assertion! Who in today's world of rational thought would venture to take the stage in any public setting and utter such naive nonsense!?

Isn't it true that only children genuinely think their parents will grant them an unrealistic but hoped-for Christmas or birthday wish? After all, aren't toddlers the only ones who think a wonderful, imagined gift will actually materialise? Who else would have this much faith in an adult, even one who is committed and loving?

Perhaps this is why Jesus said, *"Unless you change and become like little children, you will never enter the kingdom of heaven."*

Faith would be foolish if our hope and conviction had no foundation in reality, but God provides us with all the reality we require and all the information we need to make an informed choice to follow Him.

God's very nature begs for such faith, and in addition, He sent His Son Jesus to embody this nature in the physical realm and to open the door to God for us all.

Throughout the centuries, millions of us have put everything on the line for the belief that God is trustworthy. This is what the ancients were praised for, according to the Scriptures.

To accept God and His Word requires faith, and Jesus said, *"Whoever comes to me, I will never drive away."*

Are you prepared to put your trust in God and to really believe what He says? Where is your hope and conviction?

April 11

Promise Keeper

I have a little book titled *10,000 Promises*. It literally contains 10,000 promises from the Bible. Whatever your specific need is, you will likely find a promise about it in the Bible. It's not even a complete list – I'm sure you could find more if you tried. However, the fact that we can read 10,000 in one book is really quite extraordinary and it reminds us Who God is.

Are you feeling tired and weak because your life has been troubling and tiring? Here is the promise: *"He gives strength to the weary and increases the power of the weak."* (Isaiah 40:29) When you read such a promise, take it back to our great God who promised it, and ask Him to fulfill His own word.

Are you seeking after Christ, and yearning for a closer relationship with Him? This promise shines like a star upon you: *"Blessed are those who hunger and thirst for righteousness, for they will be filled."* (Matthew 5:6). Take that promise to God's throne continually. Do not plead anything else, but go to God over and over again, praying, *"Lord, You have said it, I humbly ask that You do as You have said."*

Are you distressed because of sin, and burdened with the heavy load of your wrongdoings? Listen to these words: *"I, even I, am he who blots out your transgressions, for my own sake, and remembers your sins no more."* (Isaiah 43:25). You have no worth of your own to deserve God's pardon but plead His written promises and He will perform them.

Are you afraid that you won't be able to persevere to the end? Do you fear that, after having thought yourself to be a child of God, you might instead be a 'castaway'? Take this word of grace to God's throne and plead it: *"Though the mountains be shaken and the hills be removed, yet my unfailing love for you will not be shaken nor my covenant of peace be removed."* (Isaiah 54:10)

April 12

Outrageous Grace

Luke 23:42-43 *Then he said, "Jesus, remember me when you come into your kingdom." Jesus answered him, "Truly I tell you, today you will be with me in paradise."*

How does this interaction between Jesus and the thief on the cross next to Him fit your theology? How does this criminal's experience of God fit the gospel you believe? From my experience, 80% of what I have seen and heard as 'the gospel' is completely obliterated by this one brief encounter.

The institutional church has gone to incredible lengths over hundreds of years now to create a very long list of qualifications or pre-requisites which people must tick off before they can legitimately say they are a disciple of Jesus and heaven bound.

But what about this thief? What religious boxes did he tick? No baptism; no communion; no confirmation; no speaking in tongues; no mission trip; no volunteerism; no financial gifts, and no church clothes; he couldn't bend his knees to pray; he didn't 'pray the sinner's prayer' and among other things, he was a convicted criminal. Jesus didn't take way his pain, heal his body, or smite his scoffers.

Yet, it was this thief who walked into paradise the same hour as Jesus - simply by believing. He had nothing more to offer other than his belief that Jesus was who He said He was.

No spin from brilliant theologians. No ego or arrogance. No shiny lights, skinny jeans, or crafty words. No smoke machine, donuts, or barista coffee in the lobby. Just a naked, dying man on a cross, unable to even fold his hands to pray.

Now *that* is the outrageous Gospel of Jesus Christ. *That* is the good News. *That* is what the Church should be preaching, living and breathing!

April 13

You are Never Alone

Hebrews 13:5 *"Keep your lives free from the love of money and be content with what you have, because God has said, "Never will I leave you; never will I forsake you."*

Loneliness is something many people frequently experience. Some people are in a pit of profound despair, whether they are socially or physically isolated. Going through the motions, battling challenging conditions, and questioning whether they are the only one having a hard time.

Unfortunately, a lot of the time when we are in situations like this, we start to believe the lie that if God permits us to travel down these lonely roads, then He is not a loving God. I would strongly encourage you to not fall for that deception.

Although Christ's gift to us at Calvary covered the cost of our sins, it did not grant us a life without suffering. We frequently encounter difficulties that God wants to use to draw us nearer to Him and to help us help others through similar situations.

If you are feeling lonely, consider the road Christ travelled to pay the ultimate price for your deliverance. You should also consider the many ways you can console others when they are suffering because this ultimately brings God glory.

Whenever you feel lonely, alone, or in need, remember that God himself lives in you by His Spirit and He is offering you all the comfort, companionship, strength, and faith that you need to persevere and press on to take hold of that which Jesus died to secure for you in this life and the next.

Some of the most important words to remember from Jesus every day are, *"Never will I leave you; never will I forsake you."*

April 14

Persevere

I was driving home from a meeting one night recently and felt tears forming in my eyes. There was no real reason – just the pressures of life at that time. It really caught me unawares. Perhaps I wasn't coping with things as well as I thought?

Can you recall such a time? You are managing everything that comes your way without getting upset; you are dealing with unforeseen problems with a cool head; sticking to the schedule; and then it happens ... you become acutely aware of just how exhausted you are physically, emotionally and perhaps even spiritually.

I guess that was me that night. I decided that driving while crying was not a good idea, so I stopped and prayed. God responded with just one word. *Persevere.*

I think it was His kind reprimand. My one word for the next year is *persevere*. I find myself thinking about it constantly now in very specific ways.

Through the challenging days that drag on for too long ... *persevere*. In holding on to optimism despite it appearing that others have given up - *persevere*. Continue to follow Jesus, particularly when you are aware that you're being attacked spiritually - *persevere*. Even when giving up seems simpler - *persevere*.

James 5:11 *"As you know, we count as blessed those who have persevered. You have heard of Job's perseverance and have seen what the Lord finally brought about. The Lord is full of compassion and mercy."*

I found solace in God's encouragement to keep going and it actually made me stronger. Once again God reminded me that pushing through the pressures in my own strength was just not sustainable. I must rely on His strength and embrace His empowering presence – every day.

April 15

Consider it all Joy

James 1:2-8 *"Consider it all joy, my brethren, when you encounter various trials, knowing that the testing of your faith produces endurance. And let endurance have its perfect result, so that you may be perfect and complete, lacking in nothing. But if any of you lacks wisdom, let him ask of God, who gives to all generously and without reproach, and it will be given to him. But he must ask in faith without any doubting, for the one who doubts is like the surf of the sea, driven and tossed by the wind. For that man ought not to expect that he will receive anything from the Lord, being a double-minded man, unstable in all his ways."*

Have you ever thought, "*He's so lucky,*" or "*Her life is so simple,*" when you are looking at someone else? In truth, nobody lives a problem-free life. The Bible says that everyone experiences difficulties in life.

James 1:2 is a tiny verse, but it offers a wealth of wisdom regarding our struggles. The fact that James employs the word *when* is significant, to start with. It is a question of when, not if, you will go through trials.

Secondly, James implies that problems will appear out of the blue when he says will *encounter* trials. There might not be enough time to plan for these problems.

Thirdly, he uses the word *various* to describe the constantly shifting, frequently unexpected ways that difficulties can manifest. James wishes to say something specific: "*Get ready. You need to get ready for trouble because it's approaching so you can handle it effectively.*"

Next time you face difficult times, ask God what He is trying to teach you and then have faith that He will use that time and your suffering for His purposes and your growth.

April 16

Jesus is Our Peace

Jesus reconciles both us and our enemies to God, because all who come to God must come through Jesus.

Ephesians 2:14-16 *"For he himself is our peace, who has made us both one and has broken down in his flesh the dividing wall of hostility by abolishing the law of commandments expressed in ordinance, that he might create in himself one new man in place of the two, so making peace, and might reconcile us both to God in one body through the cross, thereby killing the hostility."*

Those who come to Jesus will experience true peace. True peace refers to reconciliation with God, which is the reason Jesus came to earth. Adam and Eve's disobedience severely impacted our connection with God. Sin ruined our intimacy with God, our friendship with others. It destroyed our peace.

Paul addressed the conflict between Jews and non-Jews in the Church in his epistle to the Ephesians. We were cut off from God's covenants, from His pledge to send a Redeemer, and from His chosen people, the nation of Israel. Our predicament was bleak - but then Christ arrived.

Jesus broke down the wall of animosity and all the barriers that separated Jews from Gentiles and kept people from interacting with one another. The sinless Jesus fulfilled the Law that no human could and then died for us - reuniting us with God.

Peace comes from Jesus and through Jesus. All who come to God must come through Jesus. To those who are close to God or far from God, Jesus teaches peace and reconciliation. In Christ we find the power to mend relationships with our relatives and former friends as well as restored intimacy with God. Jesus brings peace to our souls.

April 17

Everything we Need

2 Peter 1:3 *"God's divine power has given us everything we need for life and godliness through our knowledge of Him who called us by His own glory and goodness."*

Isn't that incredible? You will have everything you need to navigate life's challenges with a godly outlook thanks to God's omnipotent strength! This means God will provide everything you need to get through everything. When the waters of life threaten to overwhelm you and you fear that you might drown in anxiety, despair, or dread, He is not promising riches and renown; rather, He is promising that you will have whatever you need. His divine authority will always intervene to save you!

God expresses the depth and breadth of everything He is for you right now, and as your understanding of Him deepens, so does your trust. As you immerse yourself in the knowledge of all that He brings to your life to support you in living in victory even in the middle of challenges, His divine power starts to work within you.

God is both huge and true! Nothing and nobody can avoid His observation. God is right here! Even in the midst of a significant struggle, you are never alone. God is love! God is unchanging. God is. His call is the persistent yearning you feel inside for something greater, for something more.

Nothing in this life will completely satisfy you. Because God has implanted eternity in your heart, nothing will satisfy you fully until your hand is securely in His hand every day as you navigate the journey of life with Him by your side.

Your faith will increase as your understanding of God deepens, and you will see His divine power at work within you as life takes on a whole new meaning.

April 18

Sleepless Nights?

Do you ever have trouble sleeping and staying asleep? There are several reasons why we might wake up and then cannot get back to sleep. Often, it is anxiety that keeps us from the rest that we need.

It is encouraging to know that sleepless nights have been the experience of God's servants for a very, very long time. Even the Apostle Paul:

2 Corinthians 6:4-6 *"Rather, as servants of God we commend ourselves in every way: in great endurance; in troubles, hardships and distresses; in beatings, imprisonments and riots; in hard work, sleepless nights and hunger; in purity, understanding, patience and kindness; in the Holy Spirit and in sincere love."*

I do not pretend to know about what Paul was going through as he penned the words above, but he does mention going through hardship, distress, and trouble and I know them!

As I read that, my attention is drawn to how Paul dealt with sleepless nights, among his other challenges: his secret was to dwell in the presence and power of the Holy Spirit. He chose an attitude of sincere love, purity, understanding, patience and kindness in response to all his challenges!

I find that praying and listening to worship music helps me. This leads to surrendering control to God, no matter what happens, knowing and believing that He is a good God. A song that has ministered to me recently is *Good, Good Father* by Chris Tomlin. Look it up on YouTube – you will be blessed.

Always remember that we all need to deal with anxiety and sleeplessness at times, but God is faithful and will never leave us or forsake us! Trust Him to give you the rest that you need!

April 19

Make a Difference!

1 Peter 4:10-11 *"As each one has received a special gift, employ it in serving one another as good stewards of the manifold grace of God. Whoever speaks, is to do so as one who is speaking the utterances of God; whoever serves is to do so as one who is serving by the strength which God supplies; so that in all things God may be glorified through Jesus Christ, to whom belongs the glory and dominion forever and ever. Amen."*

In calling believers to carry out His task on earth, the Lord has given us an amazing responsibility. How amazing that the All-Powerful God, Who is able to accomplish anything and everything, encourages us to take part in bringing people to Him, assisting His children to reach spiritual maturity, and providing for those in need.

Being the Lord's helper entails submitting to His authority, paying attention to His guidance, and obeying His directives. This job is beyond our capacity, but when we submit to God and depend upon His Holy Spirit within us, He will provide all that we require to fulfill His will and our purpose in life.

God is always preparing His children. He starts by moulding us into Christ. Then, as we work together with His Spirit, God changes a self-centred heart into a serving heart that takes great joy in providing for others. Additionally, the Lord grants each of us the spiritual gifts necessary for any task He has given us to complete.

The strength and capability are offered, and the request is extended. The most thrilling journey on earth can be experienced with just a few eager servants. Use those spiritual gifts the Lord has given to the Church through you; join the Lord in His work and influence this world for Christ.

April 20

Finding Peace in the Mess

Is it possible to find calm in the midst of the storm? When you hear the word *peace,* what picture comes to mind? Perhaps it's a serene setting like a lush meadow beside a flowing creek, the birds are chirping, the sun is shining, everything is immaculate. Maybe all that is missing is the chaos. Perhaps that is how you wish your life was right now.

What sort of peace do you seek? The lack of difficulty and hardship? This kind of peace will always be just out of our grasp. Your fingers will lose it like sand. What if peace was a safe place during a furious storm? Could it be that the peace Jesus brings is the peace we receive in the midst of our turmoil and not the absence of conflict, heartache, and brokenness?

I really love these two verses tucked away in the obscure book of Habakkuk: found near the end of the Old Testament. They take my breath away when I read them sometimes.

Habakkuk 3:17-18 *"Even though the fig trees have no blossoms, and there are no grapes on the vines; even though the olive crop fails, and the fields lie empty and barren; even though the flocks die in the fields, and the cattle barns are empty, yet I will rejoice in the LORD! I will be joyful in the God of my salvation!"*

I believe the author of Habakkuk is telling us where true peace is found. It is not in the absence of chaos, but rather knowing where to go for sanctuary in the middle of it. This kind of peace is easier to grasp in the difficult times if we have made a habit of being with our Lord in the easy times through prayer, Bible reading, and quiet times alone with Him.

Are you willing to embrace the peace that Jesus offers - shelter in a time of storm, refuge in the chaos, and sanctuary in the middle of the mess? It has always been there for you.

April 21

To Those Who Mourn

Isaiah 61:1-3 *"The Spirit of the Sovereign LORD is on me, because the LORD has anointed me ... He has sent me to bind up the brokenhearted ... to comfort all who mourn and provide for those who grieve in Zion - to bestow on them a crown of beauty instead of ashes, the oil of gladness instead of mourning, and a garment of praise instead of a spirit of despair."*

Your Heavenly Father is faithful to comfort you in your grief. Be blessed to trust that God is good and kind even if it doesn't feel like it in this moment. Hear His gentle invitation to come to Him and receive His love, comfort, and guidance.

The indwelling Christ is anointed in your life to bring good news to you, to bind up your broken heart. He hears all your prayers and sees all your tears when there are no words.

Receive the covering of His sweet presence and the peace that passes all understanding. Be blessed with His strength and courage as you face the days ahead. You are not alone.

He is your Mighty Warrior and contends with those forces that are contending with you (Isaiah 42:13; Psalm 35:1). May you be at peace with a still heart, while He fights for you (Exodus 14:14; Psalm 46:10).

Be blessed in His covenant of love, knowing that can never be taken from you (Romans 8:35, 38-39). He will never leave you. His promises can never be broken. He never loses sight of who He uniquely created you to be.

Bring Him your grief and pain as often as you need to and receive His crown of beauty and oil of gladness. Allow Him to heal all your wounded places and restore you with His love. He is more than enough for your every need, every day.

April 22

When Life Gets Tough

Romans 8:37-39 *"Yet in all these things we are more than conquerors through Him who loved us. For I am persuaded that neither death nor life, nor angels nor principalities nor powers, nor things present nor things to come, nor height nor depth, nor any other created thing, shall be able to separate us from the love of God which is in Christ Jesus our Lord."*

We all go through difficult times and if we don't hold fast to the truth, such times make us feel unstable. Let me give you three reassurances to keep in mind when difficulty comes.

Firstly, God will always provide for our necessities. This does not mean He gives us everything we ask for. Instead, the Lord will grant us all we need to accomplish His purpose for our lives. His aim is to purify us, not just to gratify our desires.

Secondly, we are never alone. God pledged to be by our side forever (Hebrews 13:5). We may feel abandoned or opposed by family and friends but until we join Him on the other side of this life, our Father has given His Spirit to remain with and be in us (John 14:16-17). He is all we require - our defender, teacher, mentor, and solace-giver.

Thirdly, God's love endures forever. He cares for us despite our circumstances and our bad choices. God is in complete control and He only permits things that would benefit His servants. We can keep in mind that God will provide for all of our needs, that He is always there for us, and that He will always love us.

Jesus warned that we would have difficulties in this world, but He also gave us hope by saying that He would ultimately triumph. Never forget that all the trials are fleeting, whereas our Father's love is constant forever. Remember that God will always meet all of our needs.

April 23

The Battle in Your Mind

Romans 12:2 *"Do not conform to the pattern of this world but be transformed by the renewing of your mind. Then you will be able to test and approve what God's will is – his good, pleasing and perfect will."*

Your mind is engaged in a fierce and constant struggle for dominance. There, the forces of heaven and earth collide, and you feel their pull on your thoughts. God gave us the ability to taste a little of heaven, but in order to do so, we must turn off the world and concentrate on being in His presence.

Our thoughts are dragged down by the outside world. We see desire, greed and cynicism in the media. We need to ask for safety and wisdom in prayer. As you travel through the wasteland of the world, remain in constant contact with Jesus.

Refuse to worry, because this form of worldliness will weigh you down and block awareness of His presence. We must remain on guard, stay alert and recognize the battle being waged against our mind as we look forward to the eternity free of strife which awaits us.

Paul tells us in Romans 8:6 that the mind of sinful man is death, but the mind controlled by the Spirit is life and peace. The Apostle John tells us to not love the world or anything in the world because the world and its desires pass away, but the one who does God's will, lives forever. (1 John 2:15,17)

How are you doing in your battle? Who is winning ... the way of the world (Satan) or the way of heaven (Jesus)? Electronic communications, the media and the grip of Satan on the world around us makes this a fierce daily battle. It is constant, but for those of us who have professed Jesus as our Lord and Saviour, we know who will win in the end.

April 24

Chill Out

Psalm 46:10 *"Be still and know that I am God."*

"Sit still! Stop wriggling!" How often have you said those words to a squirmy child in the back seat of the car? How often have you whispered something similar to yourself as you mentally fidget while reading the Bible or praying? Or, more likely, when disease or disaster strikes?

Scholars agree that the words of Psalm 46 probably were not written while God's beloved children roamed green pastures or rested beside still waters. It is more likely that they were escaping yet another enemy who wanted to wipe them out. Even nature seemed to conspire against them with quaking mountains and roaring waters.

After describing these horrors, the writer extols the glory and power of God and finally slips in, *"Be still!"*, or more literally, *"Cease, relax, quit striving, chill out!"* How is this possible and how do I learn to live like this every day?

Paul, writing to Christians under similar conditions, gives this encouraging advice:

Philippians 4:4-7 *"Rejoice! Don't be anxious! Pray with thanksgiving about everything! Then the peace of God which is beyond human understanding will calm your fears and give you mental quiet."*

It's this practice of joy-filled living, intentional prayer, and increased understanding of the nature of God that leads to and feeds the important practice of stillness.

This doesn't happen casually or overnight. It takes a daily surrender over the irritating minutiae of life and our agreement with a loving God that He has purpose and plan for each of us.

April 25

Reflected Glory

Recently I woke in the middle of the night and found myself squinting! As I pried my eyes open, I realised why. It was a really hot night and so I had the blinds and window open to cool the room overnight. There was a full moon that night and it had moved from when I went to sleep and was now shining directly in my face like a spotlight! I looked around the room and I could see everything like it was daytime.

As I rolled over and tried to get back to sleep, I was reminded once more that the moon was not shining on me at all. The moon has no capacity to shine. It is only as it catches the glow from the sun that is radiates so magnificently in the night sky. The glory of the moon is all reflected glory from the sun.

Have you ever noticed a blinding glimmer of light coming from a tiny object that just so happens to be aligned with the sun that it reflects more light than we could well conceive coming from such a small object? A watch face on a person's arm often serves as a reflector of light from the sun and if that reflection hits your eyes as a person's arm moves, it can be incredibly bright and even painful. The light is not coming from the watch face – it is reflected light from the sun.

I saw a sign once above the pulpit in a church which read, *'Let them see Christ.'* It serves as a crucial reminder to that Church's preachers, worship leaders and congregation that they should reflect Christ's glory rather than their own. Each of us should keep this challenge in mind as we go about our daily lives in this evil and broken world as Christ-bearers.

So next time you see a full moon light up the whole night sky and everything around you, remember that you are seeing the reflected glory of the sun – just as those around you are meant to see the reflected glory of God's Son in you.

April 26

Waiting With Purpose

Isaiah 40:31 *"They that wait upon the LORD shall renew their strength ..."*

Have you ever questioned why prolonged periods of waiting tend to exhaust us, when waiting on the Lord is supposed to replenish our strength? What appears to be a passive activity often requires a significant amount of emotional and spiritual energy. Waiting, however, is meant to be much more than passive. God is never inactive while we wait, and neither should we be. In the Bible, the word 'wait' actually carries the idea of 'actively standing under.'

The Psalmist would occasionally cry out, "*How long, O Lord, how long!?*" while he painfully waits for God to act. According to Bob Sorge's book *The Fire of Delayed Answers*, when God wants to do His greatest work in us, He urges us to wait. This is because we are forced into a greater dependence upon Him, His might, His timing, and His sovereign control when there is nothing we can do but wait. This builds faith in us.

Waiting can be both painful and exhausting. God is aware of this, which is why He devotes so much time in the Bible to motivating us as we wait. But we can lessen the agony of these moments by changing the way we think as we endure.

We need to accept the wisdom of God's command to wait and pay close attention to what God may be saying to us and doing in us during this waiting time.

We may even come to realise that, while all of creation waits for the Son to experience His ultimate glory and usher in a new age of heaven and earth, we share in the great Wait of heaven. Our waiting is never meant to be passive. Our waiting should always be purposeful and may we never forget – we don't wait alone.

April 27

God so Loves

We only catch a brief glimpse of God's love as it passes us, hidden in a rock crevice. Our ability to offer and receive love, which is frequently based on human selfishness, limits how much we can really grasp love.

This is why in Ephesians 3:17-19, the Apostle Paul asks for a divine revelation so that we can grasp God's unfathomable love - something that is largely beyond our comprehension.

God desires to challenge our constrained understandings of love and help us view things from His vantage point.

"Greater love has no one than this, that he offers up his life for his friends," He says, describing love as a sacrifice.

"If you love Me, you will obey My commandments," He says while discussing love in relation to obedience.

He says, *"If you say you love God and hate your brother, you are a liar and the love of God is not in you."* He also says that we should love everyone, including those who have wronged us.

Too often, we find it simpler to identify with the Psalmist's condemnations of his adversaries than with Jesus' statement of forgiveness on the cross, or with His instructions to love our adversaries, bless those who curse us, and pray for those who use and persecute us out of retaliation.

Seeing individuals who hurt us through God's eyes - the same eyes that loved us when we hurt Him - is really quite tough for us, but it is incredibly important.

Wouldn't it be more enlightening for us to view our enemy from God's viewpoint as His beloved but misbehaving child who needs to re-establish a relationship with Him and with us? Would this make it easier for us to love as God loves and to pray with compassion and an open heart? Perhaps.

April 28

Better Together

*"Christian community is not an ideal which we must realize;
it is rather a reality created by God in Christ in
which we may participate."*

(Dietrich Bonhoeffer, Life Together, p. 30)

It was never God's intention that we travel by ourselves. We shall always need God, people, and community as we seek to navigate through this life.

Dietrich Bonhoeffer called it *'Space Sharing.'* He was referring to how, as we live our lives, we share space with God and other people in a sense of community.

God is a triune God – three in one – there is a relationship between the persons within the Trinity. Whilst we may not fully understand that - we know it is true.

We also know that we are created in God's image and as such, we are created to be in relationship, in community.

God is always present in every breath we take, and through interacting with other Christians, we can all share in a sense of spiritual community. Spend time with God and others whenever possible.

Think how can you serve the community and the people in it? Who can you meet for coffee or invite over for lunch so you may encourage and bless one another while sharing life, praying, and conversing.

We embrace the fullness of God within us when we are together in community.

Psalm 133:1 *"Behold how good and how pleasant it is for brethren to dwell together in unity."*

April 29

Cheer Up!

John 16:33 *"I have told you all this so that you will have peace of heart and mind. Here on earth, you will have many sorrows and trials; but cheer up, for I have overcome the world."*

There aren't many promises in the entire Bible that provide more comfort and encouragement than the one above.

The apostle Paul spread the gospel far and wide throughout the known world. He was a tenacious soldier of God. He played a significant role in God's plan to broaden the boundaries of the growing Church, but Paul accomplished everything he did in the name of Christ and under the direction and strength of the Holy Spirit.

Paul's ministry faced stiff opposition. He appeared to be at the epicentre of spiritual conflict as a result. He was aware of his adversaries' cunning tricks, including those used by Satan and the world. He endured numerous forms of persecution during his Christian life, including stoning, beatings, and incarceration. Yet despite that, Paul could write:

Philippians 4:4 *"Rejoice in the Lord always; again, I will say, rejoice."*

About 61 or 62 A.D., while Paul was imprisoned in Rome, he sent a letter to the Ephesian Church. His letter's main subject is supernatural living, and he discusses the spiritual conflict faced by Christians. He explains that the conflict we engage in is not with other people but with Satan and the powers of spiritual wickedness.

In times of struggle, trial and even persecution, the apostle Paul experienced the miraculous peace of heart and mind that Jesus promised, a promise that we too can enjoy today.

April 30

God is Faithful

We can trust God's promises even though we cannot see them. Consider the story of Judah, where Jehoshaphat's choice to intermarry with the family of Ahab carried their homicidal character and nurture into the house of David, ultimately leading to the daughter of Ahab usurping the kingdom. After her son killed all of his brothers, 'mummy dearest' slaughtered all her grandchildren and every other contender for the kingdom!

If you had been a devout follower of God at that time, you would have been curious about God's assurance to David that he would always have a ruler over Judah. How is this even possible? Why had God's word fallen short?

Have you been there before? Have you ever examined your circumstances and wondered if God's promises have been broken or if they simply don't apply to you since you can't see them being fulfilled in your life? Maybe you question whether you misinterpreted them? Any little doubt can be used by the enemy to fuel serious despondency.

However, God had a secret, which is the rest of the story. A young child who was a descendant of King David had been secreted away by him. For the following six years, the child served as a symbol of God's fidelity to His word. God always honours His promises, but He doesn't always do it in a way which is obvious to us. Our faith has a role in this. God frequently asks us to trust in the dark, much like Abraham did when he accepted God's promise despite the fact that everything around him contradicted his expectations.

Hold onto your confidence in God. If He has made a promise to you, then be assured that you can depend on Him to keep His promise, in spite of the circumstances in which you might find yourself at the moment.

May 1

Holy Spirit, Come

Recent findings from George Barna Research don't paint a very positive picture for the future of the Christian Church in the western world. Particularly among younger generations, there has been a significant decline in theological literacy, and the gap between one's spirituality and other aspects of their life has grown.

Also, the pervasive post-modern emphasis on tolerance has infected the Church to the extent that many Christians no longer have the confidence to speak out for moral principles.

Further, an increasing majority of people believe that the Holy Spirit is a sign of God's presence or power, but not a live entity, not actually a real Person. A number of Christians are downplaying the Holy Spirit's role as a source of power. It is understandable why the Christian faith is being marginalised more and more, when in the lives of many believers, the third member of the Triune God is missing in action!

The purpose of the Holy Spirit, according to Wayne Grudem in his *Systematic Theology*, is to make known God's active presence in the world, particularly in the Church. As we live our lives as individuals and as the Church, the Holy Spirit is God residing within us. Denying His presence entails not just grieving Him but also completely quenching the Spirit.

The Apostle Paul exhorted us to always pray in the Spirit on all occasions, live by the Spirit (Galatians 5:16), walk in the Spirit (Galatians 5:25), and be consistently filled with (ruled and affected by) the Holy Spirit (Ephesians 5:18). Denying the Holy Spirit means cutting off our hearts' access to the most powerful spiritual tool we have at our disposal for living in Christ. God the Holy Spirit is the crucial link that will enable you to make a stand for Jesus in every area of your life.

May 2

Seeing is Not Believing

We occasionally need reminding of some of the fundamental realities underlying our Christian beliefs. The above heading makes reference to one of these truths. Even though it should be evident, we frequently choose sight over faith when we are confronted with a significant or threatening situation.

We want some reassurances that the thing God is calling us to will result in anything good or pleasant. Before we proceed, we want to *see* that God is providing for us.

The issue with that is, in the truest definition of the word, seeing is not believing. In addition, *before* performing many of His magnificent and amazing deeds, God asks us to have confidence and faith.

The Priests carrying the Ark were directed to proceed down to the river as the Israelites approached it to pass over into the Promised Land. The river divided when their big hairy toes touched the water, not when they waited on the shore!

God often only provides us with enough for each day, always in proportion to our daily trust and obedience, just as He told the Israelites to go out each day and gather manna in the wilderness.

This does not imply that I think everything will happen if I have enough faith, or that I have faith in faith. True faith is always in response to a call from the Lord to obedience, and it is based on His assurance that He will give us the ability to carry out everything which He calls us to do. God's bidding is God' enabling.

So, I encourage you have faith, take that initial step, knowing that He will provide the power and resources for the rest, since He never asks something that He cannot make possible.

May 3

Never Stop Learning

Matthew 11:29 *"Take my yoke upon you, and learn from me, for I am gentle and lowly in heart, and you will find rest for your souls."*

Throughout the last few decades, western culture has stressed the value of lifelong learning - a deliberate and continuous growth in knowledge and understanding, both practical and theoretical, as opposed to limiting education just to those formal school settings.

Jesus instructed His disciples to become lifelong learners of Him thousands of years before our modern style of thinking. Jesus referred to this as discipleship. The Gospel authors repeatedly quote Jesus as saying, *"Follow me."* Jesus urged people of all ages to follow His way of life and carry out the Father's desire.

As Christians in the 21st century, our goal is really the same. Jesus must be our primary source of lifelong learning. We must examine and imitate Jesus' surrender to the Father, accept God's teachings on sin, repentance, and forgiveness, and embrace the Spirit's guidance on righteousness, justice and love.

Too frequently, we emphasise making disciples but neglect to practise discipleship. We cannot make disciples of Jesus until we first become disciples of Jesus. It has to start with us.

The Apostle Paul said, *"Follow my example, as I follow the example of Christ,"* (1 Corinthians 11:1). In another translation that reads, *"Be imitators of me, as I am of Christ."*

We don't always follow Jesus exactly, but as He transforms us through the power of the Holy Spirit, we learn from Him and grow closer to Him through time. So, talk to Jesus frequently throughout the day and listen to Him.

May 4

God Will Never Leave Us

How frequently have people let you down? Many people assure you that they will support you no matter what may happen. They assure you that they will follow you closely. However, when danger arises, the majority of them are so far behind you that a telescope is required to view them!

Therefore, it is consoling to know that we have a God Who never deserted us even in the face of shifting circumstances or being let down by someone. He stated, *"Never will I leave you; never will I forsake you."* (Hebrews 13:5). The Lord your God will always goes before you; He will never abandon you nor forsake you.

What evolving conditions are you now dealing with? How are you handling those changes? Has fear taken hold of you? Do you think of God as being distant? Our God never leaves us, especially during those trying times.

I recall hearing a story of a family whose home was destroyed by fire. The young daughter who was holding the father's hand broke away from his embrace and raced upstairs to collect her teddy bear as each parent hurried to grab a few possessions and a child's hand to flee the house as quickly as possible. But as she tried to descend the stairs, she discovered that the engulfing flames had imprisoned her. As a result, she sprinted to the upper window and yelled for her father to intervene and save her.

The father responded by yelling, "*Jump down; I'll catch you.*" However, the young girl cried, "*I'm terrified to jump daddy, I can't see you through the smoke.*" Her dad replied, *"Don't worry honey, you just jump, I'm right underneath you, and I'll catch you. I can see you, even though you can't see me."* We are always in clear sight of our heavenly Father. He won't ever leave us! He will always catch us when we fall or jump at His request!

May 5

Believing is not Enough

Conversion is one of the key tenets of evangelical Church life. Evangelicals have given a very high priority to the point of conversion in all of their outreach efforts, from traditional revivals to seeker-sensitive Church services to post-modern outreach techniques.

This practise is grounded in theology; it is not just a strategy to entice individuals to join the Church. However, a common worry with this perspective is that we would turn conversion into 'believism.' That is, you are 'in' if there's a moment when you are certain that you have accepted the correct beliefs or doctrines regarding Jesus, the cross, and the resurrection. If not, then we should doubt the certainty of your faith.

This is the reason many Churches attach such importance to people coming to believe in Jesus and why the time when sinners raise their hands or approach the altar to confess their faith in Jesus is celebrated so highly. It is believed that this one-time event is their submission to Jesus as Lord.

The truth is that merely acknowledging Jesus as Lord does not transform me into a follower of Jesus any more than believing Kim Jong-un is the leader of North Korea makes me his follower. I would have to give my life to Kim Jong-un and become a North Korean citizen for him ever to be my leader. Similarly, in order for Jesus to be my Lord, I must submit to Him and embrace His Kingdom rule and reign.

It is a simple fact that my obedience to Jesus has no effect on the fact that He is the Lord of all creation. Until I choose to surrender to Him as *my* Lord, His Lordship will have no effect on my life. What you think and believe is not the crucial issue.

It's what you ultimately choose to do, moment by moment, based on your beliefs that really matters.

May 6

God's Goal

In a world where everything is bleak and gloomy; when there never seems to be enough; in the midst of messages telling us how we are falling short; in a time when we are more focused on whether we may acquire the latest iPhone than how we can help the underprivileged; and even in a Church that is battling, quarrelling, and suffering from 'friendly fire' ... God is still working among us.

All creation is being drawn towards redemption by a steady stream of hope that runs beneath the surface. A rock-solid truth runs through history amid sensationalist jabs, assaults, and news of conflict; we cannot disregard this truth lest our souls suffer.

A powerful prayer Jesus uttered soon before His crucifixion neatly sums up the whole purpose of creation:

John 17:19-21 *"For them I sanctify myself, that they too may be truly sanctified. My prayer is not for them alone. I pray also for those who will believe in me through their message, that all of them may be one, Father, just as you are in me and I am in you. May they also be in us so that the world may believe that you have sent me."*

Jesus pleaded for His followers to be as unified as He and the Father are. The Trinity's loving unity should be reflected in the Church's loving unity. As stated in "*As you are in me and I am in you, may they also be in us,*" the loving unity of the Church partakes in the loving unity of the Trinity. We *reflect* God's loving oneness as we *share in* God's loving oneness.

As God gives His life to us, we demonstrate the fullness of His life by affirming the infinite worth we ourselves have as a result of what God has done for us in Christ (self-love); and we affirm the infinite worth others have as a result of what Christ has done for them (neighbour-love). That's God's goal.

May 7

Where Would we Go?

Sometimes I just cannot comprehend God! In all honesty, it happens a lot of times. Why won't He make Himself known to me more clearly? Why does He frequently leave me in the dark about what He is doing or thinking? I have high hopes for God and what He can and ought to achieve and when I observe Him acting differently from how I believe my God should act, I can become confused and frustrated.

We all have experienced loss, tragedy and grief. The death of a baby; the horror of cancer taking a wife or husband; the senseless destruction of an avoidable car accident, crippling someone we love for life; the rebellion of our child as they run away from God. We cry out to God for Him to save them and reveal Himself to them and we see no change.

Why would God act that way? Why does our Lord not feel obligated to live up to our demands? Because He is God! You'd think He'd be out and about demonstrating who He is and what He can do because He wants everyone to come to Him. Why then does He not do that?

Then God reminded me of something. Jesus once asked His twelve disciples whether they were going to forsake Him as well after many of His followers abandoned Him one day. Peter responded:

John 6:68–69 *"Simon Peter answered him, "Lord, to whom shall we go? You have the words of eternal life. We have come to believe and to know that you are the Holy One of God."*

Peter is essentially saying, *"We will trust You even though we don't comprehend You, even though you don't fit our idea of what a Messiah should be, even if we can't see the Way – we will follow You."* So, when I'm discouraged because God is not living up to my expectations, I humbled myself and choose to believe and to have faith in the goodness of His plan.

May 8

Waiting in Faith

Isaiah 40:31 *"But those who wait on the Lord shall renew their strength; They shall mount up with wings like eagles, They shall run and not be weary, They shall walk and not faint."*

We are not always patient while we wait. We don't know the outcome, so waiting is usually difficult. We also don't know when the solution will come – our timing is rarely God's timing. However, the knowledge that God already has the solution, transforms our waiting into trust. Therefore, faith gives us new patience and because our spiritual journey will involve a lot of waiting, we will need a lot of strength.

Every action we take is based on faith. As faith gives us the ability to trust and wait, it also strengthens our faith so that we can wait on Him for the outcomes. Many times, those outcomes take a very long time to manifest, yet the process still demands faith.

Our journey is really more about how we face the unknown than it is about the outcome. Will we persevere if we become dejected? Will we put our faith in Him to restore our strength and carry us from our despair to a new place of calm and hope? According to my experience, when I cry out to God in a disheartened state, He is consistently faithful to help me recover, allowing me to once again rest in the knowledge that He is in charge and whatever I am facing, He's all over it!

So, faith is a journey of waiting; faith is not an intellectual journey; faith is not a knowing journey; faith is knowing Him, not knowing what the future holds, but knowing the One Who holds the future; knowing God is God and we are not; knowing He is Sovereign.

We will be better able to wait if we choose to trust. Our faith will deepen as a result of this decision.

May 9

Overcoming Discouragement

Psalm 42:1-5 *"As the deer pants for streams of water, so my soul pants for you, my God. My soul thirsts for God, for the living God. When can I go and meet with God? My tears have been my food day and night, while people say to me all day long, "Where is your God?" These things I remember as I pour out my soul: how I used to go to the house of God under the protection of the Mighty One with shouts of joy and praise among the festive throng. Why, my soul, are you downcast? Why so disturbed within me? Put your hope in God, for I will yet praise him, my Saviour and my God."*

Everybody has goals and dreams, and when they are not fulfilled, we are disappointed. As long as we don't allow it to turn into paralysing dread, there's nothing wrong with feeling this way, but such a mindset can often cause us to let our circumstances rule us, which can result in bad choices.

For instance, we might feel like God has let us down and we are effectively then arguing that the Lord ought to have handled the matter in the way we would have preferred. Do you recognise the arrogance in such thinking? He certainly doesn't expect that we will be happy despite our difficulties. But despite how challenging it may be, we must submit to His sovereign rule and acknowledge that He has authority over both our joys and our sorrows. This mindset is possible once we understand that everything that occurs can ultimately be for our benefit so that we can grow closer to Christ and better fulfill His mission and purpose.

So, turn your attention away from your circumstances and towards the Lord when life throws you a curve ball or your soul is in despair. Put your trust in Him, understanding that trials and pain are passing experiences. Very soon you will praise Him gladly once more on earth, as all of His children will do forever in heaven.

May 10

The 'Try Harder' Falicy

So much social media interaction is shaped by conversations about what people should or should not do and how people should or should not think. This seems to be even worse within Christian social media. What impact does this have?

"You ought to." "You need to." "You've got to." "You're supposed to." "You'd better." Do they sound familiar? They should because they reflect the prevalent western Christian belief that a person's character can be made more Christ-like, more fruitful, simply by trying harder. They reflect the frequently held assumption that any lack of the fruit of the Spirit in our lives, any deficiency of love, joy, peace, or patience, is primarily the result of a lack of effort on our part.

The 'try harder' solution is popular because it's simple and seems so sensible. Just let people know what they're supposed to do and motivate them to do it. It's that simple. Not only that, but the 'try harder' solution often seems to produce immediate results. In the long term, however, the 'try harder' solution never works. Trying harder will never produce the fruit of the Spirit. We cannot just will ourselves to be more loving, joyful, peaceful, patient, kind, generous, faithful, gentle, and self-controlled.

The fruit of the Spirit is not first and foremost about how we act; it is about who we are. It is not about our behaviour, it is about our heart, our soul, our innermost disposition. The fruit of the Spirit is not something we should strive to produce by our own effort. The fruit of the Spirit is not a goal we must seek to attain. Indeed, it is called the fruit of the Spirit precisely because it is the fruit of the Spirit and not the product of our own effort.

Let's get off the 'do more, try harder treadmill' and rest in presence of Christ as He transforms us from the inside out.

May 11

This Way – That Way

Proverbs 3:5-6 *"Trust the Lord with all your heart and lean not on your own understanding. In all your ways acknowledge Him and He will direct your path."*

Maybe you have this where you live too but in my town, there is one street that has two different names. It's a fairly busy street with lots of traffic and so for the newcomers to town it can present quite a challenge. You can be driving up this street and suddenly you realize you aren't on the same one as before. Some streets are cut in half by a railway line and have no crossing. So you reach a dead end.

Isn't that the way it often is on this road we call life? It is so easy to think we are heading in the right direction, on God's path. Then something subtle changes. We look up and see signs telling us we are headed a new way, even if we did not realize anything had changed. Or we a brought to a dead-end stop with nowhere to go and yet we know this path has not ended yet – we just can't find our way back onto the same road. How did we get here and how do we get on the right path again?

Of course, there are times when we become distracted by a song on the radio or our passenger's conversation and we miss a turn or take the wrong exit. In those times it's easy to see we have messed up and figure out how to turn around. But life can be more subtle than that. Sometimes we didn't make a wrong turn or select the wrong road – things just change around us and we lose our bearings.

So how can we know we are on the correct path, even if it seems to have changed names? By letting someone else drive … His name is Jesus.

May 12

We Will Not Fear

Psalm 46:1-2 *"God is our refuge and strength, a very present help in trouble. Therefore, we will not fear, even though the earth be removed, and though the mountains be carried into the midst of the sea."*

Living in such a wonderful country as Australia, I am constantly reminded of the might and presence of our Creator. As I drove out of town recently, I was again drawn to the majestic mountain range in the distance - its beauty and its steadfast presence brought these verses to mind: *"We will not fear. . . though the mountains be carried into the midst of the sea."*

My imagination began to run wild. What if something as sure and steadfast as a mountain did uproot and was suddenly hurled into the Pacific Ocean? A mountain dropped in the sea would cause an alarm greater than its splash. Fear would be the most natural result.

If that were to happen, what would we do? Scripture says, *"We will not fear."* If we will not fear, even if the most terrifying natural disaster were to occur, then will we fear in financial uncertainty, political upheaval, an unknown future, or a scary diagnosis?

"We will not fear" is not a mantra to be recited continuously until we convince ourselves. It is the response of faith in the character of God – a God more steadfast than the greatest mountains and more present than our troubles.

We are exhorted in the Bible well over 300 times, do not fear, do not be anxious, do not worry etc. God is pretty committed to us living without fear! So, let' make a fresh commitment today: we will not fear! Why? Because *"God is our refuge and strength, a very present help in trouble."*

May 13

Risky Obedience

Luke 19:26 (MSG) *"Risk your life and get more than you ever dreamed of."*

If God tells you to take a step of faith but you hesitate to take it until He shows you what the second step will be, you're not waiting on God. He's waiting on you.

God uses risks, large and small, to push us into a deeper faith. He wants us to step forward in faith, even if we don't know where the second step will take us. The 'not knowing' is what requires faith, and the 'not knowing' compels us to rely on God to guide us forward.

Regardless of what we see on the other side of a God-directed risk, the reality is God is there. What seems to be a no-guarantee situation actually comes with the greatest guarantee of all - a God-guarantee - that He's working in your life.

With this guarantee from God: you can enter into the risky obedience of attempting things that are impossible unless God gives you His strength to do them.

With this guarantee from God: you can enter into the risky obedience of loving other believers so deeply and so richly that you prove to the world that God's love is flowing through you.

With this guarantee from God: you can enter into the risky obedience of loving your unlovable neighbours just as God loved you, even when you seemed unlovable.

With this guarantee from God: you can enter into the risky obedience of changing your priorities to match God's priorities, sacrificing, in faith, what you cannot keep for the things that can never be taken away.

May 14

Pressing 'Undo'

Many items of computer software have an 'undo' feature. It allows you to erase your most recent action and redo it the way you first intended or should have intended. It allows you to undo mistakes and proceed as if nothing wrong had happened. It also allows you to restore something you mistakenly deleted. Real life is not that simple.

You can't un-cook a cake or take back and forever erase words you have said and things you have done. We all make wrong decisions at some point in our lives. What's worse is that no matter how much we repent and ask God for His forgiveness, what's done is done and cannot be undone. While God has already forgiven us in the kingdom of heaven, the consequences on earth are very real and cannot be reversed.

Many of us feel condemned by what we have done. We fail to understand that when God forgives our sins, He also forgets them. He cannot condemn us for something He has already forgiven. What many of us do not understand, however, is the fact that while God's forgiveness erases our offences from His sight, we still have to face the consequences of our wrong decisions. Life is not as easy as a computer program.

One thing a pilot learns is to always be looking for a place to land. Life is like that. Whenever we make mistakes, we should always be looking for how to right our wrongs as best we can. Sometimes it is embarrassing, or expensive, but it is always the right thing to do and God's forgiveness is always there.

God's forgiveness is free; it's complete and it's unconditional. We do not earn our forgiveness. We do not pay for our forgiveness. Jesus died and secured our forgiveness before we were even born. Never forget the truth that love keeps no record of wrongs – and God is love.

May 15

Unfailing Love

Psalm 13:5-6 *"But I trust in your unfailing love. I will rejoice because you have rescued me. I will sing to the LORD because he is good to me."*

We humans have a tendency to question God's unwavering love. Love is not perfect and is quite fallible in its natural state. The love of others frequently betrays us, leaving wounds.

Therefore, we can think of God's love in the same way, always anticipating that it would eventually let us down just as past loves have let us down.

But this way of thinking is completely false and will lead us only to despair. God's love is not just unwavering, God's love is also consistently devoted. The love that God has for us will never be altered by our deeds, sins, or bad decisions. What act of love is greater than the self-sacrifice of the Creator of all life for His much-loved creation?

God's acts, not ours, are what demonstrate His love for us. His love is founded not on our character but on His. He has already paid far more for our sin debt than we could ever pay. In our place, he offered up his own life.

It is because of this example of constant love that we are able to transcend our own dysfunctional conception of love and transform, becoming capable of loving even those who do not reciprocate our affection. Because of His love, we join David in singing, *"The Lord is good to me."*

What is holding you back from trusting completely in God's love? If any doubts or scars come to mind, bring those to God in prayer and ask for help to grow in trust.

Take some time to reflect on God's love today.

May 16

Find Rest My Soul in God Alone

Psalm 62:5 *"Find rest, Oh my soul, in God alone; my hope comes from Him."*

Are you one of those people who is always trying to engineer the world, especially as it pertains to you? Do you worry and fret over things that may not even happen and magnify the significance of those that do?

Do you sometimes have to sit back and scold yourself for all the time and energy you waste worrying about such things, knowing the God is in control of both the major and minor events of your life. Hear His calming word to you today:

"Rest in Me, My child. Give your mind a break from planning and trying to anticipate what will happen. Pray continually, asking My Spirit to take charge of the details of this day. Remember that you are on a journey with Me. When you try to peer into the future and plan every possibility, you ignore your constant Companion who sustains you moment by moment. As you gaze anxiously into the distance, you don't even feel the strong grip of My hand holding yours."

How foolish we are when we try to get in God's way and take over the running of our lives. Remembrance of Him is a daily discipline and we should never lose sight of His constant and continual presence with us. We should rest in Him all day, every day. Only in God can we find true rest.

As His love streams through us, it washes away fear and distrust. He is always there and never leaves and is just a prayer away at all times and in all things. Because of that, we never have to face any situation alone. His presence is all around us. Don't worry about messing things up. He is always in control and He is more concerned with our persistence than our perfection.

May 17

Contentment

Philippians 4:11-13 *"Not that I am speaking of being in need, for I have learned in whatever situation I am to be content. I know how to be brought low, and I know how to abound. In any and every circumstance, I have learned the secret of facing plenty and hunger, abundance and need. I can do all things through him who strengthens me."*

How do you know if you are content? Have you ever thought about the meaning of the word contentment? What does it mean to be content in one's circumstances? Does it mean we sit still and wait for deliverance from our dire circumstances? Does it mean that we can never ask God for deliverance?

Contentment is an all-encompassing category that applies to every believer, no matter their life stage. To be content is to be fulfilled in Christ regardless of circumstances. It doesn't mean that we won't be sad now and then about our circumstances, but it means that in the midst of our pain we will be able to rejoice because Christ is our source of joy, not our circumstances. It means that our circumstances don't have control over our joy. Praying for deliverance isn't wrong- it's our attitude about our situation that is most important.

Sometimes sitting still and waiting on God to work for us is what is needed. Other times, waiting on God includes taking action on our part as the Holy Spirit leads us. Contentment is a hard character trait to cultivate, but when we look to Christ as Paul did, we will be able to face any dire circumstance with restful assurance and perseverance, whether that be financially, spiritually, or physically.

Examine your heart to see whether you are content or not. Is your joy coming from circumstances or from the Lord?

May 18

Put God First

If I had the opportunity to speak to my younger self, here's what I would say: Put God first in your life. Of course, this starts with embracing Christ as your Lord. Then it means following Him. Jesus summed it up this way:

Matthew 6:33 *"But seek first the kingdom of God and His righteousness, and all these things shall be added to you."*

Now, what did Jesus mean by *"all these things"*? We find the answer in the earlier verses, where He said,

Matthew 6:31-32 *"So don't worry about these things, saying, 'What will we eat? What will we drink? What will we wear?' These things dominate the thoughts of unbelievers, but your heavenly Father already knows all your needs."*

At times we seem obsessed with what we'll eat, drink, and wear. These are not necessarily bad things to think about, but Jesus is saying that we shouldn't make them the focus of our lives. Instead, we should put God first. We should seek first the kingdom of God: the rule and reign of Christ in our lives.

One day, we will enter the kingdom of Heaven in its fullness, but when the Bible tells us to seek the kingdom first, that means putting Jesus first in our lives, here and now.

Think about God's will when you make decisions. Don't put money first, career first, politics first, or even ministry first. Put God first in your life, and the rest will be blessed.

This doesn't mean that God will make you incredibly wealthy. What it means is that God will *"supply all your needs according to His riches in glory by Christ Jesus."* So put God first in everything and see what happens to your life.

May 19

Taking out the Trash

It seems as though there's some unwritten law of the universe that men must take out the trash. I don't know why, but that's our job. For some reason I put it off at my house even though it's really not that hard. Our trash cans have wheels and a handle, so all I need to do is drag them out front. Then someone comes along and picks up the trash.

They do their job, and they do it well. I'm glad about that because if they decided not to pick up our trash for a month, we'd have a serious situation. Now, what I'm about to say might seem a little odd: Jesus, in effect, wants to pick up your trash. Let me explain. Jesus said:

Matthew 11:28 *"Come to me, all of you who are weary and carry heavy burdens, and I will give you rest."*

In other words, *"Please bring your cares to Me. Please bring your anxieties and your worries and your problems and your burdens to Me. When you do that, I will give you rest."*

That's quite a promise because we all have cares and anxieties and worries that weigh us down. You know the feeling. Just when you lay your head down at night, here they come. What about this crisis? What about that uncertainty? Sometimes you're able to give them over to the Lord, but then they'll pop back into your head again. It feels like a lot of weight on your shoulders. Here's what the Bible says we should do:

1 Peter 5:7 *"Give all your worries and cares to God, for he cares about you."*

We need to put our worries into God's hands. When your burdens pile up, bring them to God. As a dear sister in Christ once told me, *"When you give God a job, don't take it back again by worrying about it!"*

May 20

No Room for Jesus

In addition to rocks, there are a lot of weeds in Israel, and weeds hinder the growth of seeds. In the parable of the Sower, Jesus talked about seeds that fell among thorns, and immediately the thorns choked them out. Then Jesus said:

Matthew 13:22 *"Now he who received seed among the thorns is he who hears the word, and the cares of this world and the deceitfulness of riches choke the word, and he becomes unfruitful."*

This describes someone who seems to be growing spiritually, but they gradually walk away because other things become more important. It isn't bad things necessarily, but it's the worries of this life, the concerns of this life, that take priority.

There's nothing wrong with being concerned about putting food on the table or a roof over your head. There's nothing wrong with thinking about the needs and necessities of life. But Jesus was describing someone who allows those things to become more important than God.

They believe it's good to read the Bible, to pray, and go to Church. It's just that they don't do it. It's a choice they're making. As someone has pointed out, *"The second best can often be the worst enemy of the best."* Jesus also said that *"the deceitfulness of riches"* choke the word. In Paul's first letter to Timothy, we find an interesting verse about wealth:

1 Timothy 6:10 *"For the love of money is a root of all kinds of evil, for which some have strayed from the faith in their greediness and pierced themselves through with many sorrows."*

You decide what money will be in your life. A thorn, or a weed, is anything that crowds Jesus out of our lives. So don't make your life about those things. Make Christ your primary focus instead.

May 21

Worry

If you want to overcome worry, it starts with right praying. The apostle Paul wrote said it clearly:

Philippians 4:6–7 *"Don't worry about anything; instead, pray about everything. Tell God what you need and thank him for all he has done. Then you will experience God's peace, which exceeds anything we can understand. His peace will guard your hearts and minds as you live in Christ Jesus."*

Paul used a military term for the word guard. He was saying, *"God's peace will stand guard around your heart and protect you."* So, when your mind is flooded with worry, you can say, *"Lord, I cast all of my care upon You because Your Word tells me that You care for me, and Your peace will guard my heart and mind."*

God's peace will stand guard over the two areas of your life that cause worry: the heart, which represents our emotions and feeling, and the mind, which refers to our thinking. Not only do we need right praying, but we also need right thinking. From the Apostle Paul again:

Philippians 4:8 *"Fix your thoughts on what is true, and honourable, and right, and pure, and lovely, and admirable. Think about things that are excellent and worthy of praise."*

The Message translation puts it this way:

"Summing it all up, friends, I'd say you'll do best by filling your minds and meditating on things true, noble, reputable, authentic, compelling, gracious – the best, not the worst; the beautiful, not the ugly; things to praise, not things to curse."

What we think about ultimately affects what we do. When we pray instead of worrying and rejoice instead of panicking, we will have peace.

May 22

God is our Provider

It seems sort of funny now, but back in the 1960s the word bread was a term for money. So, if someone said, *"You got any bread, man?"* that's what they were talking about.

In Luke 11:3 Jesus taught us to pray, *"Give us this day our daily bread..."* Bread was a staple of the first-century diet, so bread in this sense, speaks of everything. It speaks of your finances, a roof over your head, and your health. It speaks of everything you need in life.

And notice that Jesus said, *"daily bread,"* not monthly bread or yearly bread. The Lord will sometimes allow things to happen in our lives that remind us we need Him every day.

You might be going through something like that right now. Suddenly you're facing a financial crisis, or you've had a health scare. Suddenly, you're dealing with things this year you'd never imagined. You're saying, *"God, help!"*

Sometimes, God allows these things to remind us that He is our provider. He provides everything we have in life. So, we need to come to Him each day, not just asking for things, but giving Him glory for the things He already has provided.

When is the last time you simply prayed a prayer of thanks? Lord, thank you for this. Thank you for providing. Thank you for my spouse. Thank you for my family.

Jesus gave us a template for prayer in what we call The Lord's Prayer, to encourage us to pray about everything and give thanks to the Lord for your joys and His constant provision. He also wants you to bring your needs before Him every day and leave them at His feet as you trust Him to deal with them in His way and in His time.

May 23

Rivers in the Wasteland

We want to live on emotional mountaintops, but the reality is that spiritual fruit does not grow on mountaintops; it grows in the valleys. It grows in times of difficulty.

Isaiah 43:19 *(God said) "For I am about to do something new. See, I have already begun! Do you not see it? I will make a pathway through the wilderness. I will create rivers in the dry wasteland."*

It's in the wasteland, in the hardships, in the difficulties that I often experience God in a way that I don't experience Him anywhere else.

James 1:2-4 *"Dear brothers and sisters, when troubles of any kind come your way, consider it an opportunity for great joy. For you know that when your faith is tested, your endurance has a chance to grow. So let it grow, for when your endurance is fully developed, you will be perfect and complete, needing nothing."*

Maybe you're facing a time of hardship right now. Maybe you've had the bottom drop out in life, and you're asking, "Why is this happening to me? I'm a Christian. I'm walking with Jesus, yet this hardship has befallen me. What have I done to deserve this?" Every Christian will face trials in life - for their own good.

John 16:33 *(Jesus said) "Here on earth you will have many trials and sorrows. But take heart, because I have overcome the world."*

1 Peter 4:12-13 *"Dear friends, don't be surprised at the fiery trials you are going through, as if something strange were happening to you. Instead, be very glad - for these trials make you partners with Christ in his suffering."*

Spiritual refreshment often comes from times of spiritual testing.

May 24

God's Work in Suffering

Romans 8:17 *"And since we are his children, we are his heirs. In fact, together with Christ we are heirs of God's glory. But if we are to share his glory, we must also share his suffering."*

A while ago I read an unusual story about a man who survived a terrible shark attack. The man actually said he was thankful that it happened. It turns out that when he went to the hospital for treatment, his doctor discovered that he had cancer. They were able to successfully remove a tumour before it was too late. If the shark hadn't attacked him, he wouldn't have known that he had cancer. Who would ever think that a shark attack could end up being a good thing?

In the same way, spiritual attacks and trials will come into our lives, but they are opportunities to turn to the Lord and trust Him. We never know how God will take a hardship and use it for our good.

James 1:2–3 *"Dear brothers and sisters, when troubles of any kind come your way, consider it an opportunity for great joy. For you know that when your faith is tested, your endurance has a chance to grow."*

From the original Greek, we could also translate the phrase *"troubles of any kind"* to read *"many-coloured trials."* You might be going through a hardship that's different from what someone else is going through. But even when things look bleak, God ultimately will work all things together for His glory. God is in control of all circumstances that us.

God knows what you can handle. He's always keeping an eye on you, and His ultimate purpose is to conform you into the image of Jesus Christ (see Romans 8:29). The big picture, then, God's endgame for you, is to make you more like Jesus.

May 25

Hardship Builds Trust

Deuteronomy 8:11–14 *"Be careful that you do not forget the Lord your God . . . Otherwise, when you eat and are satisfied, when you build fine houses and settle down, and when your herds and flocks grow large and your silver and gold increase and all you have is multiplied, then your heart will become proud and you will forget the Lord your God, who brought you out of Egypt, out of the land of slavery."*

As they were (at long last) poised to enter the Promised Land, God warned the Israelites that the real danger to their lives had only just begun. Prior to this point, Israel had wandered in a desolate wilderness for forty years, dependent on God for everything. Every day they would step outside their little tents, and there would be manna waiting for them. God gave them fresh water to drink, a cloud to guide them and shade them by day, and a pillar of fire to light their camp by night.

Yes, wilderness living came with plenty of hardships. But those very difficulties compelled them to look to the Lord every day, depending on Him for everything. But then He brought them to the brink of the Promised Land, and they could look across the Jordan and see lush green hills, rippling fields of wheat, flowing rivers, and trees loaded with fruit. They could hardly wait to get in! But God was saying, *"Be careful! Watch out, or you'll get fat and impudent and forget all about Me."*

We've all experienced it: we are hit with uncertainty, danger, or pain, we fall to our knees and cry out to God. God can use adversity to bring us closer to Him - which is actually where we will experience the greatest blessings of life.

C. S. Lewis wrote: *"God whispers to us in our pleasures, speaks in our conscience, but shouts in our pains: it is His megaphone to rouse a deaf world."*

May 26

Infiltrating Culture

Ephesians 5:15–16 *"See then that you walk circumspectly, not as fools but as wise, redeeming the time, because the days are evil."*

There never was a dull day for the first-century followers of Jesus. In fact, it seems that wherever Paul went, there was either a conversion or a riot. The early Church didn't have modern technology at their disposal. Yet in a relatively short time, these believers changed their world. They permeated their entire culture.

Tertullian, a Christian leader and a contemporary of these early followers of Christ, said this of the Church: *"We are but of yesterday, and we have filled every place among you - cities, islands, fortresses, towns, marketplaces, the very camp, tribes, companies, palace, senate, forum - we have left nothing to you but the temples of your gods."*

The Church had infiltrated everything. You could even find Christians in the palace of Caesar! This is what we need today. We need Christians to go out and make a difference. We need Christians involved in the arts, making great films and creating graphic design. We need Christians in places of authority because the Bible says that when the righteous rule, the people rejoice (Proverbs 29:2). We need Christian doctors, lawyers, tradespeople and businesspeople. We need believers to let their light shine right through this culture today.

G. Campbell Morgan once said, *"Organized Christianity which fails to make a disturbance is dead."* Believers in the first century made a disturbance because they understood that God had called them to do their part. They took risks.

Sadly, it seems that the world is doing a far better job of infiltrating the Church than the other way around.

May 27

Courage

Great things in the world are usually only accomplished through courage. Plenty of people have great intentions, but great intentions only come to fruition through courage. For most of us, courage is something we have to learn and develop.

What we learn in Daniel 3 is that courage is an essential quality of those who would shine in Babylon. In the story of Shadrach, Meshach, and Abednego, we see the soul of Christian courage - both its substance and the fuel that sustains it. Christian courage believes that God can.

Shadrach, Meshach, and Abednego's answer to King Nebuchadnezzar's threat shows us that these three Hebrew teenage boys had no doubt who the biggest daddy in this little drama is:

Daniel 3:17 *"... our God whom we serve is able to deliver us from the burning fiery furnace ..."*

This is where courage begins: God is bigger. He's bigger than cancer or a lost job or a broken marriage. He's bigger than your sin and shame, bigger than the grave. And if you are His child, nothing happens to you without His permission. Not even a hair from your head falls without His knowledge. So, the hymn-writer asks:

Why should I feel discouraged? Why should the shadows come?
Why should my heart be lonely, and long for heaven and home,
When Jesus is my portion? My constant friend is he.
His eye is on the sparrow, and I know he watches me.

Christian courage believes that God can. Christian courage expects that God will.

May 28

Are You Unoffendable?

When we study what Jesus taught, it is obvious that He came to make us unoffendable. Consider: He says that if someone slaps you on one cheek, offer him the other (Luke 6:29). He said to love our enemies and bless those who curse us (Luke 6:27-28). What He's really doing is showing us how a heart of love which cannot be offended will overcome all adversity.

We ask the Lord to change us and to answer that prayer He sometimes puts us in situations that offend us. The offense itself awakens our need of grace.

Thus, the Lord precipitates change by first offending the area of our soul He desires to transform.
God does not expect us to merely survive adversity but to become Christlike in the midst of adversity.

Ask Joseph in the Old Testament: his offense became the path to his anointing and power because he possessed an unoffendable heart. He never stopped trusting God in spite of the injustices and trials he faced.

The destiny God has for us unfolds or withers at the junction of offense. How we handle offense is the key to our tomorrow.

Psalm 119:165 *"Those who love God's law have great peace, and nothing causes them to stumble."*

Let us pray that the Lord will grant us that new creation heart that can walk as Jesus walked through a world of offenses without stumbling.

May we see everything as an opportunity to pray and to become Christlike. May be always interpret offenses as opportunities that lead to transformation. May we embrace the pulse and beat of Christ's unoffendable heart within us.

May 29

Embracing Change

Hebrews 13:8 *"Jesus Christ is the same yesterday and today and forever."*

I am someone who embraces change better than most and I usually know how to make the most of the circumstances which come my way. However, I would never say I love change. I really don't know anyone who loves change. Whether it's sudden, like the loss of a job, or expected, like a child leaving home to build their own life, change can be difficult, and adjusting to change takes time.

With change comes unknowns and what-ifs. What was normal no longer is, and a new normal has yet to settle in. That's why I find the above verse in Hebrews so reassuring. When everything else in life can change in a moment, Jesus doesn't change. He is our solid foundation in a world of upheaval and unknowns.

Despite whatever change we're going through; Jesus will be there. Whether or not we reach out to Him is another story. We have the choice to rely on ourselves and our own abilities, but when change comes, it can rock our confidence and leave us anxious and unsettled. Jesus is a constant presence when nothing else makes sense. Change doesn't surprise Him like it does us. Jesus is the same yesterday, today, and tomorrow. He stands firm, and when we keep our focus on Him, He is our lifeline. When we rely on Jesus, He brings peace.

Hebrews 12:1-2 *"… let us run with perseverance the race marked out for us, fixing our eyes on Jesus, the pioneer and perfecter of faith."*

When you're facing transition and unexpected changes, keep your focus on Jesus - the One who doesn't change.

May 30

Our Future Hope

Romans 5:1-5 *"Therefore, since we have been justified through faith, we have peace with God through our Lord Jesus Christ, through whom we have gained access by faith into this grace in which we now stand. And we boast in the hope of the glory of God. Not only so, but we also glory in our sufferings, because we know that suffering produces perseverance; perseverance, character; and character, hope. And hope does not put us to shame, because God's love has been poured out into our hearts through the Holy Spirit, who has been given to us."*

Sometimes when we're wrestling with difficult circumstances such as the loss of a family member, a diagnosis of cancer, or the loss of a job, it's hard to be able to rest in God and trust Him. It's so much easier to trust Him when things are going well. We can't always see the 'why' of a situation, so we tend to doubt and wonder if the light will ever shine in the tunnel.

But God created the earth so that light would always overcome darkness and that the sun will always rise when you wake up; His creation is the promise of something better and gives us just a hint of what is to come.

God wants us to rest in Him knowing that at the end of our situation, it will ultimately be better, whether we see our problems resolved here on earth or in Heaven. We have the promise of future hope, joy, and peace.

God doesn't want us to worry about our current problems but to have our focus geared towards the future. When we keep the future in mind and know where we are headed and who we are becoming, we are better able to handle the present.

Are you anxious about something? Trying to find peace? Whatever the situation, remember your future hope and keep the bigger picture in mind, even if you can't see the end result.

May 31

I Can do This!

Philippians 4:12-13 *"I know what it is to be in need, and I know what it is to have plenty. I have learned the secret of being content in any and every situation, whether well fed or hungry, whether living in plenty or in want. I can do all this through him who gives me strength."*

"God, when is it going to be my turn?" How many times has that question come into your mind over the years? It can be really hard when the life you long for is constantly overwhelmed by the life you have; as you are forced to deal with what is whilst dreaming about what could be and maybe, your think, what should be!

Perhaps you have known the pain of betrayal, loss, persecution or just can't get your head above the water as the pressures of life overpower you. Perhaps your mind and your heart seem constantly restless? It doesn't have to be that way.

God does not want you to feel short-changed or overwhelmed by circumstances you never asked for and feel powerless to overcome. He wants you to rise above that and embrace the many blessings you have right now. He wants you to embrace what is and not fret about what isn't.

We all struggle with life's circumstances. Very few of us have the life we imagined when we were young. But, like the Apostle Paul, we can find our peace in knowing that God is in control and that His plan for us is perfect.

We live like the circumstances in which we find ourselves is the only reality we have. God and His love for us is a far greater reality and the only one which should matter in the final analysis. Read Paul's words above again, and ask God to give you that same faith and assurance.

June 1

Enough

Perhaps the deepest longing of every human heart is to find adequacy in everything that defines life for us.

We want an adequate car, an adequate house, an adequate income. And we want the people in our lives to be enough. The word *"adequate"* means *"sufficient for a specific requirement."*

The problem is. . . we often choose what that "requirement" is. One we have laid out for ourselves. What we think will be "just enough."

When nothing seems to be sufficient, we often listen to the cries around us that say, *"I am enough. You don't have to put up with less than sufficient. Try me."* So, we try what these various voices offer. But they eventually come up short. Less than we require. Never enough.

Why? Why are we tempted to feel short-changed in life? Do we have contentment issues? Is it simply living in an imperfect world?

Or could it be we're looking in the wrong places?

Are we looking at the wrong things to be our *"Enough"*?

If there was one person who had enough, it was King David. Not because he was a king, won wars, and was given amazing promises. He had enough, because of Who his Shepherd was.

Psalm 23:1 *"The LORD is my shepherd; I shall not want."*

He never suggested that his possessions or his wonderful accomplishments were enough. His Shepherd was Enough. His God was adequate. So, nothing was missing in his life.

June 2

What Rules Your Heart?

Colossians 3:15 *"Let the peace of Christ rule in your hearts, since as members of one body you were called to peace. And be thankful."*

Busy, breathless, things seem a little crazy lately? Most of us know that kind of running. It just happens. Life happens. As things pile up, things fall behind. As we run, our quiet peace becomes a quickened pace. Our relationships start to show a frayed edge. The bank account of calm that we have carefully invested in, slowly gets drawn down until it's in the red. Concern and unrest begin to rule our hearts and our minds and our behaviour begins to show the edginess of impatience and irritation.

There is a prescription for just such times in our life. It's an age-old formula that works to restore peace to the centre of our lives. It's a way we can live in peace and confidence even when life swirls around us at a crazy pace.

The wisdom God reveals in the Bible is foundational wisdom that can carry us through our days and right through life. When it is applied, the power and strength behind it will amaze you. It will change your day-to-day living. This transformation is always only a choice away: Choose peace.

Allowing God's peace to rule your inner being is a choice that involves being intentional about two things: living in harmony with other believers and being thankful.

Living in harmony doesn't mean overlooking differences or living without boundaries. No, it means being willing to be a *peacemaker*, not simply a *peacekeeper*. It means looking with gratitude at the situations and people around you and, from that platform of gratitude and harmony, create solutions with the help of God's Holy Spirit.

June 3

God's Perfect Design

God's design for us is that we live in perfect harmony with Him and that we live and move and have our very being in Christ, through Christ and for Christ. All that comes as a free gift. That free gift comes to us in love, with no strings attached, no requirements, no religious hoops we have to jump through – it is a wonderful, outrageous and dangerously free gift.

So, your favour before God and your right standing with God is not in any way determined by your personal performance – and just as well – because if it was, then your performance would have to be absolute 100% perfect, because even the tiniest sin would destroy you in the presence of God.

Your eternal relationship with God, has been secured by God Himself. He wouldn't trust you with something so important to Him. On our smart phones and computers today, we have an option to reset the device and 'restore factory settings.' Well, that is exactly what God did for us and only God could do it. He restored our default settings; our original design; our intended purpose - and He did it all in and through the life, death and resurrection of Jesus Christ.

This is the gospel! Believe it, receive it and watch it transform your entire life. This is why every man, woman and young person on this planet pays homage to this Christ every time they write the date. This is why all our schools, our hospitals, our judicial system, our governments all have their roots in the community of faith which this one Man birthed.

Only the One Who made us and designed us could press that reset button and He did that through the most outrageous, unbelievable act of love and grace.

2 Corinthians 5:21 *"For He made Him who knew no sin to be sin for us, that we might become the righteousness of God in Him."*

June 4

Believe

John 11:40 *"Did I not tell you that if you believed, you would see the glory of God?"*

Belief is necessary for glory to be seen.

A host of people were standing around Lazarus' tomb. Some were friendly to Jesus, some were opposed, all were interested in what He was about to do.

Few had much faith, none could expect what was going to happen, but even the tiniest seeds of faith can move mountains and the rudiments of belief were all that was necessary to see God's glory.

Those who believed in Jesus that day still had a faith limited by what they understood to be possible. When Jesus had not acted within the grid of those expectations by healing Lazarus or getting there in time to raise him before they believed his spirit had departed, they were disappointed.

But Jesus didn't explain. He didn't vindicate to His disciples His decision to wait. He didn't comfort the grieving sisters with a preview of His plan. He just said if they would believe they would see the glory of God. He still calls us to do that.

When we're disappointed because He doesn't act in ways that we can conceive; when He seems too late; when our heads swim with grief and unmet expectations; we need to heed His call to simply believe and let Him take our faith to that next level of understanding and the experience of His glory.

John 11:40 *"Did I not tell you that if you believed, you would see the glory of God?"*

June 5

What Would Happen If ...?

What would happen if ... we really believed that Jesus will never leave us or forsake us. (Hebrews 13:5)? Maybe we would stop praying that God would, "be with us" and accept that He is always with us. Maybe we would stop asking God to be with others when we intercede for them and just pray that they might know that He is already with them.

What would happen if ... we really believed that it is God Who arranges the parts of the Body of Christ (1 Corinthians 12:18) and that our Pastor, Elders, leaders and fellow worshippers in the local Church are placed there by God to speak into our lives? Maybe we would embrace the teaching from our own Church more than we do.

What would happen if ... we really believed that He that is in us is greater than he that is in the world. (1 John 1:4)? Maybe we would stop living in fear of the enemy ... stop looking for the work of Satan and start believing that Jesus has conquered the enemy once and for all time so that we can live in victory and safety every day.

What would happen if ... we really believed that the Holy Spirit inspired what was left out of the Bible as well as what is included? Maybe then we would not get caught up in all the 'end-times' speculation about the antichrist, the mark of the beast, the time of the Lord's second coming and the ministry of Satan.

What would happen if ... we really believed that God has given us everything we need for a Godly life through our knowledge of Him Who called us by His own glory and goodness. (2 Peter 1:3)? Maybe then we would stop asking God for what is already ours and start trusting in what He has already given us.

June 6

The Clarity of Scripture

On May 3, 1997, world chess champion Gary Kasparov pitted his strategic brilliance against the IBM supercomputer, Deep Blue. From the outset, Kasparov's superiority was evident. But Move 44 from Deep Blue changed everything.

The supercomputer made a move that was so remarkably amateur and seemingly suicidal it spooked Kasparov. He could not believe what he just witnessed, attributing Move 44 to "superior intelligence," just assuming Deep Blue had set up a complicated trap.

Out-thinking himself, Kasparov abandoned his normal winning strategy and proceeded to make a series of unorthodox and disastrous plays that led to the triumph of machine over man. It was only in the aftermath of victory that the IBM programmers revealed Move 44 was due to a bug in Deep Blue's software.

Tragically, many people make the same error when it comes to interpreting Scripture. Rejecting the plain, clear, simple meaning of the text, they chase after some complex, deeper, mysterious truth buried within. They treat the Bible like a coded message, resorting to all sorts of exotic techniques to unlock its meaning - everything from numerology to allegory to postmodern deconstruction.

The Bible is not an ancient riddle, and biblical exegesis is not a treasure hunt. There is no fundamental Christian doctrine that hasn't been plainly revealed in Scripture. And yet much of modern scholarship is overrun with people who are so busy excavating deeper meaning that they end up burying the truth right under their noses. We should be thankful that God has chosen to communicate clearly with fallen humanity; that He isn't into smokescreens. He says what He means and means what He says.

June 7

My Sheep Hear My Voice

Jesus distinguished His true followers from the rest of the world with this simple statement:

John 10:27 *"My sheep hear My voice…"*

So how do you know you're hearing from Him? How can you be sure? There's no shortage of people today who claim to hear all sorts of things from God. For some, God gives them clear impressions on what they need to do. Others gain personal reassurance after hearing a divine voice. There are even those who claim to receive specific information from God about other people and their futures.

It has been said that time and truth go hand in hand. And time has invariably revealed that many who claim to hear from God are clearly mistaken. The God of truth is incapable of communicating an erroneous message. We need a means of hearing from God that doesn't leave us vulnerable to our own subjective impressions.

The greatest grace gift given to us, of course, is salvation. But we would know nothing about that salvation were it not for Scripture. So, in reality, the greatest grace gift is divine revelation. Nothing is more important than divine truth. You have to have the truth in order to embrace the gift of salvation in Christ. The greatest thing we have is the Word of God. This is the divine revelation – the written Word, the Bible and the Living Word, Jesus Christ.

Alongside that, the distinguishing characteristic of true Christians is that they listen to the Word of God. They hear the Word. They believe the Word. They love the Word. They obey the Word. That's what distinguishes a Christian.

June 8

Facing Trials

Patience doesn't come naturally to the carnal mind. But even the mind renewed by the Spirit of God can find patience to be an elusive virtue - especially in the face of trials.

That is why Peter had to remind his readers that suffering patiently is pleasing to God (1 Peter 2:20). We, too, need to be reminded because trials are inevitable for those who remain faithful to Christ. Christians will always encounter distinct forms of hardship.

There is the unique kind of trouble that Christians have, and that's the trouble of persecution for the sake of truth. We are persecuted because of Christ. That is a kind of suffering that the rest of the world does not experience or endure. We have to face the rejection of a hostile society who rejects the gospel. True Christians will certainly face trials and hostility from an unbelieving world. Jesus promised as much:

John 15:18–19 *"If the world hates you, keep in mind that it hated me first. If you belonged to the world, it would love you as its own. As it is, you do not belong to the world, but I have chosen you out of the world. That is why the world hates you."*

The question isn't will we face trials, but rather how will we respond when trials invariably come. The book of James in the New Testament provides the proper eternal perspective on Christian suffering. It is a powerful reminder concerning how we view and understand the trials we face.

James 5:7–11 *"Be patient, then, brothers and sisters, until the Lord's coming. See how the farmer waits for the land to yield its valuable crop, patiently waiting for the autumn and spring rains. You too, be patient and stand firm, because the Lord's coming is near."*

June 9

No Worries, Mate!

Matthew 6:25 *"Therefore I say to you, do not worry about your life, what you will eat or what you will drink; nor about your body, what you will put on. Is not life more than food and the body more than clothing?"*

In Australia we have many great 'Aussie' expressions. Two of my favourites, which are often said together are, *"No worries, mate!"* and *"She'll be right!"* I think that nicely sums up the point Jesus was making in the verse above.

When we worry, essentially, we are not trusting God. In fact, the word worry originates from a term that actually means 'to strangle' and that's exactly what worry does to us. It strangles us. It chokes us.

Worry is the interest that we pay on troubles before they're due. It comes down to this: We need to trust in the providence of God and the sovereignty of God. Simply put, that means that we accept the truth that God is in control of our lives as followers of Jesus.

You may not understand why you're dealing with a hardship right now, but God has allowed it for some reason. Nothing touches us that has not first passed through God's loving hands. He's in control. So instead of worrying, let's put God first in our lives. Hear the words of Jesus again and again:

Matthew 6:33 *"Seek first the kingdom of God and His righteousness, and all these things shall be added to you."*

The word *seek* speaks of persistence. Let's imagine that you dropped a $100 note on the ground, and a little breeze picked it up and took it away. Would you go looking for it? Would you seek something that valuable? Of course, you would. Well, how does that even compare to the kingdom of God – the rule and reign of Jesus Christ in our lives?

June 10

Your Thoughts Matter

Isaiah 26:3 *"You will keep in perfect peace all who trust in you, all whose thoughts are fixed on you!"*

Maintaining personal peace involves both the heart and the mind. Why do our thoughts matter? It is because what we think about ultimately affects what we do.

Proverbs 23:7 *"For as he thinks in his heart, so is he."* (NKJV)

It is therefore important to guard your mind – to protect it. Think about what you're going to watch or what you're going to download and listen to. Ask yourself whether what you're going to do will build you up or tear you down spiritually, because ultimately it will affect your actions. The apostle Paul wrote this to the believers in Philippi:

Philippians 4:8 *"Finally, brothers and sisters, whatever is true, whatever is noble, whatever is right, whatever is pure, whatever is lovely, whatever is admirable – if anything is excellent or praiseworthy – think about such things."*

We need to think about godly things more, and we need to think biblically. Replace those thoughts of anxiety, worry, and panic with godly thoughts. Turn your panic into prayer. Pray for little things and big things. Pray for everything.

Philippians 4:6–7 *"Don't worry about anything; instead, pray about everything. Tell God what you need and thank him for all he has done. Then you will experience God's peace, which exceeds anything we can understand. His peace will guard your hearts and minds as you live in Christ Jesus."*

When you face tough times, your thoughts will be like a rudder which steers a mighty ship. So, fill your mind with the Word of God.

June 11

How Bright is Your Light?

Matthew 5:14-15 *"You are the light of the world - like a city on a hilltop that cannot be hidden. No one lights a lamp and then puts it under a basket. Instead, a lamp is placed on a stand, where it gives light to everyone in the house."*

I recently saw a satellite image of our world - taken at night. Places in Europe were lit up like a Christmas tree but other places like China and North Korea were completely dark.

As I marvelled at this photo, I found myself wondering: if we were to take a spiritual satellite image of our world, where would the light and darkness be? Would the light be bright where we live? How bright is my own light? Is it glowing brightly enough for others to see? Or is it a dull radiance that is barely perceived?

I believe many of us know a lot *about* God. We know about God like we know about our favourite actor, singer, or band member. We may even pride ourselves on our knowledge of God. We've loaded up on information about God through Bible studies, sermons and books, but have we neglected to develop an intimate, personal relationship with Him? We may quote verses, tell others how they should live but neglect to live in close relationship with God ourselves.

We live self-centred, self-serving lives. Where is our light? Is our life just meaningless words or are we truly living what we say we believe? How bright is your light?

Think of a part of your life that you have kept dim; maybe it's the side of you that comes out at your child's sporting events or when you take a night off with your friends, or even your workplace. Intentionally bring a little light into those places this week by using positive speech, unconditional love, and the presence of Jesus!

June 12

A Fiery Sermon

A member of a certain Church, who previously had been attending services regularly, stopped going. After a few weeks, the Pastor decided to visit him.

It was a chilly evening. The Pastor found the man at home alone, sitting before a blazing fire. Guessing the reason for his Pastor's visit, the man welcomed him, led him to a big chair near the fireplace and waited.

The Pastor made himself comfortable but said nothing. In the grave silence, he contemplated the play of the flames around the burning logs.

After some minutes, the Pastor stood to his feet, then took hold of the fire tongs, carefully picking up a brightly burning ember and placed it to one side of the hearth all alone. Then he sat back in his chair, still silent.

The host watched all this in quiet fascination.

Many more minutes passed – in silence - as the one lone ember's flame diminished, there was a momentary glow and then its fire was no more. Soon it was cold and as 'dead as a doornail.'

Not a word had been spoken since the initial greeting. After more silence - the Pastor decided it was time for him to leave, but before he did, the Pastor went over to the fireplace, picked up the cold, dead ember and placed it back in the middle of the fire. Immediately it began to glow once more with the light and warmth of all the burning coals around it.

As the Pastor reached the door to leave, his host said, "*Thank you so much for your visit, Pastor - and especially for the fiery sermon. I shall see you next Sunday in Church.*"

June 13

Finding Stillness

It is so hard to get through even one day without hearing some bad news. If you connect with any news bulletin you will certainly be bombarded. If you are like me, sometimes you will feel the impulse to push away bad news of any kind. But it seems excessive to simply ignore what is going on. Certainly, this world needs our prayers and assistance. Didn't God call us to do more than bury our heads in the sand? Absolutely. Jesus told us many times that we are to care for each other. Therefore, it is vital to be aware of what's going on, but crucial to remain steadfast in Him.

In Psalm 46, we are taught that God is our refuge and strength and that we can have hope for the future. While the Psalm contains reminders of God's might and descriptions of what we can withstand when God is our focus, the key to peace is near the end of the chapter.

The final verses remind us of how God alone is our safe place. We are also given a beautiful call to action that reminds us that even in the midst of turmoil, we can experience peace. God simply prompts us to be still - stop talking, questioning, and arguing, and just listen. He prompts us to know - stop doubting and have faith. What does God prompt us to know? That He is God. He is the Almighty Refuge Who is in control. He will guide us, protect us and lead us to everlasting life.

Lord, it is so easy for me to get consumed by fear when the world seems to be falling apart. When my heart and mind are overwhelmed, help me to be still and to remember that you alone created this world; nothing in it is beyond your control!

So today, I want to encourage you to pause and be still before God and remember who He is, responding with worship, praise and thanksgiving.

June 14

Fighting Fear

The stronger our trust is in God, the greater our power over fear. Have you ever noticed how quickly fear can sneak up on us and sweep us up into a whirlwind of anxious thoughts spiralling out of control? Have you also noticed that fear often rolls in like storm clouds that darken every thought in every corner of our soul?

This is the work of the enemy of God – he does this often, he loves this scare tactic, because sadly, it works almost every time. Sometimes a very small circumstance that is troubling us becomes huge in an instant and fills us with fear, and we don't even know how it happened so suddenly.

That's the nature of fear. It eats away at peace and stability in our lives. It threatens to invade every waking moment of our day. Fear takes on a life of its own and undermines our faith and trust in God.

God has not given us a spirit of fear. God gives us courage, boldness, and strength. That is His nature and it is what He desires for us through His strength within us.

Our enemy, Satan, wants us to always walk in fear. God, our heavenly Father Who loves us with an everlasting love calls us to cast out all fear and walk in power, love, and with a sound mind. When we do this, fear is conquered in us! We overcome what the enemy brings against us through fear.

When we learn to fight fear and receive God's strength to do so, we will face fear as a challenge we know we can overcome, instead of letting it overcome us.

2 Timothy 1:7 *"For God has not given us a spirit of fear, but of power and of love and of a sound mind."*

June 15

Knowing God's Love

Galatians 1:15 *"But when he who had set me apart before I was born, and who called me by his grace."*

You may remember the old love ballad by the band called Foreigner called *"I want to know what love is."* It is one of their most popular songs. I thought about this song when I read Galatians 1:15. It is such a glorious fact about the God Who I worship that He *"set me apart before I was born"* and *"called me by His grace."* That is a love that I cannot fully understand. It continues to amaze me when I think about how God loves me.

In my earthly reasoning, I am sure I love things or people that help me or bring me joy. I love family and friends because they support me and love me even when I am not so lovely. I love riding my Harley Davidson because it allows me to forget about life for a while as the wind rushes past me. Or maybe I love to eat a good meal because it satisfies my taste buds. The love we show for people and things often brings benefit to us. That isn't a bad thing necessarily - it just seems to be how our mind works when using earthly wisdom.

That is what is so amazing about the above verse and the love of God. God chose me. God loved me, before I was born. He chose to love me so much even though He knew that I would be a sinner and would put things and even people before Him. Yet, He choose to love me and give me His grace.

Have you thought about the love of God today? Did you thank Him today for His love and grace in your life? Galatians 1:15 is a verse that humbles me again today. It makes me think of the cross. It makes me think about Jesus dying for me. My prayer is that you will reflect on God's grace in your life today and be able to show love to those around you and in doing so, bring honour and worship to God.

June 16

Love Your Enemies

We talk a lot about rights these days. Yet the attention given to human entitlements hasn't brought about much corporate or personal freedom. Instead, most people are prisoners of jealousy (you have greater rights than I do!), greed (I deserve more!), or bitterness (my rights have been violated!).

Instead of focusing on the privileges due to us, we should take the biblical perspective of loving our enemies and forgiving our persecutors (Matthew 5:44). Believers should lay down their rights so they can take up the cause of God's kingdom.

That doesn't mean that we let people trample on us. Rather, we offer a proper response according to biblical principles. In short, believers should be more concerned about showing God's love to those who wrong them than about demanding their rights.

Maybe you're thinking, *"But he doesn't know how I've been mistreated."* I certainly do not. But what I do know is how Jesus, our example, reacted to terrible abuse. He was betrayed by His friends, persecuted by His people, condemned by His peers, and crucified for our sins. Yet some of His last words were, *"Father, forgive them."* (Luke 23:34).

Before assuming that Jesus' capacity for forgiveness and love is out of reach for mere human beings, remember that His Spirit dwells in all believers. We can choose to give away our rights and let God's love work through us.

In Luke 6:29 we are exhorted to turn the other cheek and give more than is asked because expressing love always outweighs exerting our rights. You can't lose when you show others the love of God. You gain His blessing, and, hopefully, someone may even come to Jesus because of your example.

June 17

A New Default Setting

Romans 8 *"Therefore, there is now no condemnation for those who are in Christ Jesus ... Those who live in accordance with the Spirit have minds set on what the Spirit desires ... You are controlled not by the sinful nature but by the Spirit, if the Spirit of God lives in you."*

Even as I depend on my computer for the activities of daily life, I am also frequently frustrated when my assumptions about what it can or should do prove to be wrong. Why do margins or indentations change? How can information I thought I inserted into a document suddenly change?

In their effort to explain this phenomenon, technology experts toss around the phrase 'default setting' all the time. They say with feigned patience, *"The computer (or all new works of technology) is just returning to its default setting,"*

Default settings are controls of a computer or software as pre-set by its manufacturer. Some types of default settings may be altered or customized by the user. A spiritual application comes to mind here. When God created us, He declared us good! His perfect default setting. But then mankind changed that setting by choosing to set themselves in opposition to God ... they sinned. Ever since that point in time, a new 'setting' has been a part of our basic nature: *"All have sinned"* (Romans 3:23) and *"sin entered the world through one man, and death through sin ... because all sinned."* (Romans 5:12).

But God, in His infinite wisdom and love, chooses to make possible a new default setting: Christ comes to not just change a few incidentals in our lives, but to make us completely new creations. He installs totally new control protocols – through the Holy Spirit within us. Perhaps it is time you reverted to God's default setting?

June 18

Finding Peace in the Storm

Colossians 3:15 *"Let the peace of Christ rule in your hearts, since as members of one body you were called to peace. And be thankful."*

Our sense of peace can be dislodged or replaced by turmoil and confusion before we even realize it. God's Word puts it simply - in order to have God's peace in our hearts we must make the choice to let His peace rule there.

As soon as you recognize irritation or turmoil taking over in your spirit, you should stop! Almost without fail you will find the peace of God gets pushed aside when anything that has "self" as its source surges forward.

Self-defence in a relationship, results in turmoil; self-pity puts you on the slippery slope of discouragement; self-seeking in business, or even ministry, allows a shallowness to creep in that pushes peace aside; self-energy: seeking to live the Christian life in our own strength, leads to defeat.

As long as self is the focus in our thoughts and actions, there is little room for God to do His work in us or through us and His peace cannot rule in our hearts.

When we choose to let Him be the focus of all we do, drawing only on His energy, His help, His wisdom, His patience, His purposes, then His peace will rule in our hearts.

Pay attention today to what is going on in your spirit. If peace is eluding you, take a look inside and see where self-focus has taken over. Let God's peace rule in your heart by bringing everything in your day under the umbrella of His care. It is the best way to live in peace! Choose to let His peace rule in your heart today. Choose to pay close attention today to what is going on deep in your spirit.

June 19

Zephaniah 3:17

Zephaniah 3:17 *"The LORD your God is with you, he is mighty to save. He will take great delight in you, he will quiet you with his love, he will rejoice over you with singing."*

Have you ever felt like you were excluded from the 'in' crowd? Maybe it happened in school when teams were being chosen or perhaps there was a family gathering and nobody told you about it. When you feel like a misfit, the feeling of not belonging can follow you for many years. I wouldn't say this was a huge problem for me as a child, but I do remember how this feels and it's horrible.

When I heard that God loves me, I figured, of course, He has to because God loves the whole world. But, as I continued to read the Bible, I began to comprehend that Jesus loves Me, personally. I was not an accident because my God created me according to a beautiful blueprint. My God watched me as I was being formed … woven together in the womb (Psalm 139:14-16). What's more, Jesus valued me enough to die for me personally so I might live through Him forever!

Romans 5:8 *"But God demonstrates his love for us in this: While we were still sinners, Christ died for us."*

Now if I receive Jesus as my Saviour and Lord, He will adopt me into His family and it has nothing to do with me being deserving; it is God's free gift. What good news! When I finally embraced the love of God and accepted Jesus and His gift of salvation, that was the beginning of a brand-new identity as a beloved child of God in whom God delights.

This good news is for you too. Just think about it, the Creator of the universe loves you! It's not love at a distance, but He's actually involved in your life. He's walking with you.

June 20

Draw Near to God

I want to be counted among those who intentionally draw near to Jesus - near to the One Who saved us, loves us, and pours immeasurable grace and mercy into our lives; the One Who leads us and guides us, strengthens us, and never leaves us alone.

I remember others long ago who are known for drawing near:

I remember Mary, at the feet of Jesus.

I remember John, leaning on the chest of Jesus

I remember David, the psalmist whose soul thirsted for God.

I remember Enoch, walking close beside Him - so close, in fact, that God just walked him right into heaven, completely bypassing death.

The list could go on and on. I want my name to be included with those who have deeply desired intimate communion and fellowship with the Lord. Don't you?

I want to draw near to the Lord who wakens me each morning and reminds me that this a brand new day which He has made - a day to be glad.

And I am glad, deep-in-my-heart glad, that I am His and He is mine. I am grateful that I have the privilege of walking in close relationship with Him.

Let's live each day for Him and with Him and be counted near. There is no better place to be than near to God.

Psalm 145:1 *"The LORD is near to all who call upon Him, to all who call upon Him in truth."*

June 21

Crying out to God

Psalm 34:15-17 *"The eyes of the Lord are toward the righteous. And His ears are open to their cry. The face of the Lord is against evildoers, to cut off the memory of them from the earth. The righteous cry, and the Lord hears and delivers them out of all their troubles."*

The Lord is ready and able to assist us when we are in need. But He needs one thing before He will intervene and pour out His heavenly force into our circumstance: a righteous heart.

Our Father does not expect us to lead faultless lives because He is aware of that impossibility. When a sinner seeks the salvation of God, He purifies their hearts from sin and gives them a new nature (2 Corinthians 5:7).

The Lord invites us to confess and repent when we fall short because even believers occasionally behave in ways that are consistent with their old flesh. He will *"cleanse us from all unrighteousness"* (1 John 1:9). He hears us, thankfully, even through our flaws, as long as we choose to follow Him.

Psalm 34 reminds us that our heavenly Father wants to hear His children's cries. We often pray in this way during difficult times - with more intensity, emotion, and sincerity. Hannah is a good illustration. She went to the temple, distraught over her infertility, and cried out to the Lord with such intensity that the priest mistook her for being intoxicated. In response to her prayer, God opened her womb (1 Samuel 1:1-20).

Jesus made it possible for you to cry out to God whenever you are in need. He will always hear and respond, either granting your desired request or offering an alternative resolution. You can always put your complete trust in Him to provide whatever He believes you need.

June 22

Hang in There!

Hebrews 19:35-36 *"So do not throw away this confident trust in the Lord. Remember the great reward it brings you! Patient endurance is what you need now, so that you will continue to do God's will. Then you will receive all that he has promised."*

When it comes to His promises to you, God is not slack. He is still thinking of you. I use the same words I've repeatedly used to motivate myself today to motivate you.

Trusting a God you cannot see is difficult. Trusting that He cares about your issues is not always simple. However, the reality is that the God we worship will always keep His word.

In the above passage we are warned to not abandon our firm faith in the Lord. The belief that something will occur based on God's character is known as confident trust.

Once more, He keeps all of His promises. Therefore, we should place our trust in His ability to fulfil His promises in His time and in His way.

So, I implore you to hold on to your fearless confidence right now, no matter how difficult it may feel to do so. Accept the patient endurance that enables us to persevere in difficult situations without giving in.

This perseverance encourages us to keep on going even when we are tired. If we just persevere, we shall eventually reap the harvest that has been promised to us. Today, I exhort you to stick with God's plan.

Until you see God's promised outcome, be committed, keep believing, keep trusting, and keep battling.

June 23

Come to Me ...

Matthew 11:28 *"Come to me, all you who are weary and burdened, and I will give you rest."*

The gentle invitation to come is the cry of the Christian faith. *"Go, step carefully on the path in which you walk,"* sternly commanded Jewish law. *"You will perish if you disobey the commandments, but you will live if you obey them."* The law compelled people to submit to it forcefully even if it was a blessing; the gospel draws people to itself with arms of love.

Jesus is the good Shepherd Who leads His sheep by walking with them, encouraging them to follow Him and beckoning them to move forwards with the inviting phrase, "*Come.*" The gospel draws while the law repels. The gospel spans that terrible abyss and carries the sinner across it; the law reveals the gap between God and mankind and demands that we bridge it alone.

"Come, come to me ..." will be the message of Christ to you from the beginning of your spiritual life until you are finally welcomed fully into heaven. Like a mother beckoning her little child to walk by holding out her finger and saying, "*Come,*" so does Jesus.

He will constantly be with you, pleading with you to follow Him just as the soldier does his captain. You will hear His sweet voice beckoning you to follow Him throughout your entire life as He always goes before you to prepare your route and clear your path. The wonderful words He will use to welcome you into the celestial realm at the solemn hour of death will be, "*Come, you who are so blessed of my Father.*"

Are you prepared to hear and obey God when He calls? How can you prepare your mind and heart today?

June 24

Inexpressible Joy

1 Peter 1:8 *"Though you have not seen Him, you love Him; and even though you do not see Him now, you believe in Him and are filled with an inexpressible and glorious joy…"*

Would you describe your life as filled with an inexpressible joy? I'm not talking about a shallow happiness or a fake-it-till-you-make-it disposition, but actual deep-down joy!

There is a sense of giddiness that can come from the joy of releasing all that you are, and everything that you have, into the hands of the One Who loves you the most. Also, there's an unshakeable confidence that He can handle any situation that should ever arise under any circumstance!

This is the kind of inexpressible and glorious joy that Peter said was characteristic of Christ's followers to whom he wrote his letter. What makes this description even more remarkable is that he wrote to believers who, unlike himself, had never seen Jesus personally. They had never witnessed any of His miracles firsthand or, even, heard a word He taught.

They had only experienced Christ, by faith, from what they had heard and were taught about Him. Still, Peter says they loved Him and believed in Him. As a result, they were transformed and filled with an inexpressible and glorious joy!

Furthermore, their joy didn't depend on their circumstances. While happiness often depends on what happens to us or around us, the joy that Jesus brings by the Holy Spirit into our hearts transcends whatever happens here and now. That's why this joy is inexpressible and glorious! Jesus offers you His joy no matter what you are going through today. So, throw all your concern on Him. Cast all your care on Him because He cares for you.

June 25

Seize the Day!

One of the characteristics of successful people is that they don't waste time. They make the most of every opportunity regardless of the circumstances. How do you do that? One of my Bible heroes is Paul, the apostle. He was a giant in the faith! When he wrote to the Christ followers in Ephesus and challenged them to make the most of every opportunity, he provided an example for them through his own life.

At the time he penned these words, he was in prison for sharing the gospel with others. Despite being chained to Roman guards, with limited or no freedom, Paul saw the opportunity before him and made the most of it. As he could no longer travel in his missionary journeys to the churches he established or pioneer new ones, he uses the time in prison to write letters to those churches that became much of our New Testament today.

And when he asked for prayer in these letters, it is striking to me that Paul never requests them to pray that he would be released from prison or that his chains would be removed, but that he would continue to speak fearlessly about Jesus.

Then, in another prison letter, to the church in Philippi, his words radiate with joy! How could he remain so joyful and find opportunities in the midst of such difficult and restricting circumstances? Being unfairly imprisoned would cause most of us to give up or become bitter, but Paul saw it as one more opportunity to share the Good News of Christ!

So, even as we pray for a change in our circumstances, we should also pray that God will accomplish His plan through us right where we are. If you want to seize the day, consider that your current circumstances are not as important as what you do with them.

June 26

The Gift of Faith

Romans 10:17 *"So then faith comes by hearing, and hearing by the word of God."*

Martin Luther said he studied his Bible in the same way he gathered apples. He admonishes us to do likewise:

"Search the Bible as a whole, shaking the whole tree. Read it rapidly, as you would any book. Then shake every limb – study book after book. Then shake every branch, giving attention to the chapters when they do not break the sense. Then shake each twig, by careful study of the paragraphs and sentences. And you will be rewarded if you will look under each leaf, by searching the meaning of the words."

Seek to know the Lord with all your heart. While you may have no difficulty in worshiping the omnipotent God, you cannot really know God unless you meditate upon His Word. The One Who spoke and caused the worlds to be framed, is waiting to reveal Himself to you personally.

Faith is not given to the undisciplined or disobedient. Faith is a gift of God which is given to those who trust and obey Him. As we embrace His Word and follow His will for us, our faith will continue to grow. It is my very strong conviction that it is just not possible to ask God for too much if our hearts and motives are pure and if we pray according to the Word and will of God.

Every time you and I open and read the Bible carefully, we are building up our storehouse of faith. When we memorize God's Word, our faith is being increased even more.

We face huge challenges in our world today and that requires a huge faith. That will only come when we are committed to hearing God's Word and acting upon it.

June 27

Great and Mighty Things

Jeremiah 33:3 *"Call to me and I will answer you and tell you great and mighty things you do not know."*

How long has it been since you prayed for great and mighty things – for the glory and praise of God? I find in God's Word at least six reasons you and I should pray for "great and mighty things": to glorify God; to communicate with God; to have fellowship with God; because of Christ's example; to obtain results; and to provide spiritual nurture.

There is a sense in which I pray without ceasing, I talk to God hundreds of times in the course of the day about everything. I pray for wisdom about the numerous decisions I must make; for the salvation of friends and strangers; the healing of the sick and the spiritual and material needs of those to whom I minister; for the needs of the many people I encounter in the news; I pray for the leaders of our nation and for those in authority over us.

But there is another sense in which there is a set-apart time each day for prayer, with the Bible open before me as I talk to God and listen for His Word. Before I begin, I ask the Holy Spirit, who inspired its writing, to make my reading of the Bible relevant, meaningful and engaging. As I'm reading, I often pause to thank God for His loving salvation and daily provision; to confess the lack in my own life revealed by the Scriptures; to ask Him for the boldness and faith His apostles displayed and to thank Him for new insights into His divine strategy for reaching the world with the gospel.

Let us all be encouraged today to call upon God, expecting Him to show us *great and mighty things* beyond anything we have ever experienced, for His glory and for the blessing of those around us, so they may know that God does mighty things in response to the faith of His children.

June 28

Jesus talks about Jesus

Luke 24:27 *"And beginning with Moses and all the Prophets, he explained to them what was said in all the Scriptures concerning himself."*

The two disciples on the road to Emmaus certainly had a rewarding journey! Their companion and teacher was the best of all tutors. His interpretation was better than all others, and in His thoughts hide all the treasures of wisdom.

Jesus humbled Himself to become a preacher of the gospel, and He was not ashamed to preach to an audience of two. Today, He's still willing and able to do the same, and won't refuse to become the teacher of even a single individual!

Although able to reveal fresh truth, Jesus preferred to explain the old truths. He knew the most instructive way of teaching, and by starting with Moses and the prophets, He showed us that the surest road to wisdom is not speculation, reasoning, or reading human books, but meditation on the Word of God.

The way to be spiritually rich in heavenly knowledge is to dig in this mine of spiritual diamonds. When Jesus wanted to enrich others, He mined the quarry of Holy Scripture. The pair on the Emmaus Road were led to consider the best of all subjects, because Jesus spoke of Jesus, and *"explained to them what was said in all the Scriptures concerning himself."* The diamond cut the diamond. What could be more admirable? The Master of the House unlocked His own doors and led His guests to His favourite table!

Our Lord spoke naturally about the sweetest of topics, and He could find none sweeter than His own divine identity and mission. We should always take the time to search the Scriptures, for there we will find the Lord Jesus, Who is at the same time both our teacher and our lesson!

June 29

Love at its Best

Did you ever stop to think about the bad hand that was dealt to Jesus when He chose us to be His bride? No one would blame Him if He gave up on us! Good thing He doesn't think like we do or He would have left this marriage a long time ago. Listening to our culture, one might get the impression that a good relationship is something for which we all have an inalienable right.

This conclusion comes from observing how quickly we look for the back door when we are in a difficult relationship, and how that exit is usually justified on the basis that the current relationship is just too hard; the assumption being, there's someone out there with whom a good relationship is a much easier proposition.

This is when you have to think of Christ's marriage to us. As Dan Haseltine, of Jars of Clay, wrote in Relevant magazine, *"Look at the marriage of Jesus - the one with the bride who sleeps around, never listens, disowns, scorns, dishonours, runs away, intentionally proves to be more interested in anything but her husband, is selfish and bears the children of every affair and the scent of every escapade. It was a marriage that killed Jesus. And it was the Gospel that brought Him back to life to love once more."*

It would be great if we thought a little more like Jesus when it comes to our relationships. He never allows Himself an out. Leaving is just not an option and when that option is off the table, it changes everything. Jesus is in this for the long haul, including whatever suffering is involved. He is able to do this because He isn't thinking about Himself or His own rights. He is thinking about us. He sees us as holy and blameless, yes, even beautiful. He makes it so. If you want to see what love over the long haul looks like - look at Jesus and His love for His bride - the Church. Now that is certainly love at its best!

June 30

Bucket List

Have you seen *The Bucket List?* It's a movie about two older men who are diagnosed with a terminal illness and decide before they 'kick the bucket' they will do all the things they ever wanted to do before departing planet earth.

A life-threatening illness, even with a good prognosis, can cause people to focus on the future with a very different perspective, but they are not likely to escape from the hospital and go on a juvenile joy ride! The point of the movie is that when faced with eminent death these two characters, played by Morgan Freeman and Jack Nicholson, look inward to themselves to satisfy all of their personal desires and to have the personal experiences they always wanted to have during their lives, before it is too late.

Contrast that with the last day of Elijah, found in 2 Kings 2. When both Elijah and Elisha knew that it would be Elijah's last day on earth, they made the most of it to create a legacy, to pass the mantle of leadership for the sake of those left behind. They took a tour and the elder showed the younger the ropes, so to speak. They focused not on worldly pleasure, but on a Godly legacy. At the end of the day. Elijah was taken up and Elisha carried on and when he parted the water, the prophets said, *"The spirit of Elijah is resting on Elijah."*

What's on your bucket list? After all, we are all terminal. Before you depart, is it your goal to have all the fun you can, or to leave a Godly heritage and a spiritual legacy in your family, your community and your Church? Who, or what, matters most to you in life? What has God called you to do in the limited amount of time you have to do it? Maybe it is time to re-think your bucket list – or prepare one if you have never done so before – and make sure the mission of Christ informs what you place on that list!

July 1

Finishing Well

Acts 20:24 *"... I consider my life worth nothing to me, if only I may finish the race and complete the task the Lord Jesus has given me the task of testifying to the gospel of God's grace."*

As I reflect on 'the race' I am seeking to finish and 'the task the Lord Jesus has given me,' I am reminded of the truly amazing moment in the Beijing Olympics when Romania's Tomescu-Dita crossed the finish line in the Women's Marathon. She not only won the gold medal, but, at 38 years of age, she became the oldest Olympian ever to do so, leaving 83 competitors in her dust.

Tomescu-Dita led the race unchallenged for more than an hour, running alone for more than half of the race. It was a remarkable achievement given the quality of the Beijing field. I watched her running along the gruelling course that snaked through the streets of Beijing from Tiananmen Square to the Bird's Nest stadium.

I watched her become energized when the stadium came into sight and then as she circled outside before entering the stadium, I was impressed with something the announcer said, declaring that: *"Entering the stadium of victory is something every marathon runner looks forward to."* Tomescu-Dita looked strong as she entered the National Stadium to a huge, rousing ovation from the crowd of over 60,000.

Life is a race and the finish line is in heaven. Paul expresses it again here when writing to the Philippian Church:

Philippians 3:13-14 *"Forgetting what is behind and straining toward what is ahead, I press on toward the goal to win the prize for which God has called me heavenward in Christ Jesus."*

Now that's what I really call running for gold.

July 2

Jesus is the Way

John 14:6 *Jesus answered, "I am the way and the truth and the life. No one comes to the Father except through me."*

Have you ever stood in a bookstore and surveyed just how many books there are which have a certain number of ways to achieve almost anything? For example: *8 Simple Workouts; 10 Mindful Steps to Happiness; 7 Principles for Making a Marriage Work; 7 Days to Whiter Teeth.* Perhaps you remember Steven Covey's global best seller years ago: *7 Habits of Highly Effective People.* He put the words *proactive* and *synergize* on the map!

I remember reading one list years ago – I still have it saved on my computer. It was titled: *50 Ways to Improve Your Life this Year.* The inclusive list covered everything from flossing your teeth to enjoying a massage to joining a singing group. It seems that everybody writes or reads books that boil anything down into precise steps to accomplish a goal. There seems to be a formula for almost everything! We live in a scientific and technological culture where people believe that every single problem can be solved by applied techniques (six steps to a better whatever).

As Christians, we also often think there's some magic formula out there to dramatically change us and make all of our problems go away overnight. Well, it isn't quite that easy. A lot of self-help guides, spiritual and otherwise, are on the shelves of local bookstores. None of them actually work.

There is only one way and it is a one step process. *Jesus said, "I am the way and the truth and the life. No one comes to the Father except through me."* I suggest that if you really want to change your life, then commit yourself to follow Jesus. In a world that tells us to conform, Jesus tells us to transform and to present ourselves as a living sacrifice before God. He does all the rest.

July 3

Never Failed me Yet

There is a quirky piece of music written and recorded by the British composer Gavin Bryars that features a continuous running tape loop of a homeless man recorded on the streets of London singing an old gospel song, *'Jesus' Blood Never Failed Me Yet.'* The old man's voice is wistful and wobbly, with a thick Cockney accent and a confidence that stands in contrast to his life situation.

> *"Jesus' blood never failed me yet, never failed me yet,*
> *Jesus blood' never failed me yet.*
> *This one thing I know, for he loves me so."*

A reporter recorded this little song by accident while he was researching a story on London's poor, and Bryars had been captivated by its simple grandeur. He was haunted by the power of the old man's sincerity and the boldness of his hope even though, by his own admission, he does not share his faith. That's when he had the idea to immortalize the man's testimony by writing an orchestral accompaniment that would weave intricately in and around the sinewy voice as it repeated, over and over again, its confidence in the never-failing love of Jesus.

Think of it: a homeless bum out on the streets in the lowest of states, carrying a hopeful message to hundreds of thousands of people about the reality of Christ's love that defies his health, his circumstances and the physical conditions that are his daily reality. Hearing him should make us view whatever we might be going through in a very different light.

Romans 8:39 *"Whether we are high above the sky or in the deepest ocean, nothing in all creation will ever be able to separate us from the love of God that is revealed in Christ Jesus our Lord."*

Or, to put it another way, whatever happens to you or me, we can always say: *"Jesus' blood never failed me yet."*

July 4

Becoming Spiritually Fit

1 Timothy 4:8 *"For physical training is of some value, but godliness has value for all things, holding promise for both the present life and the life to come."*

A recent online article caught my eye: *'Can exercise slow aging?'* It would seem that active people have cells that look younger on a molecular level than those of us who may be couch potatoes. The bottom line is confronting: there is strong evidence now documented to show that exercise may stave off the effects of aging.

The Apostle Paul spoke about physical training in his first letter to Timothy and noted that while physical training has some value, godliness is of even greater value. He was talking about the exercise of being close to God.

Pastors who talk about 'Church growth' are usually referring to numerical growth - getting more members for the Church. But I believe that when the Bible talks about 'Church growth' it refers to spiritual growth. We are directed to grow in our knowledge of God and faith in God. Our individual task of growth with Jesus comes through worship, prayer and study of God's Word. This is our 'spiritual exercise.'

In today's world there is much emphasis on being physically fit. Perhaps many of you have been influenced by the call to 'get into shape.' The benefits of entering into a physical fitness program are many, but it's even better to focus on spiritual training. We are not only physical beings, but we also have a spiritual dimension to our lives. With good physical fitness we will live longer and ultimately die with a healthier body, but spiritual fitness impacts our life beyond the grave.

Is 'spiritual fitness' a priority for you? Give it some thought.

July 5

Once and for All

Did Jesus actually accomplish a once-and-for-all atonement and, as a result, set sinners everywhere right with God? Or did Jesus' work merely make it possible for sinners to enjoy this atonement if they follow through, correctly and precisely, so that they complete what Jesus only started? Paul answers:

2 Corinthians 5:19 *"God was reconciling the world to himself in Christ …"*

From the moment man sinned, restoring a right relationship between sinners and God was God's top priority. This job was too important to delegate it to any angel, much less to any mere mortal. God assigned this task to Jesus of Nazareth, His anointed Servant and incarnate Son. And when Jesus carried out this job, He accomplished it once and for all.

God has set the world at-one with himself through Jesus, urging hearers not to *"receive the grace of God in vain"* but *to "be reconciled to God."* (2 Corinthians 5:20; 6:1).

Some Christians struggle with the 'once-and-for-all' reality of our salvation. Deep down, I believe that's because we want to have come say in own salvation. We are happy to give God 99% of the credit for our new life in Christ, but our fallen nature still cries out to hang on to the 1% and believe that we had something to do with this incredible transformation.

Our salvation and reconciled relationship with God is a free gift, effected by the life, death and resurrection of Jesus Christ. Either we believe that and receive the reality of that gift – or we don't. We didn't deserve it; we didn't earn it; we didn't barter for it with our obedience or repentance; everything was a gift from God, by His grace and for His glory – achieved once and for all, by Jesus. That's why they call it good news!

July 6

The Shocking Truth

If you have been awake and observant over the past decade you will have seen a significant shift in public opinion against the Church. We have always been a minority voice, but there was a time when that minority was respected and our opinion held significant weight in the world around us. Not anymore!

Into that cesspool of rejection, antagonism and indifference, allow me to now drop some very inconvenient truth bombs!

- Modern science as we know it is essentially the result of the Christian message. Every founder of every major branch of modern science was a Bible-believing Christian.

- Modern medicine as we know it is essentially the result of the Christian message. Hospitals themselves were a Christian 'invention' in response to the healing ministry of Jesus.

- Modern education as we know it is essentially the result of the Christian message. The concept of the university itself, and the great early universities of Europe, were all created in response to the Christian message that, as revealed by Jesus Christ, God was both knowable and rational, and so was His creation.

- The concept of "atheism" was only possible because of the Christian message of human free will and liberty. Before Christ, although some people chose to mock or ignore the gods, there was no philosophical option to be an atheist. "Atheism" only exists because of Christianity!

- Therefore, western civilisation as we know it today is essentially the result of the Christian message.

The truth is always confrontational. Deal with it.

July 7

Righteousness vs. Rightness

Matthew 23:2-3 *"The teachers of the law and the Pharisees sit in Moses' seat. So, you must be careful to do everything they tell you. But do not do what they do, for they do not practice what they preach."*

In effect Jesus told them to practice and observe whatever the religious leaders tell you - but not to do what they do. For they preach, but do not practice. What Jesus was warning them about was to not confuse rightness with righteousness.

The problem with the teachers of the law and the Pharisees was not that they were wrong; they were right in many things. And so, Jesus said, *"By all means respect them. Listen to then carefully, and do what they teach you."* But while they were right, they were not righteous. They didn't do what their own teaching said they ought to be doing.

The whole focus of the teachers of the law and the Pharisees was on being right, and they thought that by being right, they would also be righteous.

Nothing much has changed. Your righteousness today has nothing to do with your rightness. It does not depend on the fact that you belong to the 'right' Church, believe the 'right' things, read the 'right' books, or understand prophecy the 'right' way. These have absolutely nothing to do with the righteousness by which you are accepted by God.

In actual fact, during His earthly ministry, Jesus commended the faith of people who knew the least – who technically were the least 'right'!

When we understand that the righteousness by which we are justified can only stand apart from us – in the person and atoning work of Jesus Christ – then will we no longer confuse rightness with righteousness.

July 8

Don't Waste Your Suffering

1 Peter 1:8-9 *"Though you have not seen Him, you love Him; and even though you do not see Him now, you believe in Him and are filled with an inexpressible and glorious joy, for you are receiving the end result of your faith, the salvation of your souls."*

At first glance, what Peter says in this passage seems out of place when you consider those to whom he is writing and what they are going through. He is addressing believers who are experiencing extreme trials and suffering. They are exiles scattered from Jerusalem throughout the Roman world due to severe persecution. He says they are suffering grief in all kinds of trials. (Vs. 6)

However, he then puts a new perspective on these problems by pointing to a faith that transforms our outlook when we face trials. In his comments on 1 Peter, author and pastor, Warren Wiersbe, says that faith carries with it a present dynamic that can turn suffering into glory today, not just one day when you die. How can you enjoy that glory now?

The first way to turn suffering into glory now is to celebrate God's love! We don't have to see Jesus, Peter says, to love Him! Faith is not based on seeing - but believing! Peter offers some insight into our problems. Problems have a purpose. Although Satan wants to use life's trials to bring out the worst in us, God uses them to bring out the best in us.

Another way we can turn suffering into glory now is by believing God. Peter says, *"... even though you do not see Him now, you believe in Him and are filled with inexpressible and glorious joy!"* That kind of faith involves trusting Christ. Love and trust go together. When you really love someone, you trust them. As you grow in that intimate relationship of love with Christ, no matter the circumstances or adversity, you are filled with an inexpressible and glorious joy!

July 9

Our Identity in Christ

In Matthew 16:13-18, Jesus asks His disciples, *"Who do you say that I am?"* And then He proceeds to reveal to His followers what is the true basis of the Church; indeed, of Christianity itself. The true basis of Christianity is the identity of Jesus Christ. Your identity as a Christian is not based on a bunch of personal opinions. It is not based on a catalogue of traditions.

Your identity is based on who Jesus is. The Church is built on the identity of Christ. Because of who Jesus is, the gates of hell will never overcome the people of God. This is a fantastic thing to grasp. We need to understand that the identity of Christ, as confirmed by His resurrection, is not just personal opinion. It is not like believing in fairies at the back of your garden. The identity of Jesus Christ is rock-solid.

Christianity is based on the life, death, and resurrection of Jesus. Christianity didn't grow because it subjugated nations with a sword, like many religions did. Christianity didn't grow because it provided an attractive philosophy – that is what religion does.

Christianity grew because there were thousands of people on the Day of Pentecost willing to stand up and testify that Jesus Christ had indeed risen from the dead. That Jesus was precisely Whom He had always said He was, *"the Christ, the Son of the Living God."*

Christianity grew because for generation after generation, thousands upon thousands of believers were willing to die as martyrs for the truth that they had seen, that their parents had seen, that their grandparents had seen in the risen Christ.

I want you to say with Peter, *"You are the Christ, the Son of the Living God!"* Your identity stands or falls on the identity of Jesus Christ. Learn to stand on that. Feel how solid it is under your feet. Learn to depend on it. Our identity is in Christ.

July 10

True Righteousness

During the time Jesus was on earth, Israel was deeply focused on pursuing righteousness. The leaders of the nation were emphasising that following the law of Moses was the greatest (and possibly the only) way to become righteous.

The teachers of the law viewed this as being so vital to the survival of the nation that it was surrounded by a complex web of regulations designed to keep people safe from breaching the law. These extra requirements were deemed so crucial that they were incorporated into God's Law.

Jesus saw these extra requirements as failing in their purpose. He did not hesitate to encourage people not to make the scribes and supposed experts in the law their benchmark for righteousness. For Him, righteousness had more to do with a person's relationship with God than conformity to a long list of rules. He pointed out that obedience to a rule fell a long way short of what God desired.

The righteousness which Jesus commended excelled that of Israel's spiritual leaders. They promoted morality with the least amount of work. Through it, a person who met all the requirements of the law may have gained the respect of his community while still harbouring hatred and jealousy within.

There is no more striking example of Jesus' teachings on this topic than His surprising commandment, "*Love your enemies.*" This morality is too complex to be encapsulated in a written or spoken directive. It transcends logic. It goes above and beyond what is required of anyone.

This is righteousness beyond comparison, it's not just the bare minimum. This is righteousness coming not from legislation but inspiration. Only the honing and polishing influence of God's love can produce such a beautiful result.

July 11

Our Forgetful God

Isaiah 43:25 *"I, even I, am he who blots out your transgressions, for my own sake, and remembers your sins no more."*

If God chooses to never think of our sins again when we've been forgiven, then why do we? It seems to be human nature to remember the things we ought to forget and forget the things we should remember. Never forget this incredible promise of God:

Jeremiah 31:34 *"I will forgive their wickedness and will remember their sins no more."*

How often do you recall the failures in your past? Are you haunted by many regrets? God underscored forgiveness by assuring us He will never again think of our sin! In other words, God chooses to forget! He chooses to never bring up the charges against us when He forgives us!

That's just the opposite with our accuser, the devil. He constantly tries to remind us of our dark past. When the devil reminds you of your past, just remind him of his future!

Too many of God's children live with crippling self-imposed limitations because of past failures. The truth is, God uses those failures to display His glory and grace. It's out of our brokenness that God brings blessing! God uses broken things. He used broken bread to feed a multitude. He used a broken life to win a Samaritan village to Christ.

When Gideon was leading his band of three hundred men against overwhelming odds, they were carrying torches and clay pots. It was only when the clay pot was broken that the light could shine through.

If God chooses to forget your sins, maybe you should too!

July 12

Your Life Matters to God

Isaiah 43:1-3 *"... the one who formed you says, 'Do not be afraid, for I have ransomed you; I have called you by name; you are mine. When you pass through the waters, I will be with you; and when you pass through the rivers, they will not sweep over you; When you walk through the fire, you will not be burned; the flames will not set you ablaze. For I am the Lord your God ..."*

If you've ever doubted how much your life matters to God, just look at the cross! God says, *"You're worth dying for!"* Even centuries before Jesus was born in Bethlehem, God revealed His thoughts about you and me.

Although the above passage in the Old Testament speaks specifically to Israel, it has a spiritual application to you and me today. It says the One Who created you cares about you!

Just consider the description of His concern for you from what Isaiah writes. *"... the One who formed you says, 'Do not be afraid, for I have ransomed you.'"* To ransom is to obtain the release of a captive by making a payment.

When we were imprisoned to our past or present hurts, habits, and hang-ups, God sent His One and only Son to offer His own life in our place as a ransom for our sins!

1 Peter 1:18-19 *"For you know that God paid a ransom to save you from the empty life you inherited from your ancestors. And the ransom He paid was not mere gold or silver. It was the precious blood of Christ, the sinless, spotless Lamb of God."*

As if that were not enough, God says, *"I have called you by name; you are Mine. ..."* That is about as clear-cut as it can be! Your life matters to God! You are special to Him! Whatever you are going through in life, God is there with you.

July 13

Making God in our own Image

People's perceptions of God are always influenced by their upbringing, culture, education, experiences in life, and mental state. It is true that humans have essentially made God in their image: legalists worship a legalistic God; little people serve a small God; narrow-minded people serve a narrow-minded God; some worship a gigantic, love-filled God whose kindness has no bounds, whose forgiveness is total, and whose company is intimate. Naturally, if you gather a bunch of people together who share your beliefs, you soon find yourself with a new denomination or religion! So, why do we humans have such different perspectives on God?

From the dawn of time, humans have attempted to make God in their own likeness. At Sinai, the children of Israel desired a God that they could comprehend, not the mighty one who thundered from the mountain and split the sea. Accordingly, they created a golden calf, something they had seen in Egypt.

In Romans 1:25, Paul describes how people would rather serve the creation than the Creator. It is only human nature to want a God who is like us, someone we can manipulate. That's what fallen, sinful, degenerate human nature does. We have control over what we make and whether we admit it or not, deep down, we want to control God.

God permanently destroyed any merit in that reasoning when He entered this world in a real, objective, temporal, and historical sense via the person of Jesus Christ - Who came in the flesh to reveal to us what God is like. God gave us an objective revelation of Himself, not in an impersonal, cerebral way, but rather by living among us as one of us for decades.

Don't fall into the trap of building an image of God based on fallen humanity. We were created in God's image and Jesus came to redeem us and restore that image in each of us!

July 14

Build on the Rock

Have you seen one of those professionally built sandcastles on the beach? You know, the ones that win awards and are just breathtaking in their detail. There is one problem with them all. They are not going to last. Eventually there will be a king tide or a serious storm and all that hard work will be gone in seconds. That's OK, I guess. There are things in life that aren't meant to last. Like ice cream, rainbows ... and sandcastles built on the beach.

However, there are things in life that you wish would last. Like real love, true beauty, and let's face it, you yourself. You want to be able to stand against the tides and the waves and the storms that you know will come. Jesus told us how we can do that with this illustration:

Matthew 7:24–27 *"Therefore everyone who hears these words of mine and puts them into practice is like a wise man who built his house on the rock. The rain came down, the streams rose, and the winds blew and beat against that house; yet it did not fall, because it had its foundation on the rock. But everyone who hears these words of mine and does not put them into practice is like a foolish man who built his house on sand. The rain came down, the streams rose, and the winds blew and beat against that house, and it fell with a great crash."*

I know that some people understand exactly what Jesus said, because they have had their actual house destroyed by storm or flood. Many of us haven't. Jesus didn't really live on the seashore. The Sea of Galilee is a lake, and not subject to tides like the ocean. But I think if Jesus had grown up in Australia, near the sea, Jesus would had built sandcastles and perhaps His illustration would have been about them instead.

Some sandcastles are very impressive - but what Jesus has built for you is far more impressive and rock-solid.

July 15

Your Authority in Christ

Luke 9:1-2,6 *"When Jesus had called the Twelve together, he gave them power and authority to drive out all demons and to cure diseases, and he sent them out to proclaim the kingdom of God and to heal the sick ... So they set out and went from village to village, proclaiming the good news and healing people everywhere."*

When Jesus released a measure of His own authority and power to the disciples, they were able to restore the Kingdom of God where there had previously been darkness.

These early training missions gave the disciples a limited experience, which was to be enlarged after Pentecost when each disciple received his own supernatural empowerment from the Holy Spirit.

Finally, after His resurrection, Jesus appeared to His disciples and said this about authority:

Matthew 28:18-20 *"All authority in heaven and on earth has been given to me. Therefore go and make disciples of all nations, baptizing them in the name of the Father and of the Son and of the Holy Spirit, and teaching them to obey everything I have commanded you. And surely I am with you always, to the very end of the age."*

Jesus was able to reclaim full authority over heaven and earth, and restore that authority to every one of His followers. When this authority is combined with the power of the Holy Spirit, the Kingdom of darkness cannot stand.

The role of the Church, our role, is to learn how to think, talk, and act with this royal authority. As children of the King, we have the legal right, power, authority and responsibility to manifest God's kingdom on earth as we live and minister in Christ, through Christ and for Christ.

July 16

Knocked Down, but not Knocked out

We all have our tough times, don't we? I think I would be right in saying that most of us complain about some of the struggles we face in life and especially in front line ministry for Christ. When I feel like complaining, the Lord usually leads me to the same passage in the Bible.

In 2 Corinthians 11:23–27, the Apostle Paul writes about how many times he has been thrown in prison, beaten, abused, flogged within an inch of his life, stoned, shipwrecked. He says that he has gone without sleep, food, drink, and warmth, and that everywhere he has faced dangers, including being backstabbed by those within his own Church.

Eventually, as a result of what smells suspiciously like a religious set-up, and after nine years in prison, Paul was executed in Rome.

Yet, incredibly, it is this same Paul who can write this:

2 Corinthians 4:8–9 *"We are hard pressed on every side, but not crushed; perplexed, but not in despair; persecuted, but not abandoned; struck down, but not destroyed."*

Paul is explaining what it means to live the Gospel life. He tells us that an absolute commitment to the proclamation of the Gospel drives everything that a true Christian does. Paul said we will often be knocked down, but not knocked out.

2 Corinthians 4:17-18 *"Therefore, we do not lose heart. Though outwardly we are wasting away, yet inwardly we are being renewed day by day. For our light and momentary troubles are achieving for us an eternal glory that far outweighs them all. So, we fix our eyes not on what is seen, but on what is unseen, since what is seen is temporary, but what is unseen is eternal."*

July 17

Is Anything too Hard for God?

Chapter 32 of Jeremiah describes a time when things were very bleak for Jeremiah and all those who loved God. The Babylonian army was besieging the city of Jerusalem and no help was coming. The city was about to fall.

The situation seemed absolutely hopeless. They would kill the inhabitants of Jerusalem and Judah and carry away those who were left into slavery. Jeremiah himself is in prison.

Just then, God comes to Jeremiah with a business proposition. He says to Jeremiah, *"I want to you to buy your cousin's field."* (v.8.) What a seemingly stupid suggestion! Who in their right mind would be buying real estate in the current situation! Surely the field was doomed! Surely it would be destroyed and made desolate by the Babylonians!

So, Jeremiah's cousin comes to the prison and sells the field to Jeremiah and Jeremiah pays the price and makes the sale official. And the Lord tells Jeremiah something that seems utterly ridiculous

"Don't worry; houses, fields, and vineyards will again be bought in this land. Don't worry, Jeremiah; the market's going to go up again. You will have your reward; I will bless my people" (v.15.)

Then Jeremiah scratches his head. He can't work out the logic behind this. And the Lord speaks to Jeremiah and says,

Jeremiah 32:27 *"I am the Lord, the God of all living things! Is anything too hard for me?"*

There will be times when it will appear as if you have no future, as if the field of your life is absolutely doomed. It is then that you will need to remember that there is Someone who has already invested in you – Jesus Christ at Calvary.

July 18

By the Grace of God, I am what I am

1 Corinthians 15:10 *"But by the grace of God I am what I am, and his grace to me was not without effect. No, I worked harder than all of them - yet not I, but the grace of God that was with me."*

Paul could have said, *"I am what I am because of my family's money."* He could have said, *"I am what I am because of my great education."* He could have said, *"I am what I am because of my position of power in society."* But no, he said, *"by the grace of God I am what I am."*

In his letter to the Philippians, Paul says this:

Philippians 3:7-8 *"These things were my assets, but I wrote them off as a loss for the sake of Christ. But even beyond that, I consider everything a loss in comparison with the superior value of knowing Christ Jesus my Lord. I have lost everything for him, but what I lost I think of as sewer trash, so that I might gain Christ."*

In 2 Corinthians 11:23-27, Paul lists off a great number of tragedies and misfortunes that he has experienced. He could have said, *"by the many things I have suffered, I am what I am."* Instead, he says, *"by the grace of God I am who I am."*

Paul refuses to be identified by the misfortunes in his life.

Paul tells us that the most important thing about him is that he is what he is - only by the grace of God. Effectively, what Paul is talking about here is the cross. It is because of the cross of Christ that Paul understands that he needs grace. And he found grace at the cross. And because of the cross, Paul became a servant of the God of grace.

Grace brings us all to the same level, because at the foot of the cross there's no economy class, and no first class; there's only kneeling class.

July 19

The Foolishness of the Cross

1 Corinthians 1:18-19 *"For the message of the cross is foolishness to those who are perishing, but to us who are being saved it is the power of God. For it is written: 'I will destroy the wisdom of the wise; the intelligence of the intelligent I will frustrate.'"*

Celsus was one of the pagan philosophers living in the second century and he wrote that the idea that a man who had been crucified should be worshiped was so unbelievably stupid, that it was worse than the fairy tales that women would tell their children!

The earliest graphical depiction of Christ apparently shows Him as a crucified man with a donkey's head, worshipped by a man called Alexamenos. This is from Rome in the second or third century. All of this mocking by unbelievers influenced even some Christians to have some very strange views.

For example, in one of the Gnostic gospels, Jesus is talking about the idea that He had been crucified, and He says, *"It was a joke, I tell you, it was a joke,"* and Jesus then mocks Christians who *"proclaim the doctrine of a dead man."*

The idea here is that Jesus played a trick on everyone by somehow projecting an image of Himself on the cross, like a hologram, but He wasn't really there at all, because He was God and He wouldn't ever let himself be crucified, would he?

Fast forward to today and we have Richard Dawkins calling the idea that God sent His Son to this earth to die for our sins, *"barking mad."*

Nothing much has changed since the time when the message of the cross was first preached to the world. The offence of the cross (see Galatians 5:11) has not ceased and yet, the cross of Jesus Christ still our only hope.

July 20

Grace Upon Grace

John 1:16–17 *"From his fullness we have all received grace upon grace; as the Law was given through Moses, so grace and truth came into being through Jesus Christ."*

The opening verses of the gospel of John are so magnificent – I am sure you know them well – and that is probably why verses 16 and 17 have been overlooked. But they are in fact the climax of the entire passage.

In these verses, John is not saying that he has a problem with Moses. Neither does he have a problem with the law. John is making a positive comparison: although the law is good, what Jesus Christ has brought to light is infinitely better.

For John, the coming of Jesus changes everything. The Old Testament pointed to the grace and truth that Jesus Christ has now brought to light. Grace and truth were never manifested in the fullness of its objective reality until Jesus Christ broke into this world.

Think of it like this, without the New Testament, without the gospel, everyone who ever lived would be doomed to the misery of guilt and a life and death without God. There would be no grace and truth in this world.

What John is saying here is that grace is not just something that exists by and of itself. Grace was actually brought into being by Jesus Christ and fully manifested for all time at Calvary. Jesus did this by His self-sacrifice through which all sin can be forgiven and every sinner accepted, restored, and maintained to a right standing with God; and by which one day all things will be fully reconciled with God.

For John, truth is never an opinion. Truth is never simply a doctrine. Truth is Jesus Christ.

July 21

Looking for Jesus

Luke 24:5-6 *"The women were frightened and bowed their faces toward the ground, but the men said to them, 'Why do you look for the living among the dead? He isn't here but has been raised.'"*

These women search for Jesus because they find it unbearable to imagine their lives without Him. The previous day, they had witnessed His murder. They didn't remember or believe what Jesus had taught them about His resurrection. Since they had witnessed His death, they weren't exactly sure what they were searching for. However, they visited the tomb in order to satisfy the void in their hearts.

We look for Jesus in our society as well. However, we search in the wrong places for Him, just like these women did. We search for Jesus in science, but it is impossible to demonstrate that Jesus Christ rose from the grave through an experiment in the lab.

We search for Jesus in contemporary culture. However, the foundation of our contemporary western society is a strong belief in naturalism and materialism in particular, as well as atheism in general. It makes no difference what you believe about Jesus - He is just not present in contemporary culture.

Some people look for Jesus in religion. The day before, after Jesus' body was lowered from the cross, the ladies who went to the tomb had prayed and carried out certain religious rites over Him. But in the end, their religion was unable to quench their desire for Jesus.

Stop wasting time looking for Jesus in all the wrong places – just relax and let Jesus find you where you are and transform your life completely – opening your eyes and your heart to His grace – His empowering presence. When that happens, you will never have to look for Jesus again!

July 22

Are we There Yet?

Every parent of little children who has travelled has heard the question *"Are we there yet?"* repeated endlessly. It seems as though the distance between our current location and our destination is, in the best-case scenario, meaningless.

All of the major creeds of Christianity affirm that Jesus will return. *"He will come again in glory to judge the living and the dead, and his kingdom will have no end,"* according to the Nicene Creed. Some Christian traditions have emphasised Jesus' second coming.

We should approach the second coming of Jesus with glad assurance and hope because it is a very significant event. However, there are Christians who ask themselves, *"Are we there yet?"* every moment of their lives. By their attitudes, actions, and religion, they pose this question as though the distance between the starting point and the final destination is meaningless. It's not just about the destination!

It is a dishonour to the Lord Jesus and a disservice to the good news of His gospel to live with the second coming as our one and only hope, to wonder constantly why Jesus hasn't returned, and to lament that we are 'not there yet.' This is a misplaced emphasis that exposes a misreading of the gospel.

Only if we are experiencing His victory in our daily lives can we fully comprehend how the story ends. The expectation of the second coming of Christ is just meaningless talk without this. The New Testament conveys this lesson and it is from this standpoint that we are urged to anticipate the day of His coming. On that day, Christ will create everything new and the righteousness that has redeemed us will spill over into every corner of our planet, from east to west, from sea to sea, and from earth to sky. Just make sure you enjoy the journey!

July 23

Passionate Faith

Matthew 24:12 *"Because of the increase of wickedness, the love of most will grow cold."*

Many Australians are known for having an unreasonable fear of emotion in exercising their spiritual faith. This is in spite the fact that they frequently overindulge during football games. When questions of meaning and conviction arise, our biggest dread of emotional exhibition surfaces. Why is it we won't allow ourselves much enthusiasm or passion when it comes to topics of great consequence?

This oddity was brought into focus during the charismatic movement in the Church in the 1970's. They have proven that expressing one's deep emotions in matters of faith is perfectly acceptable. Do we keep enthusiasm and faith apart because showing our passion indicates that we have everything riding on the issues that are very important to us?

Are we worried that our cause won't succeed; that our zeal will still make us look foolish; or that our faith won't materialise into sight? Do we not want the world to know how strong our beliefs are?

Exhibiting enthusiasm and passion is akin to promoting one's desires, principles, and aspirations. This will require guts! Detachment has less hazards. Being attached makes you vulnerable. But no babies are born without passion; poetry cannot be created without passion or excitement; excellent music requires arousal to be created. Our emotions are what transform a lifeless, colourless existence into one that is vibrant and warm and alive!

The love of God is the greatest thing in the whole world. If your experience of God's love does not arouse in you genuine and deep passion, then I suggest you check your pulse!

July 24

The Light that Never Dims

I remember as a child waiting in anticipation for my birthday or for Christmas Day to arrive. Time moved slowly and the waiting dragged on forever.

As an adult, that time moves much more quickly. It seems like Christmas is around the corner again before last year's gifts are put away. And waiting for birthdays isn't quite as exciting anymore.

But waiting on God is hard too. Some days it feels impossible. And sometimes it takes me right to my knees in tears and frustration. Perhaps you're waiting on God now …

- … for physical healing.
- … for employment.
- … for a child to come home.
- … for a relationship to be restored.
- … for a loved one to come to faith.

Whatever it might be, there will be days when waiting on God is just too hard; days when you think you cannot do it one more day. You can't wait patiently without worry and fear. On those days, peace gets edged out. In its place are anxiety, nausea, tears, depression, anger, and despair. Hopelessness seems to cover the world in darkness, but never completely, because darkness can never extinguish the Light.

John 12:46 *"I have come as a light to shine in this dark world, so that all who put their trust in me will no longer remain in the dark."*

Jesus came into this world to show us the Light - His Light that never dims. It never goes out. We may become blinded to it at times, but it's there, shining like a beacon - a symbol of hope, always leading us back to Him.

July 25

There is Only one You

There is only one you. I don't say that to boost your self-esteem – but to help you better serve others by being more confident about your God-given role in life. No one else fits your shape. No one else has your blend of gifts, talents and natural abilities making you very important in the whole scheme of things. As it is with the human body, so it is with the Body of Christ, the corporate collection of all who believe.

1 Corinthians 12:18 *"But in fact God has placed the parts in the body, every one of them, just as he wanted them to be."*

This uniqueness goes beyond giftedness; it reaches well into the depths of each of our experiences in life. No one else has lived your life. No one else has experienced your pain, your hardship, your joys and your sorrows. Everything in life shapes us and we are shaped by everything for a reason: so that we can touch others in a unique way based upon who we are and what we've been through.

Every piece of our lives and all our experiences can be used by God to touch someone else. We were made for each other; we live for each other; we even die for each other. We die with hope so that others who live might see the reality of Christ in us - even the darkest of hours. God uses everything.

Are you just getting by, or are you living for a reason? Think about your unique gifts and ask yourself how those gifts are benefiting others. What specific ways is God using you to touch others in the Body of Christ? Do you seem to have an extra measure of wisdom, or mercy, or discernment, or maybe knowledge, or administration, or a desire to serve?

There are some things which God can only achieve through you, because there is only one you!

July 26

All we Have is Now

Worrying about your past won't change it any more than worrying about the future will control it. It just messes with your head and ruins the present! Worry causes a paralysis of analysis. It forfeits us from living life in the moment. Because God is not limited by time and space, He is already in our future as well as our present, and He says:

Matthew 6:27 *"Who of you by worrying can add a single hour to his life?"*

Look at Israel as an example. When Jeremiah wrote them his prophetic letter, he was letting them in on what God had planned for their future.

They were living in exile under an enemy in the foreign land of Babylon. The future didn't look good. False prophets were sending mixed messages that this was the end of their nation, while others suggested things would turn around soon and that they would go home. They were stuck and didn't know what to do or who to believe. In his letter, Jeremiah gives them (and us) some wise insight on living in the moment.

Jeremiah 29:4-6 *"This is what the LORD Almighty, the God of Israel, says to all those I carried into exile from Jerusalem to Babylon: 'Build houses and settle down; plant gardens and eat what they produce. Marry and have sons and daughters; find wives for your sons and give your daughters in marriage, so that they too may have sons and daughters. Increase in number there; do not decrease.'"*

God's message to His people was that they would be there for some time. It would be a time of discipline and would last for 70 years – but it wasn't the end. God is saying, *"Don't let your fears about the future keep you from living in the present."*

July 27

Living by Faith

Hebrews 11:8 *"By faith Abraham, when called to go to a place he would later receive as his inheritance, obeyed and went, even though he did not know where he was going."*

Would you do it? Would you, like Abraham, leave all the security of where you were and set out on a journey, if you did not know where you were going? Sounds absurd, doesn't it? That's the kind of faith that pleases God!

To do what Abraham did, you would have to be absolutely convinced that the God who called you, also loved you and was able to sustain you and lead you on the correct path.

Faith is an adventure because it risks it all in obedience to Him. Abraham didn't set out on his own. It wasn't even his idea. He didn't wake up one morning and say, *"God, I'm ready to move and I need you to lead me to another place."* The Bible says, *"By faith, Abraham, when called to go …"* It was God's initiative from the beginning, yet God didn't explain much upfront! When you live by faith, you will discover a truth: Sometimes, the path is not clear until you start the journey.

When God is all you have, you discover that God is all you need! The God of Abraham is the same God today. Jesus described the kind of faith that pleases God like this:

Matthew 6:31-33 *"So do not worry, saying, 'What shall we eat?' or 'What shall we drink?' or 'What shall we wear?' For the pagans run after all these things, and your heavenly Father knows that you need them. But seek first His kingdom and His righteousness, and all these things will be given to you as well."*

You will not know all the answers. All you will need to know is that God does! That's the adventure of living by faith!

July 28

Who to Believe?

One of the fallouts from the recent Covid pandemic has been confusion over who to believe and what to believe! One day 'science' says this is the thing to do and the next day it's different. Then there are the 'prognosticators' who forecast everything from the stock market to the end of the world. What about your personal future? Who do you listen to? What do you believe?

Only one person knows the future. He is the One Who has been there! God is the One Who was, and is, and is to come! He is the God of your past, present, and future! You can trust your future to the God who is already there!

When Israel was in captivity after the fall of Jerusalem, lots of people were calling themselves prophets and they sent mixed messages to the people they claimed were from God. One group offered a doomsday message with no hope. Another group offered false hope that Israel's captivity in Babylon would be brief and that they would soon find deliverance. But there was one prophet who was truly from God. His name was Jeremiah, and his counsel gave them real hope. He spoke on behalf of the Lord Almighty.

Jeremiah 29:8-9 *"This is what the LORD Almighty, the God of Israel, says: 'Do not let the prophets and diviners among you deceive you. Do not listen to the dreams you encourage them to have. They are prophesying lies to you in My name. I have not sent them,' declares the LORD."*

When you are worried about the future and don't know who to believe, trust God's Word over man's opinion. God alone knows the future, and He tells us it is a hope-filled future! You can listen to the world and be filled with panic and fear, or you can listen to God's Word and find peace and confidence.

July 29

I Can

Psalm 3:2 *"Many are they who say of me, 'There is no help.'"*

Maybe you have repeatedly heard the words *"You can't"* throughout your life. Many people like to tell others what they cannot do.

Even people you wouldn't automatically consider to be against you, like teachers, coaches, parents, family, friends, and Church leaders, who often fail to realize the power of their words over young lives.

Many of us grew up thinking, *"I can't,"* when that wasn't true at all. No matter how often you have heard someone say, *"You can't,"* you can stand on God's Word and say, *"Yes, I can!"* We can do everything we need to do through Christ who is our strength. (Philippians 4:13)

God believes in you, and it's time for you to also believe in you. This is a new day! Put the past and all its disheartening remarks behind you. Words that speak of failure come from the enemy, not God, so decide right now that you will not allow the power of *"you can't"* to affect impact you any longer.

God's Spirit always encourages you and will do everything to urge you forward toward success in all areas of life. Facing the challenges of the promised land, God told Joshua three times, *"Be of good courage."*

Always remember that if you feel *dis-couraged,* it's from the Devil and if you feel *en-couraged,* it's from God. Decide today to agree with God and say to yourself, *"I can!"*

Let the power of God's Word dominate the power of every negative word that has ever been spoken to you or about you.

July 30

Integrity

Proverbs 10:9 *"He who walks with integrity walks securely, but he who perverts his ways will become known."*

What do you say is the single most important characteristic of a person who wants to be successful and make a difference in the world? Some would say *intelligence*. After all, knowledge is power in numerous ways.

Others would argue that it is *intensity*, that spirit of conquest supplemented with a passion that becomes contagious. Yet others propose that it is *insight*, good old common sense accompanied by the ability to clearly perceive certain issues.

The Bible suggests that the most important quality in success is no *intelligence, intensity* or *insight,* it is *integrity.* You will eventually become known by your integrity or the lack of it. We have all known people along life's road who possess extraordinary intelligence but no integrity, and they are no longer in the race. Others with great intensity and passion but little integrity have ended up the same way. The same result is true of people with great insight but no integrity.

The thesaurus equates integrity with such words as *honesty, completeness,* and *incorruptibility.* Integrity begins in your private world; the part of you that's known only to God and yourself. Then it shows up in your personal world; the part of you that you reveal to a small circle of family members and possibly a few friends. After that comes your professional world. Here people know you by your product, your work ethic, or your skill set. And they all ask the same question: *"Can I trust you?"* Finally, your integrity shows up in your public world where everyone gets to see you as you really are.

So here is the question: Do you have integrity?

July 31

Choose Forgiveness

Matthew 18:21-22 *"Then Peter came to Jesus and asked, "Lord, how many times shall I forgive my brother or sister who sins against me? Up to seven times?" Jesus answered, "I tell you, not seven times, but seventy-seven times."*

Peter must have felt so spiritual when he suggested forgiving someone up to seven times. After all, the rabbis taught that three times was sufficient. But Jesus shocked him when He responded, *"No, not seven times, but seventy times seven!"* That's 490 times! Who could keep count of that many sins? Maybe that was the point Jesus was trying to make. By the time you've forgiven someone 490 times, you've developed a habit of forgiving. Forgiveness comes from a heart of love:

1 Corinthians 13:5 *"Love keeps no record of wrongs."*

The forgiveness Jesus spoke of was never meant to be careless or shallow. Sometimes, we fail to forgive because we don't understand what forgiveness really means.

Forgiveness is a choice of the will. It isn't a matter of feelings. No one *feels* like forgiving. It is a supernatural choice that is intentional and repetitive. Every time the hurt comes to mind from an offense, you choose to forgive again.

Forgiveness is not minimizing the hurt, living in denial, or pretending that it's no big deal. The hurt is real, and the pain can linger. Forgiveness is preventing the hurt from turning into hate and becoming a prisoner to bitterness.

So how are you doing in the area of forgiveness? Are you holding on to some hurt? Make the choice today to forgive and release the pain to God. Let Him heal the hurt in your heart and release the offender to the God who judges justly.

August 1

Celebrate Freedom

Galatians 5:1 *"It is for freedom that Christ has set us free. Stand firm, then, and do not let yourselves be burdened again by a yoke of slavery."*

Are you free? We are fortunate and blessed to live in a 'free' country. We should never forget the price that others paid for the freedoms we enjoy. It's tragic that so many today live in a free nation and yet, are not free themselves. They are bound by hurts, habits, and hang-ups that enslave them. Others are bound by legalism, trying to earn God's favour through their achievements and performance.

The above verse was written to a people who didn't have the privilege of living in a free nation like ours. Many to whom this letter was written were slaves at worst and politically oppressed at best. They were hoping for a Messiah to come that would be a military king and liberate them from Roman oppression, restoring the glory days when King David ruled Israel. Despite the political constraints, the Bible says we have freedom now. That's the Good News of the Gospel!

John 8:36 *"If the Son sets you free, you will be free indeed!"*

The shackles of the past have been broken! You are free in Christ! How is that possible? He set you free by breaking the power of sin that enslaved you and condemned you! The power of the cross sets the captives free! It was there that our souls were set free! But sadly, we can willingly come under bondage again which is why Paul warned the Galatians to remain living in their freedom.

If you find yourself slipping back into that works-based religion, shake off those shackles and stand strong in the freedom by which Christ has made you free!

August 2

God's Love Endures Forever

Romans 8:35 *"Can anything separate us from the love of Christ? Can trouble, suffering, and hard times, or hunger and nakedness, or danger and death?"*

It is easy for us to wonder where God is when we are hurting. Our pain can deceive us into thinking that somehow God has abandoned us. Even the heroes of faith in the Bible questioned where God was in times of suffering. King David was one of those who struggled at times:

Psalm 69:3 *"My eyes fail, looking for my God ... Where can I find Him?"*

In Paul's letter to the Romans, he deals with the struggles and trials of life we all encounter whether it is because of human, natural or supernatural causes. Regardless of the cause, the promise is clear – absolutely nothing can separate us from the love of Christ!

Romans 8:37-39 *"No, in all these things we are more than conquerors through Him who loved us. For I am convinced that neither death nor life, neither angels nor demons, neither the present nor the future, nor any powers, neither height nor depth, nor anything else in all creation, will be able to separate us from the love of God that is in Christ Jesus our Lord."*

In the painful times of life when you feel so alone - claim His promise. Nothing can separate you from the love of God. You cannot do anything that would cause God to love you less, nor can you do anything to make Him love you more!

God is *for* you. His love will never leave you nor forsake you. You may not understand the trials of life, but you can always know you are deeply loved by God forever!

August 3

A New Heart

Ezekiel 36:26 *"I will give you a new heart and put a new spirit in you; I will remove from you your heart of stone and give you a heart of flesh."*

As a follower of Christ, you have been given a new heart. He didn't come to just patch up the old one. Your natural heart is described as a *"heart of stone."* Another translation describes it as a heart that is *"self-willed."* Your new heart has new and right desires. It is aligned with God's heart. Have you noticed the changes God is making in you? You have a new Spirit in you. Your desires and attitudes have changed.

You are no longer called a 'sinner' in Scripture. You are now called a 'saint.' Satan can do nothing about your position in Christ. But, if he can get you to believe you are no different from an unbeliever, then that's the way you will live.

If you still think of yourself as a failing sinner, you will continue to live a defeated life. You will lack the assurance of the salvation Christ died to give you.

Stop trying to *become* a saint as a Christian – you *are* a saint! Trying to become a saint is like trying to become a person. You either are a person or you are not. We are not trying to become children of God; we are children of God who are in the process of becoming like Christ.

Your inner change happened when God gave you a new heart and a new Spirit. It happened the moment you trusted Christ as your Saviour. Are you trying to become something you already are?

Being a saint doesn't mean you won't ever sin. It means you don't have to sin. You have a new heart now and the power to really live because Christ lives in you now.

August 4

Faith over Feelings

John 13:17 *"Now that you know these things, you will be blessed if you do them."*

Do you live by faith or by feelings? As a Christ-follower, the Bible says we are supposed to live by faith. What's the difference? Author and counsellor, Neil Anderson, noted this:

"If you believe what you feel, instead of believing the truth, your walk will be as inconsistent as your feelings. If what you believe does not reflect the truth, then what you feel does not reflect reality. The order of Scripture is to live by faith according to what God says is true. Your emotions will follow … We don't feel our way into good behaviour; we behave our way into good feeling."

In other words, don't wait until you feel like it to obey God's Word. When you obey what you know to be true, your feelings will eventually catch up with your actions.

In the verse above, Jesus is saying that if you wait until you feel like doing what is right, you may never do it. But, if you do what is right, you will feel good about it. Your feelings will catch up when you act on the truth you know to be right.

So, what do you do when your feelings do not reflect the truth? It takes the pressure off when you understand that your feelings are neither right nor wrong. You don't have to feel guilty about your emotions. They are an important part of your being, but they are not the determining factor of your life and your emotions can often lie to you!

Learning to acknowledge our emotions is a critical part of our freedom and maturity. You can't be right with God and not be real. Don't repress your feelings. Learn to express them to God. Revealing how you are feeling is the first step to healing. Tell God exactly how you feel.

August 5

Working out what God has Worked in

Philippians 2:12-13 *"Therefore, my dear friends, as you have always obeyed - not only in my presence, but now much more in my absence - continue to work out your salvation with fear and trembling, for it is God who works in you to will and to act in order to fulfill his good purpose."*

God desires that we reach our full potential. He designed us and began a good work in us when we received Christ. The challenge is to work out what God has worked in! This does not mean we work *for* our salvation, but that we work to show the results of our salvation. How? Through obedience and deep reverence and respect for God.

The verb 'work hard' or 'work out' carries the meaning of working to full completion. In the New Testament it was also used to describe mining, so that you could get out of the mine all the valuable ore possible or working a field to harvest the most crops possible.

God's desire is for us to be conformed to the image of His Son; that we would begin to live and act like Christ. As the very life of Christ is formed within us, the Holy Spirit is at work in our hearts and minds enabling us to work out what He is working in that we may reach our full God-given potential in Christ! For God to accomplish His greater work through us, He must do a deeper work within us.

Working out what God has worked in, then, isn't the result of strenuous effort or striving alone. Paul tells us, *".. for it is God who works in you to will and to act in order to fulfill his good purpose."* Aren't you glad it's not a matter of willpower but God's power? And not only does God give us the power to do what pleases Him but He also gives us the desire to do it.

August 6

World - Changers

1 Timothy 2:1-3 *"I urge, then, first of all, that petitions, prayers, intercession and thanksgiving be made for all people - for kings and all those in authority, that we may live peaceful and quiet lives in all godliness and holiness. This is good, and pleases God our Saviour, who wants all people to be saved and to come to a knowledge of the truth. For there is one God and one mediator between God and mankind, the man Christ Jesus, who gave himself as a ransom for all people."*

God's strategy for the Church to reach a lost and hurting world begins with prayer. Before we talk to people about God, God says we are to talk to Him about people - all people. Notice the priority in this passage. It's a simple strategy for bringing good news to a bad news world.

We are urged first of all to pray for all people. Then Paul tells us what to pray. We are to ask God to help them; to intercede on their behalf, and to give thanks for them. People may not be open to a discussion about God, but prayer will unleash the Spirit of God to soften and prepare their hearts

Then Paul instructs Timothy to have the Church pray for all those who are in authority. This was remarkable considering that he was living at a time of extreme persecution under the notoriously cruel emperor, Nero!

The command to pray for leaders didn't depend on whether they were good or evil. The point was so that Christ followers could live peaceful and quiet lives marked by godliness and dignity.

How much of a priority is prayer in your life? When was the last time you prayed for political leaders? It's so much easier to find fault than to pray.

August 7

In the Potter's Hands

Philippians 1:6 *"And I am certain that God, who began the good work within you, will continue His work until it is finally finished on the day when Christ Jesus returns."*

God began a good work within you the moment you received the Lord Jesus! His life became yours by faith!

Colossians 2:6 *"So then, just as you received Christ Jesus as Lord, continue to live your lives in Him…"*

This is a key to a living, dynamic faith! How did you receive Christ? By faith. It wasn't a matter of your good works or human effort, but faith in the marvellous grace of God offered to you in Christ! And it will take the same faith to continue to live your life in Him that it took to begin!

The problem is that often we begin by faith, receiving that which we could never achieve on our own, but then we start to act as if we must sustain our faith through our own strenuous effort. Very soon we become utterly exhausted and lose the joy of our salvation.

If that describes your Christian experience, I have some good news for you! Just as it was God who began the good work in you, only God can complete it!

No amount of striving on your part will enable you to be more acceptable to God. The very God who began a good work in you will continue that work throughout your lifetime until it is finally finished on the day when Christ Jesus returns!

There are three amazing parts to God's work in our lives. He works *for* us, He works *in* us, and He works *through* us! You are in the Potter's hands and He has not finished with you yet!

August 8

The Everlasting Arms

Deuteronomy 33:27 *"The eternal God is your refuge, and underneath are the everlasting arms."*

What is your refuge? Where do you go for safety, to find rest and peace? In his final song, Moses would teach a whole new generation of Israelites where their true refuge can be found.

Moses' song declares that the eternal God is our refuge! Is He your refuge? Your shelter? Your hiding place? Or do you seek refuge in your own strength, brilliance, money, or career? All of those things are temporary and can be taken away. The only refuge that is eternal is God. He never changes!

Psalm 73:26 *"My flesh and my heart may fail, but God is the strength of my heart and my portion forever."*

The Psalmist knew that when all else failed, God would never fail! Our only true refuge is the eternal God, Who always holds us and will also catch us when the shaky supports of life collapse, and we fall.

Not only can we rest in that security, but we can take greater risks of faith as we lean on His strength and press on with His resources. To some, living for God may seem like the riskier path to take in this world, but in reality, it is those without God who are on the shakiest ground. One mistake could wipe them out. But when the eternal God is our refuge and His everlasting arms are under us, we can dare to be bold!

What is it you've hesitated to be obedient in doing that God has prompted you about? What step of faith is God leading you to take, but fear is holding you back? Perhaps today is the day when you are going to step out in faith and trust those everlasting arms …?

August 9

Seeds

Our thought-world is vitally important. It touches our entire life. God's Word is like a seed planted in our hearts that bears the fruit of love and peace and strength.

As the psalmist focuses on the fundamentals of life in Psalm 119, he shares that he has hidden God's Word in his heart and rejoices in it as one does great riches.

It is like a seed planted that gives strength and power to live a fruitful and fulfilling life. When you plant God's Word in your heart, it begins to nourish your heart and will take root and grow. You will find a new strength for living and a deep abiding joy.

So today, I encourage you to let your heart be refreshed and strengthened with God's Word.

Here are some selections from Psalm 119:

"How can a young person keep his or her way pure? By living according to your word. I seek you with all my heart; Do not let me stray from your commands. I have hidden your word in my heart that I might not sin against you. Praise be to you, O Lord; teach me your decrees ...I rejoice in following your statues as one rejoices in great riches. I meditate on your precepts and consider your ways. I delight in your decrees; I will not neglect your word."

Ask God today to help you find His plan and purpose for your life and allow it to take root in your heart and life and bear the fruit of a deep, rich and abiding faith, and remember these powerful words from Helen Keller:

"Character cannot be developed in ease and quiet. Only through experience of trial and suffering can the soul be strengthened, ambition inspired, and success achieved."

August 10

Breaking Tradition

Preoccupation with a religious tradition can often be a way of sheltering from the far-reaching claims of the love of God.

Mark 7:9 *"You have a fine way of setting aside the commands of God in order to observe your own traditions!"*

Jesus is not talking to heathens here. He is talking with people whose life mission is to do the will of God and thereby prove that they are God's people.

But Jesus is unequivocal. He says that the Pharisees attention to various traditional observances fails to achieve its aim. He clearly saw their religion as a farce, a swindle. Jesus then illustrate what He means:

Mark 7:10-11 *"Moses said, honour your father and mother ... but you say that if a man says to his father or mother, "Whatever help you might otherwise have received from me is Corban, then you no longer let him do anything for his father or mother."*

Moses taught that God expected a man to honour his parents, but according to the Pharisees, a man could dedicate his property to God by using a form of words called Corban, and so avoid his responsibility to his parents. By dedicating his assets to the temple, he could place them beyond the reach of his parents needs while still using them for himself.

By their zeal for one of the precepts of the law, the Pharisees made it possible for some to regard themselves as Godly, even though their so-called obedience left their aged parents destitute. In their religious zeal, they completely ignored love.

May the love of God shine into your heart and mine, driving out useless piety and planting responsibility and compassion.

August 11

I Can do Nothing on My Own

John 5:30 *"I can do nothing on my own. As I hear, I judge, and my judgment is just, because I seek not my own will but the will of him who sent me."*

Incredibly - though He was divine, eternal, and one with the Father, Jesus initiated nothing on His own throughout His time on earth. Instead, He listened to the Father and carried out the Father's will at all times. Isaiah foretold that the Spirit would reside in the Messiah.

Isaiah 11:2 *"And the Spirit of the LORD shall rest upon him, the Spirit of wisdom and understanding, the Spirit of counsel and might, the Spirit of knowledge and the fear of the LORD."*

Jesus fulfilled that prophecy. So, while on earth, the Eternal Son of God didn't base His decisions on His human abilities - though no human had greater understanding. He didn't look at the facts or listen to the various sides of the argument to make a judgment (Isaiah 11:3). Rather, because Jesus knew His Father to be perfectly wise, perfectly just, and perfectly good, He trusted Him completely and did what He wanted.

Thanks to His perfect obedience, His Spirit now indwells all believers in Christ who have opened their heart to Him. If Jesus could do nothing on His own, then neither can we. We shouldn't even try.

The Holy Spirit's primary role isn't simply to help us make decisions. Just as Jesus came to reveal God to the world, now, the Holy Spirit reveals God to us. Therefore, through the Holy Spirit, we come to know God's will by coming to know God Himself, in Christ. By revealing God's character and by reminding us of God's commands, the Spirit guides us to do nothing on our own, but only the will of the Father.

August 12

Finding Jesus in the Fog

Come with me for a moment, back in time, to witness what was perhaps the foggiest, darkest night in all human history. The scene is very simple; you'll recognize it immediately. A grove of twisted olive trees; the ground cluttered with large rocks; a low stone fence; a dark, almost eerie night.

Now, look into the picture. Look closely through the shadowy foliage; see that person; see that solitary figure. What is he doing? He is flat on the ground; His face is stained with dirt and tears; His fists are pounding the hard earth; His eyes are wide as He fears what is to come; His hair is matted with salty sweat. Is that blood you see on his forehead? Then you realise that this is Jesus – He's in the Garden of Gethsemane.

Maybe you've seen the classic portrait of Christ in the garden, kneeling beside a rock; in a snow-white robe; His hands peacefully folded in prayer; there's a look of serenity on His face; halo over His head; a spotlight from heaven illuminating His golden-brown hair. I don't claim to be an artist, but I can tell you one thing - the man who painted that picture didn't use the gospel of Mark as his source! When Mark wrote about that painful night, he used phrases like these: *"Horror and dismay came over him ... My heart is ready to break with grief ... He went a little forward and threw himself on the ground."*

Does this look like the picture of a saintly Jesus resting in the palm of God? Hardly. Mark used black paint to describe this scene. We see an agonizing, straining, struggling Jesus. We see the *"man of sorrows."* (Isaiah 53:3) We see a man who is struggling with fear; He's wrestling with commitment, and yearning for relief. We see Jesus in the fog of a broken heart.

The next time you are called to suffer, pay attention. It may be the closest you'll ever get to God.

August 13

It's Time to Recharge!

Ephesians 6:10 *"Finally, be strong in the Lord and in his mighty power."*

Ever had one of those days when you felt as though you had nothing left in you; no motivation, no passion, no desire to move forward? Feelings of worthlessness begin to surface and it seems as though you are headed backwards instead of forward. What happened to the fervour and the passion?

If this is you today, I have a word of encouragement: The Lord wants you to know that He is still working in you and for you. Sometimes handling life's challenges can drain us of our power and our drive to keep going. Some of us are just in need of a good re-charge!

I am reminded of the passage in 1 Kings 19 where Elijah was on the run from Jezebel after defeating 850 prophets of Baal. This was a great victory for Elijah and many other great feats followed. What caught my attention in this story however was that Elijah became fearful when Jezebel sent him a message about what she would do to him.

Elijah came to rest under a tree and prayed that he might die. Upon falling asleep, he was visited by an angel of the Lord. Elijah was given bread and water and told to eat because the journey ahead of him was great. That speaks volumes to me.

As Christians, we need to stay connected to our power source. When our mobile phone dies or our battery is low, we connect it to the power source. Why not do the same spiritually? Just like a battery needs to be recharged by being plugged in, so too do we as children of God.

Only then can we *"be strong in the Lord and in his mighty power."*

August 14

Time and Attention

God doesn't desire more of our time now and then; He desires more of our *attention* all the time! Do you ever feel frustrated because you hear messages about getting closer to God and you definitely desire this for yourself, but you are inundated with so much to do already that this only makes you feel guilty because you are too busy for God?

I think we all feel this at one time or another, but carving more time out of your busy schedule to be with God isn't necessarily the only answer. Look at the following scriptures:

Psalm 16:8 *"I have set the Lord always before me."*

Psalm 25:15 *"My eyes are ever on the Lord."*

Psalm 34:1 *"I will extol the Lord at all times; His praise will always be on my lips."*

Reading these verses makes you wonder if these are the words of a monk who had nothing else to do but devote time to God. Actually, they are the words of David, King of Israel, a great ruler and warrior. How did he manage to run a nation at war, lead his troops in battle and keep his eyes on the Lord at all times? The only conclusion is that he did this while he did everything else. We need a continual awareness of God, not necessarily more time devoted to spiritual pursuits.

God is Who you pay attention to and You can pay attention to God while you are doing everything else. It's all about doing everything for God and seeing God in everything we do. It's about bringing God into the boardroom, the exercise room, the living room, the bedroom, the office, the garden.

Now of course He's already in all these places but we are talking about being aware of His presence there at all times. That's what it means to set the Lord *always* before us.

August 15

A Good Example

1 Thessalonians 1: 6-7 *"You became imitators of us and of the Lord, for you welcomed the message in the midst of severe suffering with the joy given by the Holy Spirit. And so you became a model to all the believers in Macedonia and in Achaia."*

I used to tell my children that we needed to be careful about what we said and did because someone was always watching us. We could be a good example and encourage others to be Christ-like, or we could be a bad example and discourage others from learning about or growing in Christ.

Now that I am older, I realize we'll never be perfect examples. Life can wear us down and suck the joy out of our hearts. But God can use us anyway.

Seeing how a sister in Christ handles her financial difficulties with a smile on her face, or how a brother faces a poor medical prognosis with courage and faith, can strengthen us during our challenging times. And that strengthening can then help others. Jesus wants believers to be an example. In the Sermon on the Mount, he said:

Matthew 5:14 *"You are the light of the world. A city set on a hill cannot be hidden."*

Even if we are not perfect, we can still be an example of faith to others if we try to reflect Jesus. What do others see in us? Do we show them how to answer grumpy people with kind words? How to bear loss and suffering with patience? How to be content when turmoil swirls all around us?

Today, let's seek to reflect the light of Christ into this dark and sinful world and give courage to people in every place we go by our example of faith, joy, and love.

August 16

Jars of Clay

2 Corinthians 4:7 *"But we have this treasure in jars of clay to show that this all-surpassing power is from God and not from us."*

Your heavenly Father wants you to be completely whole in belonging and worth, in identity and legitimacy. Be blessed to know without question what a treasure you are to Him. Be blessed to live as the special treasure you are. As you know who you are, you will understand the 'why' of what you do. Be blessed with knowing your purpose and the specific blessings which God has stored up for you.

Be blessed in the name of the One who is all-surpassing power. Be blessed with knowing experientially that Jesus is the 'how' of everything you are and all you do. Paul asked the rhetorical question, *"What do you have that you did not receive?"* (1 Corinthians 4:7) and the answer is *nothing*.

God is your competence (2 Corinthians 3:5). Know that it is *"not by might nor by power, but by my Spirit," says the LORD Almighty* (Zechariah 4:6). You can be confident, knowing that apart from Him you can do nothing (John 15:5), but in Him you can do everything (Philippians 4:13).

You can be confident in the core of your being in following God's will, not your own; in speaking His words, not your own; in doing His work, as He does His work of intimately revealing Himself to you.

Thank God today for your God-given competence, but don't allow your competence to become your identity. Be blessed with healing in your deepest doubts and your deepest wounds of identity, so that you do not have to strive to prove that you are worthy, legitimate, significant, and deserving of honour. Be blessed in everything He designed you to be to fulfill His purpose on the earth.

August 17

To God be the Glory!

Romans 11:36 *"To Him be the glory forever! Amen."*

This should be the single desire of all Christians. Everything else must come second to this. As a Christian we may wish for prosperity in our business, but only insofar as it may help us to give God more glory!

We may desire to attain more gifts and more graces, but it should only be so we can give God all the glory! You are not acting as you ought to when you are moved by any other motive than to give glory to your Lord.

Charles Spurgeon put it best when he said:

"Let nothing ever set your heart beating so mightily as love for God. Let this ambition fire your soul; let it become the foundation of everything you do, and become your sustaining motive whenever your passion grows cold. Make God your only goal."

When I depend on myself, sorrow begins; but my joy will be complete when God becomes my supreme delight. Let your desire for God's glory be a growing, daily desire.

Has God prospered your business? Give Him more as He has given you more.

Has God given you great experiences? Praise Him by stronger faith than you exercised at first.

Does your knowledge grow? Then sing more sweetly.

Do you enjoy happier times than you once had? Have you been healed from sickness, and has your sorrow been turned into peace and joy? Then give God more music; increase the thankful fervour of your praise. Give Him honour in every part of your life. To God be the glory, today and every day!

August 18

My Peace I Give You

Trials, commotion, fear of the unknown, suffering, death, evil amongst others characterizes our society today. We seem to constantly move from one evil event to the other. Joblessness, marital wars, terrorism, natural disasters, famine, war… the endless struggle for survival continues. The hearts of many are failing them; the younger ones are faced with a daunting, bleak future and there is uncertainty everywhere.

In the face of these storms of life, many are being misguided and they are not seeking helping in the right place. The more they run faster than their shadows, the more entangled they become with disappointment.

Some resort to alcohol, hard drugs, immorality etc. to manage the stress and hard breaks. The truth is, those things can never solve any problem, they aggravate the issues and create new challenges because evil can never be used to fight evil.

In the midst of all these alarming disorders, there is only one place where you can find abiding peace which lasts forever; that is in Jesus. It is only in Christ that you can find real peace which flows like a river, the best rest for your aching soul. So, receive the words of Jesus afresh today:

John 14:27 *"Peace I leave with you, my peace I give unto you: not as the world gives, give I unto you. Let not your heart be troubled, neither let it be afraid."*

You can only experience this peace when you accept Jesus into your life as your Lord, personal Saviour and Friend. He is the answer to all of your questions. Jesus is the only reason for living and without Him, life is absolutely meaningless.

So, what are you waiting for? Give Jesus a chance in your life today – and embrace that peace which only He can give you.

August 19

Don't Lose Hope

Hebrews 10:23 *"Let us hold unswervingly to the hope we profess, for he who promised is faithful."*

Hope is such a small word but without it, we humans are doomed. Whether we know it or not, hope is what gets us up every morning and draws us into another day. However, my observation is that recently we are facing an unprecedent wave of hopelessness. So many people are losing hope during these troubled times.

As Christians, we know how easy it is to lose hope when we lose sight of Christ. In Hebrews 10, the writer reminds us to live out our faith rooted in hope. There is never a reason we cannot put our trust in our Saviour, persevering even when things seem bleak. That is our right and our responsibility as believers in Christ, because He will never fail us.

Hope in Jesus is never in vain. When it looks impossible that help will arrive in time, we can count on Him to save us. He is ready to send in a cavalry of faithful believers or provide another surprising way to rescue us. Yes, we might feel like giving up sometimes because we do not know what to expect anymore. But our Saviour's love and compassion should really inspire us to press on. God is always with us and His promises endure forever. We can lean on His Word with complete confidence.

There is no other way to learn the power of hope than to place our complete trust in God when confronted with seemingly insurmountable challenges; holding tight until the last hour; persevering and trusting a blessing is coming our way. Don't lose hope. Keep hope alive, and do not be afraid (Mark 5:36), trusting God to lead us out of the darkness into His light, leading us through a new door of new opportunities.

August 20

Time

How often does our preoccupation with living make us forget that we are always in the presence of God? We try and cram more and more into each day and often become so stressed and anxious that we don't have enough time to do everything. Sometimes it is the things that we put off doing until another day that wear us down the most.

Yet it is in our everyday living that we should place God first as we continue with our work and our play. How often do we become so caught up in the 'everyday' that we find we do not have enough time for God?

Our moods so often depend on how much time we have. If we work all day and come home tired and stressed because we didn't have time to finish all that was on our desk; or there was not enough time to finish the housework or complete the gardening or do the shopping; all these things affect the way we react to those around us.

I believe that happiness is not something for which we should ever search. It is like a butterfly that is so elusive when we try to catch it, and yet when we don't try, one may just come to rest on our shoulder. We can come to know true happiness only by living the life that the Lord would have us lead – by serving and showing unconditional love to others. It is taking the time to slow down and listen to the still, small voice that gives us the patience and the courage to take each moment and know that we are surrounded by God's grace.

John 10:10 *"The thief comes only to steal and kill and destroy; I have come that they may have life and have it to the full."*

Is our life full in the way Jesus promises in that verse? We should think of time as the thief, and so if we make time for God, the rest of our lives will come into perspective.

August 21

It's Not That Simple

Proverbs 9:6 *"Leave your simple ways and you will live; walk in the way of insight."*

Has anyone ever told you being a Christian is easy? Did you laugh in response? If you have been a believer for more than fifteen minutes, you probably have realized it's not simple.

Becoming a Christian seems simple enough: just accept the fact that you cannot save yourself or ever earn your way into Heaven. Instead receive the free gift Christ already purchased for you. And yet, for many of us it becomes difficult because our pride, scepticism, or feelings of unworthiness snag us.

In a strange way, the world's method is the simpler one. The world says you have to *"make it on your own"* with blood, sweat, and tears! *"Every man for himself." "The one with the most toys wins." "Be all you can be." "Just do it."* You know all the slogans – they bombard us every day.

But Christ tells us to open our hands and hearts to receive that which *His* blood, sweat, and tears provide. Be servants, not masters. Put others first. Die so that you can live. In your weakness, there will be immeasurable strength.

And the world scratches its head and claims this is either too foolish or just too hard. The Apostle Paul understood this dichotomy way back in the first century.

1 Corinthians 1:25 *"For the foolishness of God is wiser than human wisdom, and the weakness of God is stronger than human strength."*

How about you? Will you give up the simple ways to embrace the deeper, richer 'foolishness' of God? You may find it is the wisest decision you ever made.

August 22

Living in the Moment

Mark 13:11 *"Whenever you are arrested and brought to trial, do not worry beforehand about what to say. Just say whatever is given you at the time, for it is not you speaking, but the Holy Spirit."*

I saw a coffee mug advertised recently and it made me smile a lot. It said, *"Hold on, let me overthink this."* How many of us spend more time preparing to do something and less time actually doing it?

At times we are we so afraid of saying or doing the wrong thing that we over-analyse or talk ourselves out of doing anything. When we do something, we often ruminate on it for ages. The desire to be perfect can be paralysing.

Jesus spoke to His disciples about what would happen to them as believers. He knew they would be persecuted for their faith. But Jesus encouraged them by promising they would never be alone. When they were asked to defend their faith, the Holy Spirit would give them the right words to say.

We should never dismiss the work of the Holy Spirit in those moments when we speak to others about Christ's salvation and His work in our lives. If the fear of saying the wrong thing overtakes us, we could possibly neglect the most important work of the Gospel - telling those who are lost about God's immeasurable love for them. Don't over-think it.

Whether we are defending our faith or sharing God's Word with someone far from Him, the Spirit within us will guide our words so that, as Mark recorded, *"... it is not you speaking, but the Holy Spirit."*

Always trust the Holy Spirit within you (and within the person you are speaking to) more than you trust yourself. He will never let you down.

August 23

Moments

In the *happy* moments - *praise* Him.

In the *difficult* moments - *seek* Him.

In the *prayerful* moments - *ask* Him.

In the *decision* moments - *follow* Him.

In the *quiet* moments - *see* Him.

In the *lonely* moments - *know* Him.

In the *listening* moments - *hear* Him.

In the *unsure* moments - *believe* Him.

In the *active* moments - *serve* Him.

In the *waiting* moments - *trust* Him.

In the *hurting* moments - *touch* Him.

In the *lovely* moments - *adore* Him.

For in all your moments, He is there
in goodness, in kindness, in love.

Proverbs 3:5-6

"Trust the Lord with all your heart and lean not on your own understanding. In all your ways acknowledge Him and He will direct your path."

August 24

The Heart of a Servant

Mark 10:45 *"For even the Son of Man did not come to be served, but to serve, and to give His life as a ransom for many."*

Being a servant in our world means being suppressed, even trod-upon. But in the Biblical context, it takes on a totally different meaning: one of freedom and devotion. It describes those who are more like Jesus.

The quality that so completely characterized the life of Jesus was His unselfish servant heart. The Apostle Paul added to this focus when he wrote:

Philippians 2:3-4 *"In humility value others above yourselves, not looking to your own interests but each of you to the interests of the others. You should have the same attitude toward one another that Christ Jesus had."*

If we, as Christians, are going to grow and mature into Christ-like character, we need to make a commitment to be daily giving of ourselves in ministry to and for others. Living with a servant heart stands opposed to the primary concerns we see today - where the focus of our culture and society is more on our own personal happiness and comfort.

The preoccupation with self today is readily seen in slogans like, *"Be all you can be."* Simply put, our modern-day society (and this includes a great number of Christians) is focused on making satisfaction the goal of life.

Serving God and others is always more important than self-fulfilment. We must be careful to not take the focus off what is truly at the heart of Christianity: knowing and loving God. Out of the infinite resources within that relationship, we are then able to live as servants of God and others in the power of the Spirit, in Christ, through Christ and for Christ.

August 25

Troubled Hearts

When children are afraid of the dark, they need someone to reassure them. The best thing to do is turn on the light so they know there's actually not a monster or other supposed threat to them under the bed. They need the reassuring words of an adult who can help them get a proper perspective.

Like little children, we often need the reassuring words of our heavenly Father to help us in times of fear or anxiety. Because no matter where you live, how much money you make, or what you do for a living, you will never be able to create a trouble-free life.

Job 5:7 *"People are born for trouble as readily as sparks fly up from a fire."*

Just when you get through that one conflict or difficulty, that one hardship or trial, another one will come. It always will be something. I don't say that to depress you but to prepare you. Understand, troubles come. We are a broken people living in a broken world – so trouble is never far away. While there are good reasons to be troubled sometimes, there is a greater reason not to be. Hear the words of Jesus:

John 14:1 *"Don't let your hearts be troubled. Trust in God, and trust also in me."*

Jesus said this to His disciples in the Upper Room, after they learned He would be crucified. Needless to say, they were very stressed. Deep anxiety and fear filled their hearts. But Jesus was saying, *"Look, I haven't brought you this far to abandon you now. I know what I'm doing. So, I'm asking you to believe. I'm asking you to trust Me."*

When a problem you're facing fills your heart with anxiety or fear, remember this: God is always bigger than your problem!

August 26

One Man's Mission

Matthew 28:19 *"Therefore go and make disciples of all nations, baptizing them in the name of the Father and of the Son and of the Holy Spirit."*

In the mid nineteenth century there was an huge economic collapse. Thousands of businesses closed and hundreds of thousands of people were unemployed. A quiet and zealous businessman by the name of Jeremiah Lanphier, took up an appointment as a City Missionary in down-town New York. Burdened by the incredible need, Jeremiah Lanphier decided to invite others to join him in a noonday prayer-meeting, to be held on Wednesdays once a week.

Accordingly at twelve noon, on September 23, 1857, the door was opened and the faithful Lanphier took his seat to await the response to his invitation. Five minutes went by. No one appeared. The missionary paced the room in a conflict of fear and faith. Fifteen minutes passed. Lanphier was still alone. Twenty minutes; twenty-five; thirty; and then at 12.30 p.m., steps were heard on the stairs, and the first person appeared, then another, and another, until six people were present, and the prayer meeting began. The following week there were forty people. Within six months, ten thousand businessmen were gathering daily for prayer in New York, and within two years, a million converts were added to the American Church.

Undoubtedly the greatest revival in New York's history was sweeping the city, and it was of such an order to make the whole nation curious. There was no fanaticism, no hysteria, simply an incredible movement of the people to pray.

Our world today needs such a movement again! Can you see how one person can make an enormous difference. Might there be another Jeremiah Lanphier today? Could it be you?

August 27

Nevertheless

2 Samuel 5:6–9 *"And the king and his men… spoke to David, saying, "You shall not come in here; but the blind and the lame will repel you," … Nevertheless David took the stronghold of Zion (that is, the City of David)."*

Did you see it? Most hurry past it. Let's not. Let me just pull out a pen now and underline this twelve-letter masterpiece: <u>Nevertheless</u>. *"Nevertheless, David took the stronghold …"*

Wouldn't you love it if God would write a *nevertheless* in your biography?

> *'Born to alcoholics, nevertheless she led a sober life.'*
>
> *'Never went to college, nevertheless he mastered a trade.'*
>
> *'Didn't read the Bible until retirement age, nevertheless he developed a deep and abiding faith.'*

We all need a *nevertheless* - and God has plenty to go around. Strongholds mean nothing to Him. Remember Paul's words? *"We use God's mighty weapons, not mere worldly weapons, to knock down the Devil's strongholds."* (2 Corinthians 10:4). You and I fight with toothpicks; God comes with battering rams and cannons. What He did for David, He can do for us. The question is, will we do what David did?

Two types of thoughts continually vie for your attention. One proclaims God's strengths; the other lists your failures. One longs to build you up; the other seeks to tear you down. And here's the great news: you get to choose which voice you hear! So, why listen to the mockers? Why heed their voices? Why give ear to pea-brains and scoffers when you can, with the same ear, listen to the voice of God?

Your *nevertheless* awaits you. What's holding you back from achieving your full potential as a reborn child of God?

August 28

On Borrowed Time

Luke 9:51-62 *"As the time approached for him to be taken up to heaven, Jesus resolutely set out for Jerusalem. And He sent messengers on ahead, who went into a Samaritan village to get things ready for Him; but the people there did not welcome Him, because He was heading for Jerusalem."*

Jesus is totally devoted to accomplishing His Father's will and finally, resolutely He begins the journey to Jerusalem. This decision is radical and final. The followers who by now have at least some sense of His plan, trudge alongside him; fear mixed with obedience. I wonder if they really understand that their Saviour is living *'on borrowed time.'*

One of the English definitions of that idiom is *"a period of uncertainty during which the inevitable consequences of a current situation are usually postponed or avoided."* If we look into the future that looms ahead of Jesus, we can see Him agonizing with His Father, asking if there could not be some other plan: *"Father, if you are willing, take this cup from me…"* Jesus' acceptance of that plan (*"yet not my will, but yours be done"*) eliminates any thought of avoiding the consequences of the situation He is facing.

Shortly after Luke describes the resolute path to Jerusalem, he records a conversation Jesus has with His friends in which He talks yet again about the cost of following the Saviour. Some who hear the cost will want to return to the assumed safety and security of what they have become accustomed to.

Others, like those trudging disciples, will follow the path to Jerusalem, not understanding all the cost, but willing to live - with Jesus - *on borrowed time.*

Are you willing to do the same today?

August 29

The Power to Change

We all fail - but here's the good news – our failure is never final! God uses our failure to teach us that we can't do it; He never said we could, but He can and always said He would! In his timely devotional, Oswald Chambers writes, *"All our promises and resolutions end in denial because we have no power to accomplish them."* How then can we ever change? Grace! Grace is the power to change! Look at what the Apostle Paul said in one of my favourite Bible verses:

1 Corinthians 15:10 *"By the grace of God I am what I am, and His grace to me was not without effect."*

God's grace to you is not without effect. That word means to cause to change. Your life changing as a follower of Christ is the result of an exchanged life! It's not about will power, but God's power. What else could have changed a man like Paul, bent on *"destroying the church,"* (Acts 8:3), into the greatest missionary of the New Testament Church age?

Paul's encounter with Christ changed his life dramatically! He met Grace on a road to Damascus, where he was headed to imprison even more believers for following Christ. What effect did grace have in his life? The same effect it will have in your life and mine: complete transformation!

Grace exchanges our sin for God's forgiveness; our emptiness for His fullness; our pain for His promises; our brokenness for His wholeness! When confronted with the truth about Jesus, shame and guilt could have overwhelmed Paul for all he had done to Christ's followers.

However, grace gave Paul hope and purpose. The man who entered that city was very different from the one who had left. Grace gives us the promise for real, permanent life change.

August 30

Shine, Jesus!

John 4:42b *"Now we believe, not just because of what you told us, but because we have heard Him (Jesus) ourselves. Now we know that He is indeed the Saviour of the world."*

When Jesus turns the light on in our lives it always produces inspiration and inspiration fuels passion! We experience life – real life, the life God intended for us to live with the Creator Himself restored as His creature, making of us a new creation in Christ! Old things will pass away and everything will become new!

This is what happened to a Samaritan woman in chapter 4 of John's Gospel. This woman was considered an outcast by the religious Jews. Jesus had no such prejudice.

This chapter reveals His love and compassion for everyone regardless of their race, religion, or morality. It demonstrates also the uncompromising power of speaking the truth in love! This unnamed woman was so impacted by the love of God, she *"left her water jar beside the well and ran back to the village, telling everyone, 'Come and see a man who told me everything I ever did! Could He possibly be the Messiah?'"* (Vs. 28-29) Love breaks through all barriers!

Curiosity must have gotten the better of the people because John said the people in the village came streaming to see Him, and many believed in Jesus because of what the woman had told them. Like that woman, your story matters! So let your light shine like she did! It is the greatest evidence for the existence of God and His redeeming love!

Whether it's your body or soul that is afflicted, Jesus is the answer. Read all of the fourth chapter of John and experience again the compassion of Jesus for those the world has written off and let His light shine on those around you.

August 31

The Challenge of Faith

Proverbs 3:5 *"Trust in the LORD with all your heart and lean not on your own understanding. ..."*

The challenge of faith is trusting when you don't understand. It's so much easier to lean on your own understanding than to trust God. Faith says, *"Even if I don't understand, I will trust in You."*

It's human nature to say, *"I'll trust when I understand it."* The sceptic says, *"I'll believe it when I see it."* God says, *"You won't see it until you believe it."*

Mary is a great example of someone who was determined to trust God even when she could not possibly understand. Whoever heard of a virgin giving birth to a child, much less the Son of God! The Angel's announcement to Mary before that first Christmas was as unbelievable as it was startling!

Luke 1:30-33 *"Don't be afraid, Mary, for you have found favour with God! You will conceive and give birth to a son, and you will name Him Jesus. He will be very great and will be called the Son of the Most High. The Lord God will give Him the throne of His ancestor David. And He will reign over Israel forever; His Kingdom will never end!"*

Talk about trusting when you don't understand it! I love Mary's response because it shows us the simple child-like faith God is looking for when He asks us to trust Him.

Luke 1:38 *"I am the Lord's servant. May everything you have said about me come true."*

Mary knew there was nothing she could do to bring this to pass apart from trusting that what God had said, He would do, in His time and in His way!

September 1

The Hope of The World

Matthew 12:18-21 *"Look at My Servant, whom I have chosen. He is My Beloved, who pleases Me. I will put My Spirit upon Him, and He will proclaim justice to the nations. He will not fight or shout or raise His voice in public. He will not crush the weakest reed or put out a flickering candle. Finally, He will cause justice to be victorious. And His name will be the hope of all the world."*

Matthew was quoting a prophecy from Isaiah 42:1-4 which described the character and nature of the coming Messiah. Matthew could recognize that character in Jesus as he followed Him and observed the way He lived and ministered to those around Him, especially in the way Jesus treated him. Being a despised tax collector, Matthew would have been overcome when Jesus called him! He immediately left his lucrative business and followed Christ. His life would never be the same. Matthew must have thought, *"How could God accept me when everyone around me despises me?"*

Matthew experienced the acceptance and love that Isaiah described of God's chosen Servant. Jesus spoke the truth in love, unlike the other religious leaders. Though Matthew felt broken and bruised and no doubt burned out with religion Jesus didn't toss him aside as irredeemable. He invited a Tax Collector to follow Him! Incredulous!

Truly, this must be the Messiah Isaiah predicted would come; one who would not crush the weakest reed or put out a flickering candle!

Maybe you feel like a weak reed or a flickering candle. Are you broken and bruised, perhaps from bad choices, and you feel useless? God is not out to step on you or toss you aside. He is calling you today, *"Follow Me."* He has a hope and future for you with purpose just as He did for Matthew.

September 2

Faith

John 4:50b *"The man believed what Jesus said and started home."*

Understanding the nature of faith will help us live by faith. Jesus' encounter with a government official in John 4 offers practical insights into the nature of faith. The official comes to Jesus in a crisis. His son is gravely ill and, apart from a miracle, will most likely die. He travels some 20 miles from Capernaum to Cana where Jesus had performed His first miracle turning water into wine at a wedding feast.

When He saw Jesus, He said, *"Lord, please come now before my little boy dies."* (John 4:49) When he addresses Jesus as Lord, he put himself under Jesus' authority even though he was a legal authority over Jesus. He believed that Jesus had the authority and power to heal his son. Faith always begins with believing that God is able to handle whatever situation we face. Not only did this government official believe, but he earnestly sought out Jesus and asked Him to come and heal his son. Rather than leaving with the man for Capernaum, Jesus told him, *"Go back home. Your son will live!"* (John 4:50a)

Notice how the man demonstrated his faith. He believed before he saw the miracle. He obeyed God before there was any evidence of God's work. Faith is trusting God no matter what happens.

Before the story ends, John adds this note: *"And he and his entire household believed in Jesus."* (John 4:53b) That's the nature of faith! Grateful for what Jesus had done, this government official gave the glory to God and his faith led his entire household to believe in Jesus.

When you put your faith in Jesus, you'll discover He is able to do immeasurably more than all you could ask or even imagine!

September 3

A Grateful Heart

Psalm 28:7 *"The LORD strengthens and protects me; I trust in Him with all my heart. I am rescued and my heart is full of joy; I will sing to Him in gratitude."*

American playwright and Pulitzer Prize-winning novelist, Thornton Wilder said, *"We can only be said to be alive in those moments when our hearts are conscious of our treasures."* Most people who know their days are numbered understand the importance of the little sensory details that we often take for granted. They know what it means to wake up each day with a grateful heart. I have seen men and women who were suffering chronic pain, smiling as they sipped their morning coffee or held the hand of their spouse. Such people are immeasurably grateful for one more day, for just another opportunity to embrace their lives in every detail.

We talk about gratitude a lot in our culture, but we find it difficult to practice. The consumer mindset instilled by media and advertising, combined with our human tendency to compare, leaves us coming up short. We are told – and often believe – that what we have isn't enough. We are conditioned to automatically accept that the next electronic gadget, the next pair of designer shoes, the next tropical vacation, or the next romantic relationship will fulfill us.

Of course, material goods, exciting experiences, and even other people can't quench the spiritual thirst in our lives. It only leaves us in the wilderness of discontentment.

Only God can satisfy our deepest thirst with His living water. Cicero once wisely observed, *"Gratitude is not only the greatest of virtues, but the parent of all the others."* When we are thankful, we become content and full of the peace that only God can provide.

September 4

Overcoming Depression

Is there anything you're going through that you feel you won't get through? Storms in life can do that; bad news can knock you to your knees; hurts and grief that never seem to heal; past pain robs us of any present joy. It could be the loss of a loved one; a habit that is controlling you; or a financial setback that you don't think you'll ever recover from. You may never get over it, but God wants you to know that you will get through it.

As a follower of Christ, you are an eternal being, but your pain is temporary. Although there are some losses in this life which we may never get over this side of heaven, we can get through them with God's power.

Elijah struggled with anxiety and depression. He was a mighty prophet of God, but he was also just a man subject to the same issues you and I face as well.

James 5:17 tells us, *"Elijah was a man with a nature just like our own...."* That's a great description because it brings these 'spiritual giants' down to our size!

The Bible doesn't hide the humanness of God's servants. So, we can easily identify with them. Like us, Elijah was just an ordinary man. Too often we tend to think God only uses superstars. But just look at the characters in the Bible that God used for a moment. They were just ordinary men and women with similar weaknesses to our own.

What is the pain you're feeling that cries out to God? God uses our greatest struggles to get our attention. Has God got your attention now in the midst of your pain, loss or infirmity? It may not feel like it but you're in a good place. Like Elijah, if God brought you to it, God will bring you through it!

September 5

The Wasteland of Worry

Philippians 4:6-7 *"Don't worry about anything; instead, pray about everything. Tell God what you need and thank Him for all He has done. Then you will experience God's peace, which exceeds anything we can understand. His peace will guard your hearts and minds as you live in Christ Jesus."*

That great theologian, Erma Bombeck once said: *"Worry is like a rocking chair: it gives you something to do but it never gets you anywhere."* The truth is, worry is utterly worthless. It's stewing without doing. It can't change your past or your future, it just wastes time today. If you've been living in the wasteland of worry, God offers you a way out - today!

God offers a promise of peace for everything that makes you anxious. Rather than just telling us not to worry, the Bible tells us what to do instead. Replace your worries with prayer. The news gets even better. You can pray about everything! There is not one concern too big or one care too small that you can't pray about. So, whatever causes you to worry can become a prayer target for you today. If it's big enough to worry about, it's big enough to pray about!

God is offering you a choice today. You can worry or you can pray. When you pray, you are giving God your worries and letting Him meet your needs. He's big enough for the job. So, make a list of the things that cause you to worry today and then commit that list to God in prayer. You can escape the wasteland of worry. Claim His promise of peace today!

After you tell God what you need, thank Him for all He has done. Thanksgiving is a declaration of faith that shifts our mind's attention from our worries to God's faithfulness. When you choose to live in the promised land of peace, God will guard your heart and mind in Christ Jesus.

September 6

Forgiveness

Luke 5:20b *"Young man, your sins are forgiven."*

Imagine this young man. Luke tells us that he was a paralytic and was carried to Jesus by some friends. They believed that if they could just get their friend to Jesus, he would be healed.

The crowd was too great for them to get near Jesus, so they took extreme measures and carried their friend to the roof. They removed some tiles from the roof and lowered him right in front of Jesus while He was teaching the crowd!

I imagine that would stop a service in progress! The focus shifted to the paralysed man on the mat suspended in the air in front of the teacher. However, what Jesus said surprised them even more. Jesus told the man his sins were forgiven.

The religious leaders in the crowd were indignant! *"Only God can forgive sin! Who does this man think He is?"* They accused Jesus of blasphemy, claiming to be God!

But then Jesus turned to the paralysed man and said, *"Stand up, pick up your mat, and go home."* (Luke 5:24b)

The man received both physical and spiritual healing. Luke tells us that he *"jumped up, picked up his mat, and went home praising God."* (Luke 5:25). Jesus went deeper than the man's physical needs. He gave him the miracle he needed most – freedom from the paralysis of sin and shame!

How often do you stop short in your prayers from asking God for what you need most? Jesus saw this man's heart. It was paralysed with guilt and sin.

The good news is that God offers the same forgiveness given to the paralytic to you and me.

September 7

Relinquishing Control

Control issues. We all have them to one extent or another. It's simply a part of human nature that we want to be in control of our lives and think that we can control our own destiny. Jeremiah recognized the problem and came to the realization that we really can't control our lives, but we can submit our lives to God's care and God's control.

Jeremiah 10:23 *"Lord, we know that people do not control their own destiny. It is not in their power to determine what will happen to them."*

One of the best illustrations of this in the New Testament is in the life of Simon Peter. Jesus taught Peter a valuable lesson about control that would prepare Peter to later follow Christ and become a great Apostle.

Peter and his partners had been fishing all night long with no success. They returned to clean their nets and that's when Jesus came challenged Peter to launch out into the deep and let down his nets for a great catch of fish. Look at Peter's response:

Luke 5:5 *"Master, we've worked hard all night and haven't caught anything. But because You say so, I will let down the nets."*

Peter expressed both respect and sarcasm in his response. He called Jesus, *"Master."* He respected the fact that Jesus was a master teacher of spiritual truths, but He obviously didn't know that much about fishing. Despite Peter's disbelief and sarcasm, he still obeyed, and because he obeyed, he would experience a miracle! The catch of fish was so great that he had to signal for his partners to help bring in all the fish!

To trust God, we must give up control first. Only then will we come under Christ's control and see the miracles of God.

September 8

The Four Invitations of Christ

The first invitation of Christ to a curious seeker is *"Come and see ..."* (John 1:39) He is never demanding or forceful. The decision is yours to investigate the claims of Christ. When you do, you will discover that God always takes the initiative first.

Luke 19:10 *"For the Son of man (Jesus) came to seek and save those who were lost."*

If God had not come to where we are first, we would never be able to go to where He is. Love reached out. Love reached down. How thankful we should be today for a love that looked beyond our faults and saw our need. Have you ever experienced a love like that? God's love is unconditional. There is nothing you could do to earn His love any more than there is anything you could do to cause Him to love you any less. What a relief!

When Jesus invites us to come to Him, His love is reaching out to embrace us with grace and acceptance. I wonder if you have responded to the first invitation of Christ - *"Come and see."* With that offer comes another invitation. *"Follow Me."* (John 1:43). Curious seekers will come and go, but disciples will follow Jesus. Are you a curious seeker? Perhaps your soul has been awakened to a new spiritual reality, the possibility of experiencing a personal relationship with Jesus that is transforming. Take the next step and follow Him. Then comes the third invitation, *"Learn from Me."* (Matthew 11:29)

As you learn from Jesus, you will then hear a final invitation, *"Abide in Me."* (John 15:4). The word *abide* means to remain, to live attached, connected to Christ. As a branch abides in the vine to receive its very life, we are to abide in Him.

So, come, follow, learn and abide. Jesus is waiting for you.

September 9

One Thing

Luke 10:42a *"Only one thing is important."*

Jesus said there was only one thing needful, only one thing is important, but very few of us operate our lives like that's true. We find ourselves preoccupied with many of life's demands. The tyranny of the urgent robs us of the one thing that is most important. What is that one thing that is so important and needful? Mary shows us in this story. It's a common story descriptive of our own experience. Two sisters and a brother, friends of Jesus, offering hospitality to a friend in His ministry as they host Him in their home.

Luke tells us (Luke 10:39) that Mary is *"sitting at Jesus feet and listening to Him teach."* Imagine that moment Mary as was enjoying being with Jesus. She is soaking in His presence with every word He speaks. She listened attentively and was the only one who seemed to gain insight into His death. That's why she would later anoint Him with expensive perfume that Jesus said she did in preparation for His burial in John 12:7.

That kind of spiritual insight comes when we do the one thing that is important, when we sit at our Saviour's feet and listen. The one thing that is important in our lives is the presence of God. It's the one thing that is most needful. We need God more than our daily bread. God designed us that way, and we are dysfunctional without Him.

Have you found yourself, like Mary's sister, Martha, so busy with life's demands that you are running on empty? Maybe you're just too busy. Stop! Don't miss the presence of God in your zeal to serve Him. Hear the loving rebuke Jesus gave to Martha: *"Mary has chosen the better thing …"*

Pause for a moment today. Do the one thing that is important. Then act on the spiritual insight you gain in His presence.

September 10

Loneliness

Psalm 25:16 *"Turn to me and have mercy on me, because I am lonely and hurting."*

Psychologist M. Scott Peck writes, "*Once we truly know that life is difficult - once we truly understand and accept it - then life is no longer difficult.*"

Have you accepted that reality? It does take some of the pressure off from thinking that somehow our life is the exception to the rule. Everyone around us seems to be doing great. What's wrong with me? The truth is, life is difficult. We are in a wilderness. This isn't heaven. We live in a fallen and sinful world. Scripture is replete with stories of great men and women of God who faced unimaginable circumstances and yet became overcomers through their faith and trust in God.

The Bible is the best *Wilderness Survival Guidebook* we can turn to. It teaches us how to thrive in the wilderness. When we think of those giants of faith like David, Moses, Abraham, or Paul it's easy to think they didn't struggle with the same issues in life we struggle with. But they did!

One of the big issues David struggled with that you and I can relate to is loneliness. You've heard the expression: It's lonely at the top! David was a King and yet he felt lonely. His popularity was off the charts, yet he prayed about being lonely.

In Psalm 25, David helps us process our pain in loneliness. If you're in the wilderness of loneliness today, spend some time reading and meditating on how David processed his pain and found comfort and hope for his faith to thrive. It provides a model for praying when you feel lonely.

As you meditate on Psalm 25, ask God to apply this Psalm in your life today.

September 11

Rejoice!

Happiness is a choice. When Paul wrote to the Philippians, he was speaking from personal experience. He said to them, *"Whatever happens my dear brothers and sisters, rejoice in the Lord. I never get tired of telling you these things, and I do it to safeguard your faith."* (Philippians 3:1)

No one was more qualified to say that than Paul. Philippi was the city where he was wrongly accused, severely beaten, and falsely imprisoned. Following that experience, Paul would later endure two years of false imprisonment in Caesarea and two more years of imprisonment in Rome, not to mention when he was stoned and left for dead in Lystra. He was even awaiting his sentence while imprisoned in Rome when he wrote this letter of Philippian Church, unsure if he would ever be released.

Despite such suffering, he writes this letter full of joy! In fact, the concept of rejoicing and joy appears sixteen times in four brief chapters, culminating with a challenge to: *"Rejoice in the Lord always. I will say it again: rejoice!"* (4:4)

It makes you wonder if he was nuts! How is it possible to rejoice no matter what happens? Paul was living proof that, when your aim is knowing Christ, your heart could be filled with inexpressible joy even in the worst of circumstances. Happiness depends on what happens and it's short-lived and hollow. When you experience sorrow and suffering, you need more than laughter to lift your spirit. You need joy! The Bible says, *"The joy of the Lord is your strength!"* (Nehemiah 8:10)

Our strength and happiness come from the joy of knowing Jesus and His presence empowering us. Knowing Christ is the one thing that changes everything! It may not change the circumstance, but it changes you in the midst of any and all circumstances which come your way!

September 12

Ready to Give up?

Psalm 142:3 *"When I am ready to give up, He knows what I should do ..."*

Have you had those days you just felt like giving up? You're not alone. Even pastors feel the same – usually on Monday mornings. In the Psalms, David records one of those *"just for today, Lord"* prayers in Psalm 142. Feeling overwhelmed and desperate, he was on the run from King Saul as a fugitive, falsely accused and condemned. Hiding in a cave to survive, he was ready to give up.

Have you been in that cave? I am sure you have.

Godly men and women throughout the Bible fell victim to such feelings. Like David, the great prophet, Elijah, also felt that way, and he too went on the run and hid in a cave to try and figure out what to do next. It was there in the solitude of the cave that God spoke to David as he cried out in despair.

When you feel that way, Psalms 142 offers wise counsel that will pull you out of the wilderness of despair and put your feet back on solid ground.

Psalm 142:1-2 *"I call to the LORD for help; I plead with Him. I bring Him all my complaints; I tell Him all my troubles."*

The difference between David, who was called *"a man after God's own heart,"* and most of us today, is where he took his complaints. David took his complaint to God. What he was enduring was not fair and didn't make sense with the destiny God had given him years before. But He trusted God.

When you feel like giving up, echo the prayer of David in Psalm 142. Instead of giving up, give it over to the God Who cares and can always see you through!

September 13

Serve With Gladness

Do you serve with gladness or have you forgotten the One Whom you are called to serve? The Psalmist reminds us, *"Serve the LORD..."* The quickest way to restore your joy in serving others is to consider that the One you're really serving is God. We best serve God by serving others.

Another way to restore our joy in serving is to love with no strings attached! I'm more apt to serve with gladness when I'm serving the Lord and loving others as Christ loves me - unconditionally! When I love with no strings attached, I can serve with gladness because my service is an act of worship! Jesus said that those who serve would be the greatest:

Matthew 20:25-28 *"Jesus called them together and said, 'You know that the rulers of the Gentiles lord it over them, and their high officials exercise authority over them. Not so with you. Instead, whoever wants to become great among you must be your servant, and whoever wants to be first must be your slave - just as the Son of Man did not come to be served, but to serve, and to give His life as a ransom for many.'"*

Serving with gladness runs contrary to our nature and our culture. We want to *be* served. Yet, as counter intuitive as it seems, real joy comes in serving, not being served. We lose our joy when the word *service* becomes *serve-us!*

Jesus' own life and ministry are a living example to us.

Matthew 20:28 *"... the Son of Man did not come to be served, but to serve, and to give His life as a ransom for many."*

We are most like Jesus when we are serving, and when we recognize that He is the One we are ultimately serving, we can serve others with gladness!

September 14

The Power of Praise

Psalm 146:1 *"Praise the Lord! Let all that I am praise the Lord."*

Are you a person of praise? Take a close look at your attitude and your conversations of late. Are they filled with praise or complaints? Are they positive in nature or more negative and fault-finding? Because we are all part of a fallen world, it's human nature to complain.

Even as disciples of Jesus, we can be pulled back into that vortex of negativity. It was what kept the people of Israel in the wilderness wandering around for forty years rather than enjoying the fruit of the promised land!

I want to challenge you to eliminate negativity in your life. It simply blocks God's blessings when you grumble, gripe and complain. The choice is before us every day: we can praise or complain. Those who praise live by faith. Complainers live by fear. Praise doesn't deny the problems you have nor the pain you feel. Praise simply lifts them up to God with the absolute confidence that He is greater than any problem and can heal any hurt with His love and power.

Will you choose to be a person of praise? It will take practice. Every time you are tempted to complain, gripe, and grumble, turn your problems into praise! Praise your problems back to God. *The problem with problems is never the problem. The problem with problems is our response to the problems!*

All our problems are temporary! When I worry about them, I'm saying, *"God, I don't think you can handle this one, so I must worry about it."* Sounds silly, doesn't it? Worry is like revving up your engine. It burns a lot of fuel but doesn't get you anywhere. Discover the power of praise in your life and choose today to become a person of praise!

September 15

Finding God in our Pain

2 Corinthians 1:4 *"He (God) comforts us every time we have trouble, so when others have trouble, we can comfort them with the same comfort God gives us."*

Where is God when it hurts? Maybe you're in a season of sorrow and His presence seems far away. Our pain often prevents us from feeling God's nearness, but the truth is, He is closer to us than we are to our own selves.

It only makes sense when we open our hearts to receive the comfort God offers. Sorrow is indiscriminate. Heartbreak and pain will visit every one of us at some time or another. When it does, we face a choice: receive God's comfort or resist it.

Our sorrows will either make us bitter or better. If we run from God, our grief can bury us. But if we run to God, pour out our sorrows before Him, we will experience the sweetness of His presence and a peace that passes understanding.

Psalm 30:5 *"Weeping may endure for a night, but joy comes in the morning."*

Cry out to the Lord. Receive the comfort of the Holy Spirit. His very name means 'Comforter.' In fact, the entire Godhead comforts us, God the Father is called *"… the Father of compassion and the God of all comfort. …"* (2 Corinthians 1:3) Then in verse five, the Bible says, *"… our comfort abounds through Christ, (God the Son)."* And in John 14, Jesus told His disciples, *"I will ask the Father and He will give you another Comforter, and He will never leave you. He is the Holy Spirit. …"* (John 14:16-17).

God the Father, God the Son and God the Holy Spirit all play a vital role in comforting us in all our troubles and thereby enable us to comfort others.

September 16

Waiting

Psalm 37:4   *"Be still in the presence of the LORD and wait patiently for Him to act."*

Waiting is certainly something I would like to be able to do better. Waiting on God and waiting for God doesn't seem to come easily. We live in a microwave and internet culture that fosters our impatience. You may have even prayed, *"Lord, give me patience, but hurry up."* The truth is, God is never in a hurry, and yet He's never late either.

Abraham waited 25 years from the time God promised him a son until Isaac was born. Moses waited 40 years before God would use him to deliver the children of Israel out of Egypt. David waited over ten years from the time he was anointed by Samuel to be the next King of Israel and then another seven and a half years before his reign included all the tribes of Israel. It's easy to interpret "not yet" as "no" when you are seeking God's guidance.

So, what's the point? Why the waiting period? Most of the time that we are waiting on God, God is really waiting on us. He is waiting for us to grow in our character as He prepares us for our next assignment. When you think about waiting like that, try and discern what God is trying to develop or mature in your character. This gives value to your waiting.

Don't waste your time in the waiting room. Learn to be still in God's presence. Knowing Him is always more important than knowing the answer! God has a plan and a path for you. He uses the waiting periods to prepare you.

If you're waiting on God, be encouraged that God is at work in your life preparing you for His purpose. Help Him complete the process by being still in His presence as you listen for His voice.

September 17

Where are we Heading?

Only 6% of Americans have a biblical worldview, according to research from notable evangelical pollster George Barna released as part of a new endeavour with the Christian advocacy organization Family Research Council (FRC).

The data found, among other things, that while 51% of American adults say they have a biblical worldview, only 6% of them actually hold this worldview.

Of the 51% who claimed they had a Biblical worldview, 49% said they believed in reincarnation! Meanwhile, only 33% said they believed that *'human beings are born with a sinful nature and can only be saved from the consequences of sin by Jesus Christ.'* Data for the research came from a national survey featuring a representative sample of 1,000 adults.

Christians have a duty to stand against the prevailing cultural tides and proclaim God's truth to a dark and wandering world. But before you stand, you need solid ground and it seems the ground beneath us is anything but sold.

The data comes as similar results have been found by other surveys in recent years. The Cultural Research Centre survey in January 2020 showed that 2% of Millennials hold a biblical worldview even though 61% identify as Christian.

In 2017, a survey from the American Culture and Faith Institute found that only 10% of Americans hold a biblical worldview even though 46% claimed to lead a Christian life.

Given Australia's tendency to follow America in almost every area of life, we need to be concerned about where are we headed and what can we expect our society to look like when its foundation has been completely eroded.

September 18

Lessons from Kindergarten

Robert Faughum once wrote an article called, *'All I Ever Needed to Know I Learned In Kindergarten'* in which he said the following:

"These are the things I learned: Share everything. Play fair. Don't hit people. Put things back where you found them. Clean up your own mess. Don't take things that aren't yours. Say you're sorry when you hurt somebody. Wash your hands before you eat. Flush! Warm biscuits and cold milk are good for you. Live a balanced life. Learn to think, draw, paint, sing and dance. Play and work a little every day. When you go out into the world, watch for traffic, hold hands and stick together."

I really can't remember much about kindergarten but most of the above seems to ring a bell in my memory. How about you? Yet somehow life seems to get increasingly complicated the further we travel along its path. If only it could be as simple as it was in kindergarten.

It seems we have this innate ability to take the simple things of life and turn them into something that we adults call *"sophisticated"* when, in fact, it may be nothing more than unnecessarily complicated.

There's a world of difference between 'childish' and 'childlike.' To be childish suggests to me a level of immaturity unbecoming for an adult. But to be childlike suggests a simplicity and faith that remains alive and fresh despite life's rat race and distorted values.

Jesus once talked about adults not being able to experience the wonder of the Kingdom of God unless they became like little children. That is not a call for immaturity, it is just the acknowledgment that, sophisticated or not, childlike faith, trust and dependence is still the only way to come to God and live each day in His presence.

September 19

The Pit of Betrayal

Betrayal in any context is painful. Betrayal in the Church is more painful because we assume that a certain level of trust, loyalty, transparency and honesty exists among the disciples of Christ. Every pastor or Church leader I have known over my forty plus years in ministry has experienced betrayal in one form or another. Yet despite its prevalence, it still seems to catch us by surprise. When you are passionately consumed in the work of loving the Bride of Christ, you just aren't expecting to be blindsided by betrayal. When that betrayal comes from a trusted colleague, a close friend or perhaps a person you looked up to and regarded as a mentor, it can break your heart and often it can plunge you into a deep pit of disappointment, pain and bewilderment.

That pit has been my home a number of times throughout my ministry and I can attest first-hand that it is a cold, dark and incredibly lonely place. Even those closest to you cannot reach you at the bottom of this pit. The only voices you hear come from God or from the demons who are celebrating your demise. Unfortunately, hearing God's voice through the pain of betrayal can be very difficult and yet God doesn't seem too concerned that you are broken, disheartened, bewildered or in pain. He can actually work with that.

What God will not allow you to be is surprised. If you try and step back from your personal situation and look at the big picture, you might be strangely comforted by the facts. Betrayal is on every page of our human story and yet God has always been there to transform our pain into growth and wisdom.

When you find yourself in the pit of betrayal, you are actually at a crossroad. You can choose the road marked bitterness or the road marked brokenness. God can only work with your brokenness. Choose bitterness and you will remain in the pit.

September 20

Called to Die

John 12:24-26 *"I tell you the truth, unless a kernel of wheat falls to the ground and dies, it remains only a single seed. But if it dies, it produces many seeds. The man who loves his life will lose it, while the man who hates his life in this world will keep it for eternal life. Whoever serves me must follow me; and where I am, my servant also will be. My Father will honour the one who serves me."*

Late at night a jeep drove into the clearing. Four men with machine guns jumped out. Inside they handcuffed the schoolteacher and pastor of the local church. He and a friend were forced into the jeep.

They were driven along a rugged road until they reached a bridge. There they pushed the pastor out of the jeep. Knowing what was going to happen he asked permission to write a few words in his diary.

He noted the time, the date, and the events, which were now transpiring. He simply wrote: *'We are going to heaven tonight.'*

Then he was told to walk to the middle of the bridge. As Pastor Yona walked along, he sang the following song loudly and joyfully:

> *There is a happy land where saints in glory stand.*
> *There's a land that is fairer than day,*
> *And by faith we can see it afar:*
> *For the Father waits over the way,*
> *To prepare us a dwelling place there.*

His song of praise ended abruptly with an ear-piercing burst of machine gun fire. His now lifeless body tumbled off the bridge into the river below as yet another postscript was written to the Book of Acts.

September 21

Kingdom Living

Our central job is not to solve the world's problems. Our job is to draw our entire life from Christ and manifest that life in the world around us. Nothing could be simpler. Nothing could be more challenging. Perhaps this partly explains why we have allowed ourselves to be taken captive by the world.

It's hard to communicate to a prostitute her unsurpassing worth by taking up a cross for her, serving her for years, gradually seeing her change on the inside, and slowing winning the trust to speak into her life (and letting her speak into our life, for we too are sinners).

Indeed, this sort of Calvary requires one to die to self. It is much easier, and more gratifying, to assume a morally superior stance and feel good about speaking against 'the sin of prostitution.'

Perhaps this explains why many Christians spend more time fighting against certain sinners in the political arena than they do sacrificing for sinners. But Jesus calls us and empowers us to follow His example by taking the more difficult, less obvious, much slower and more painful road - the Calvary road. It is the road of self-sacrificial love.

When we return to the simplicity and difficulty of kingdom living, the question that defines us is, "How do we reflect the extravagant love of God in Christ? When love is placed above all kingdom-of-the-world concerns (Col. 3:14; 1 Peter 4:8), the kingdom-of-the-world options placed before us will rapidly dwindle in significance.

Kingdom living always requires that we bleed for others, and for just this reason, kingdom living accomplishes something kingdom-of-the-world activities will never accomplish. It may not adjust people's behaviour at first, but in time it will transform people's hearts and therefore transform society.

September 22

Barriers and Bridges

John 5:6 *"When Jesus saw him lying there and learned that he had been in this condition for a long time, He asked him, 'Do you want to get well?'"*

Have you ever felt stuck, praying for a barrier to be removed but seeing no change? It can be frustrating, but what if that barrier is actually a pathway to your greatest blessing?

Sometimes, it may seem like God isn't listening or doesn't care, but the truth is that there is always a bridge between the new beginnings God wants for us and the blessings He has in store.

A powerful example of this can be found in the story of Jesus healing a lame man in John chapter five. In this chapter, Jesus poses a seemingly insensitive question to the man who had been an invalid for 38 years: *"Do you want to get well?"*

At first glance, it may appear unkind, but if we dig deeper, we can uncover the wisdom behind this question.

Take a moment to reflect on the barriers in your own life that prevent you from moving forward. What excuses do you lean on? What is it that you truly desire God to do in your life?

As we revisit this story in John 5, we discover the reasons for the man's condition and as we shift our perspective, we begin to see what empowered Jesus to perform the miracle.

When the light of God shines into our lives, it illuminates our barriers and reveals them as bridges to blessings. Once the lame man recognized who Jesus was, he no longer needed to rely on others for help. His disability became an opportunity for him to experience the transformative power of God.

September 23

Transformed

We are transformed as we gaze upon the beauty and glory of God. Paul put it this way:

2 Corinthians 3:18 *"And we all, who with unveiled faces contemplate the Lord's glory, are being transformed into his image with ever-increasing glory, which comes from the Lord, who is the Spirit."*

This occurs as we cease striving and rest in the unconditional love of Christ and as a result, our soul begins to be nourished and restored. It is only then that we can experience a worth that embraces God's acceptance of us just as we are, that genuine growth from the inside out can really occur.

What our souls need more than anything else is rest. Maybe you are wounded because of your sin; weary because you have been too busy; or hungry because you have been trying to find your source of life in things other than God.

The primary way the hunger of our soul is satisfied is by feasting on the spiritual food it was created to enjoy. The primary way the sickness of the soul is cured is by resting in the health and life of its Creator. We grow healthy as we rest, in the midst of all our brokenness, in the unconditional love and acceptance of Christ.

This requires faith in God's grace. Resting in God does not take work, but it does take faith to trust that your standing before God is not based on works or your effort. If you view your 'doing' as establishing your right to be in His presence, then you will never rest and you'll fall short of His glory.

Only when we can rest and experience God's love for us as we are, can we ever be empowered to genuinely become better than we ever hoped we could be!

September 24

Faith is Spiritualised Imagination

Have you seen that quote before by Henry Ward Beecher? 'Faith is spiritualised imagination' When I first read it many years ago, I recall having a negative reaction. I felt I needed to push back for some reason – but I am not sure I knew why. However, I have come to realise that our imagination matters and it's part of us as image-bearers of God. Let's ponder this.

One of the most fundamental problems with contemporary Western Christianity is that we have lost the positive spiritual use of our imagination. So many of us only know Christ intellectually. We know and experience the web of deception imaginatively and vividly, but often this is not how we experience our Christianity.

For many, faith is little more than intellectual assent to certain propositions and a commitment to live a certain way. So, is it surprising that our experienced self-identity continues to reflect more the pattern of this world rather than conformity to Jesus Christ? It is surprising that our old self seems more real than all the incredible things Scripture says about our new self.

If our faith is going to be powerful and transformative, it is going to have to be imaginative and experiential. St. Ignatius, founder of the Jesuits, wrote, *"It is not knowing a lot but grasping things intimately and savouring them that fills and satisfies the soul."* Memories shape us profoundly because we grasp them and savour them not as information. This is the manner in which we need to embrace our faith if it is to satisfy our souls and transform our lives.

This involves the imagination. We always need to be engaged imaginatively in the unconditional love of God; only then can it break our flesh's need to hide and set our soul free!

September 25

Simple Faith

Hebrews 11:1 *"Now faith is confidence in what we hope for and assurance about what we do not see."*

It is all about simple ... not getting duped by the complex theories, herculean hypotheses and advanced equations of genius conjectures.

It is all about simple ... not joining the madness of consumerism and collectivism.

It is all about simple ... not looking left or right or up or down, trembling, then constructing your own bomb shelter of safety.

It is all about simple ... not getting involved in the wars of deep-seated theology that are bound to leave relational battle-wounds, simply, unrepairable.

It is all about simple ... not counting the pennies of another, while staring at your possibly empty piggy bank.

The simpler our faith, the more abundant our life.

The simpler our reliance, the more wisdom we accrue.

1 Corinthians 1:25 *"For the foolishness of God is wiser than human wisdom, and the weakness of God is stronger than human strength."*

Galatians 5:6 *"The only thing that counts is faith expressing itself through love."*

Simple faith ... which leads to simple love.

It's that simple!

September 26

Conflict

It is that thing that pretty much all of us hate. It's what we would rather run from than run straight into. It's what makes us speak accusations instead of affirmations. It's what drives us bat crazy, feeling like we are chasing a shifting shadow of ever-changing goals and needs. It's what sends us to mindsets of sin rather than pastures of holiness.

Conflict.

It is that thing that we don't know why, we as Christians have to deal with, but, we do. Somehow and sometimes, we just hit it. And as ugly as it is, we often stand, right in the midst of it, wondering how something so yucky and so unsavoury, could exist in one who is trying to pursue God?

How a God-seeker could turn into more of a raging lunatic than a calming saint? How this very growth of mould could threaten to swallow God's very light shining on it? But, yet, if we stop and think, sometimes our heart actually lands at the truth, doesn't it?

God's light is still shining – even when our heart is not.

There is no amount of disgrace, shame and darkness that can remove the ray of light shining on you. Like the rays that follow your tin can of transport, so does God. Like the light that reflect off the tiny pieces of dirt on the side of the road, so does God. Like the moon that shines even in the darkness, so does God. You can't stop the places His light shines.

God's light shines hope into every endless pit of death and decay – it can't help but make things grow. Conflict is painful, ugly, destructive and difficult to navigate. But it's not a match for God's light! Always bring every conflict in the light - and be amazed at how quickly God can give you what you need.

September 27

Undiluted Grace

For a long time, I believed a lie which is threatening the very heartbeat of the Church today. It sneaks in like a slow poison and its symptoms are often loss of joy, endless activity and little time for meaningful relationships. It doesn't announce itself with brazen warning signs or even seem evident in the sanctuary on Sunday morning. But it's there, endangering the gospel message which Christ died to bring to the lost.

It pollutes the hope of our Redeemer and plants the seed of doubt. It says we can never do enough, be enough or work enough. *It is the message of striving.*

It may be presented with splashes of so-called grace along with it, but at the core it is unchanged because grace cannot be watered down. The gospel doesn't say it is by grace plus works that you are saved through faith. No, God doesn't need us, but through His love He chooses to use us.

Romans 11:6 *"And if by grace, then it cannot be based on works; if it were, grace would no longer be grace."*

The message of striving says, *"God's grace saves you, but you must also do this."* It whispers, *"If you were really a Christian and a good church attendee, you would serve on this committee."*

I know the voice because I listened to it a lot many years ago. I went on an endless chase for God, not realizing He was right beside me all along. I strived, I compared, I looked at other's lives and works, measuring mine against theirs because after all, I wanted to please God.

Then the truth set me free. God the Holy Spirit brought me wisdom, peace and discernment, not a slavery of endless striving.

Galatians 5:1 *"It is for freedom that Christ has set us free."*

September 28

More than Enough

Do you remember when you purchased your first home? Probably, no matter the price, you put the bulk of your saved money into the deposit. That's how it worked for us. It was a tiny house and our furniture was the cheapest we could find in the shop. But it was home.

Compared to so many around us it was really not enough. But God has a way of taking our *"not enough"* and exchanging it for *"more than enough."* He always seems to do that when we are looking, seeking and praying after His will, doesn't He?

The word *insufficient* just doesn't reside in Jesus' vocabulary, because He entirely defines the word *sufficient*. If we have Jesus, we have the all-encompassing sufficient answer to every one of life's problems. It can just be very hard to see in the whirlwind of pain. He understands this and, in many cases, gently brings us right into His fold, when we are ready.

I look back at that tiny first home with great affection now. We have owned homes since that are four times the size, and yet that first home was where I learned about the 'more than enough' provision of God. When we look for Jesus, no matter what our situation – we will always find Him.

Jesus is always the access point to greater things. If you have walked through Jesus' door of salvation, you are saved. Not just saved for eternity's joys but saved to enjoy Christ's present ones today. Are you seeking them? If you have walked through Jesus' door, you are gaining access to your calling and mission. Are you using your gifts, talents and finances for his glory?

When we look for Him, we realize we have – and always have had – more than enough!

September 29

We Need Revival

Even with truth living in and around me, somehow the lie came along too. I believed in Jesus quite young. No major questions, just a big *Yes, I believe*. I don't ever remember saying yes to the lie, but it followed me anyway. It's the oldest lie on the books, the same lie that poisoned the garden of Eden. It wears the mask of something more, something better. But it spoils, after it weasels in and takes root in our hearts.

God's love is not enough. You need more.

That's the lie! Did you know that we can hold the truth in one hand, whilst reaching for something 'better' with the other hand? We live in such a broken place, but we still build our towers to the skies. We fill ourselves up, at least we try. Even when we are given the truth, we can still be living under the influence of the lies.

We need to remember, every day of our lives - **God loves us.** God loves us so much that He made a way to rescue us. While we were still sinners, Christ died for us. He who came not to condemn the world, but to save it, is our Saviour!

Not only that, but also - **Jesus is enough.** He didn't only die; He was raised to life for us. He is life, and He wants to create new life in us. So why do we still look for life in other places?

The root of all our sin is that we desire created things more than we desire the Creator. We are idolaters, of the hidden kind. We need to remember Who God is, and we need to remember who we are. And then, the only way for us, is to repent and embrace all that God has for us again.

We really need revival. We need the life of Jesus poured into us - right now, right here, wherever we are. We need revival in the Church, in the whole world, but first and foremost, we must have revival in our own hearts!

September 30

Running the Race

God doesn't answer based on what we *want*, He answers based on what we *need*. We may think we need peace and He says no, you need trials. We may think blessings – He says endurance. We may think money – He says contentment. We may think appreciation – He says love.

There will be many times in your life and mine when we hit a wall or face a difficult circumstance and we are crying out for encouragement and support. At those times in my life, I have often been led to the same verse:

Hebrews 12:1 *"Therefore, since we are surrounded by such a huge crowd of witnesses to the life of faith, let us strip off every weight that slows us down, especially the sin that so easily trips us up. And let us run with endurance the race God has set before us."*

Running a good race is always our goal but this verse reminds us that as disciples of Jesus Christ, the only race we should be running is the race *"God has set before us."*

It is easy to want joy, peace, contentment and blessings. It is easy to want encouragement and motivation, but God is operating from the throne of all knowledge, all power and all sovereignty. From His unique vantage point, God sees yesterday, today and tomorrow. He knows precisely what you need to finish your race. He also knows precisely what will hold you back from finishing your race well.

God wants you to be a champion. He wants you to run with speed and power and strength. He wants you to finish strong and joyful.

What baggage holds you back? What do you need to confess? What trials might God be using to train you, shape you and transform you into the image of His Son, our Saviour, Jesus Christ?

October 1

Real Faith

We all face them – tough times. Some more than others. It's only a matter of time before life falls apart. The loss of a job; a diagnosis of cancer; an unfaithful spouse; abuse from a leader; the betrayal of a friend. It doesn't matter how comfortable our lives are at the moment, if we haven't already, we will all come face-to-face with the tragic. Suffering is the common human experience; our ability to relate to each other's grief and sorrow binds us together.

Too often, faith and suffering are linked in a cause-and-effect relationship. In some circles, suffering is seen as the effect caused by a lack of faith; or faith is the cause that gets us out of suffering; or faith re-orients our perspective towards suffering. In all those cases, the implicit message is the same: Faith is necessary to make it through the moments when life falls apart. But how do you know if you have enough faith to make it through the arduous journey unfolding before you?

The truth is, you cannot know how wide and deep your faith runs until life falls apart. We have every reason to place faith in a good and loving God when life is blessed. We have every reason to trust God's goodness when our marriage is strong, our bank accounts full, our health is great, and our kids flourish. Yet our faith is left untested during these times.

It's easy to believe God is in control when life is full of joy. It's when the wheels of life fall off that we begin asking the questions. At that point, the only place to go is to God.

Taking our complaint to God doesn't show a lack of faith. Instead, it shows a deep trust that God will keep His promise. Without this trust, there would be no reason to come to God at all. Real faith comes from an honest admission that we can't do this alone – we need God – and God is always there for us.

October 2

Selfishness

One of the greatest threats to a healthy Church is selfishness. In fact, I would go so far as to say that selfishness is perhaps the greatest threat to society at large and the root cause of the vast majority of problems in the world today. We live in a world where our own selfish desires, wants and perceived needs are nurtured, encouraged and allowed to dominate most of our choices each day.

This produces a very sick and sad world ... but it filters back into the Church and destroys the very fabric of the Body of Christ on earth. Selfishness is the No.1 enemy to the fulfilment of God's purposes on earth. Selfishness is the root cause of 99% of tensions, disputes and divisions within the Church.

The need to identify, confess and eradicate selfishness in our attitudes and actions should be our highest priority ... not only if we want to grow a healthy Church ... but if we want to grow a healthy society also.

Matthew 16:24-25 *"If any man would come after me, let him deny himself, and take up his cross, and follow me. For whoever would save his life shall lose it: and whoever shall lose his life for my sake shall find it."*

These are the words of Jesus, words in which He points out that we must renounce self in order to be His devoted disciple. Notice the expression, *"If any man would come after me, let him deny himself."* The denial of self is one of our most difficult problems and it has been with us from birth. Christ not only taught against selfishness, He gave a perfect cure for it. That cure is love. The centre of Christ's teachings is love.

True love and selfishness cannot co-exist in a person. One will always destroy the other. Each day we must choose whether love or selfishness define our lives.

October 3

All You Need is Love

I truly believe that our primary purpose, when boiled right down, is to receive and to give love and that's why everyone can be a huge success in life regardless of age, race, gender, intellect, physical ability or status.

We are all given the opportunity to receive love and to extend love to others and from my experience over the years, I can promise you that if you sincerely connect with this truth then God can and will re-vitalise, re-new, revive, restore and re-focus your life and bring clarity and power to your ministry in the Kingdom of God.

In fact, I will go even further out on the limb here and say that a fuller Biblical understanding of love is one of the greatest needs in the Church of Jesus Christ. The Church is in crisis across our nation and throughout the world. Hundreds of congregations are closing every week. Countless hours have been poured into Church growth conferences, books, courses, training programs, evangelism initiatives and strategies to 'fix' the Church.

There has been a nauseating number of committees, task forces and councils convened to discuss the problem and the result is always the same: so much precious oxygen and time are consumed as we knock down another thousand trees to produce the paper on which our strategic plans and vision statements are printed and then filed in a drawer somewhere and forgotten!

Love truly does make the world go 'round and a fuller understanding of the priority and place of love is certainly what is needed for the Church to grow and touch our nation for Christ. It is confronting in its simplicity but revolutionary in its effect when finally grasp this thing called love!

October 4

Beyond Cultural Relevance

I don't really care if the Church is culturally relevant. Of course, I don't want us to wallow in some old-time, glory days that probably never existed. But cultural relevance is not the answer. It's better to be relevant than stale but being relevant isn't enough. Trying to be culturally relevant is turning the Church into followers instead of leaders.

A relevant Church may be following slightly ahead of others, but we're still following. Too often that makes our Churches look too much the same in ways we ought to be different – from each other and from the culture around us.

Chasing cultural relevance can give us a false sense of success because it can be learned by reading the right books and watching a couple of the latest TV shows. But thinking I can reach the youth of my community because I read a book on postmodernism and wear the latest clothes, is a delusion. So, if not cultural relevance, then what?

We need to stop worrying about being culturally relevant and start being contextually real. Contextually real - that's our goal! Ministry is not about relevance, it's about reality. It's not about the culture, it's about our context. It's about living my real life in the context of other people's real lives.

Jesus was real and He adapted to the reality of whatever context He found Himself in. One city at a time, one crowd at a time, one person at a time. And He did it without ever betraying His core reality or mission.

Dealing with people rather than trends takes a little longer. But it's well worth it and it's the only way we can really earn people's trust so that they'll allow us to share the deeper reality that's only found in Jesus. A reality that fits any context and any culture at any time!

October 5

Stupid Prayers

Why doesn't God answer all my prayers? The short answer is because some of them are stupid! God doesn't do stupid things, regardless of how many times we say please; no matter how much faith we have; no matter how hard we pray.

God does strange things; hard-to-understand things; even things that can seem totally messed up and cruel from our limited vantage point. But God never does stupid things.

I've come to believe that the main reason for my unanswered prayers is that I keep praying stupid prayers, asking God to do stupid things. I can hear some objections already. *"There are no stupid prayers!"* But there are. I know. I've prayed them!

Jesus introduced the Lord's Prayer by telling the disciples not to pray stupid prayers. In fact, Jesus introduced the Lord's Prayer by telling the disciples not to pray the stupid prayers of the hypocrites and pagans. (Matthew 5:6-7)

People regularly ask God for stupid things:

"Help me lose weight while I eat whatever I want"
"Bless me now, even though I've been ignoring you for years"
"Help me pass the test I didn't study for"

Then we get mad when God says no to our stupid prayers. Sincere, but stupid. Prayer may be the most overlooked aspect of Christian life and pastoral ministry. Even though we know it's the most important. We need to become better at prayer - but how? Try starting with prayers guaranteed to get a 'yes.'

- ➢ *That God's kingdom would take greater hold in my heart*
- ➢ *That God's will would be done in me, like it is in heaven*
- ➢ *That God would supply my needs (not my wants) for today*

October 6

Following Jesus is the Goal

What if the members of our Churches started sharing their faith, but it wasn't in a way that brought more people to our congregation? Would we celebrate and encourage that? If not, then perhaps we are not as committed to kingdom growth as we think we are.

As people use social media more, aspects of our lives are happening without regard to geography. From crying with a friend going through a divorce, to celebrating the joy of childbirth, many of our most intimate moments are being lived through online platforms.

More people who share their faith are doing it online, too. Which means that the friends and family they're sharing it with are less likely to be together in the one place.

This has great potential for our Church's participation in kingdom growth, even if it doesn't always result in the numerical growth in our local congregation. In the western Church, we have become so skilled at tethering evangelism to our Church's program and attendance that we can forget they are not the same thing.

What if a Church was teaching and practicing evangelism in such a way that people shared their faith in Jesus at work, in their neighbourhoods, with their families and online, not necessarily as part of a Church program, but as a natural outflow of their faith?

We must always remember that, while Church attendance is a vital element in our spiritual growth, Church attendance isn't the goal of evangelism. Following Jesus is the goal – even if it means they attend a different Church than ours. Making disciples always comes first.

October 7

Calling all Boomers!

What's wrong with today's younger generations? I hear that question often - especially from my fellow Baby Boomers. The quick answer? Nothing! Nothing is wrong with the current and upcoming generations that hasn't been wrong with every previous generation - with one possible exception. They don't have the elders and mentors that almost every previous generation before them has enjoyed.

And why is that? Because (I hate to say it) my generation of Boomers is not discipling the next generation as well as the previous generations did for us. Calling all Boomers - it's time to become elders! If you, like me, are a Christian and a Boomer (born between 1946 and 1964) you need to know that our primary mission at this stage of our lives is to become the elders and mentors that every generation needs. Instead, too many of us stand back and complain that Millennials are entitled, they're lazy, they're loud, they're disrespectful etc.

But that is no truer of this generation than of our generation. In fact, I'm convinced that the biggest 'sin' millennials have committed in the eyes of many of my Boomer colleagues is not wanting to do Church exactly the way we did it. But no generation should do Church exactly the way anyone else did, because they're not like anyone else. Each generation needs to honour and worship God, follow Jesus, disciple believers, reach their community and teach the unchangeable truths of God's Word in the way God leads - not in the way their parents or grandparents are comfortable with.

Like every generation that preceded them, today's young believers need the wisdom, kindness and counsel of previous generations to become the mature disciples they want to be. The choice is ours: we can whine about the new generation or we mentor and support them – but we can't do both.

October 8

A Prison Without Doors

I recall many years ago a Pastor friend of ours was visiting our Church from interstate and I happened to be preaching on grace that day. At the end of the service, he came to me and shared a vision he believed God gave him during the service. The picture he described was as simple as it was confronting. He saw a group of people in a prison cell and it looked like they had been there for some time and were very familiar with their surroundings. They were not stressed or trying to get out or protesting their lot in life. They actually seemed resigned to their fate. But when he looked closer into this vision, he could not believe what he saw. This prison had no doors! They had been ripped off and there was this gaping hole where they used to be. Everyone was therefore free to leave this prison and yet they were so used to life behind bars, they either didn't notice there were no longer any doors or they did notice but were too afraid to step into the unknown and embrace their freedom.

I have never forgotten that vision and over the following decade in that Congregation I had the incredible privilege of seeing hundreds of people finally venture out of that prison into the freedom which Christ died to give them. That prison is religion. That prison is what the visible Church will always become when God is not given free reign.

From the day the Church was born and thousands of people were set free from the chains of religion and brought into the freedom of a relationship with God through Jesus Christ, the enemy of God, Satan, has been running a relentless campaign to drag God's people back under the bondage of the law. He has blinded so many believers to the spiritual reality that lies beneath much of the religious activity that can consume our time, energy and focus. Many of us need to be set free again so we can respond to God's amazing grace.

October 9

Grace IS the Gospel

Grace is not a part of the Gospel story – grace is the gospel. The gospel is grace! Grace is to the Christian faith what air is to the earth's atmosphere. If Christianity was a motor vehicle, grace would be the motor! If we do not have a firm grasp on grace; if grace has not had its effect within us, then all we have is a facade, a shell, a Christian faith with no power, no motivation and no real ability to fulfil our purpose. A car without a motor is, at best, an attractive display. It can never achieve what its designer and creator desired and intended.

So too with our journey in Christ. Unless we have a firm understanding of God's amazing grace; unless His grace permeates all that we think, say and do every day – then our Christian lives will lack substance, vitality, truth and power. Each of us must get to the point of saying with Paul:

1 Corinthians 15:10 *"… by the grace of God I am what I am, and his grace to me was not without effect. No, I worked harder than all of them – yet not I, but the grace of God that was with me."*

You may think you already know all about grace. Prior to my awakening to God's amazing grace, I used to think that too. That is also what our brothers and sisters in Galatia thought. We read in Galatians 3 what happened to them when they lost sight of grace! That's why Paul preached about grace over and over and over again. He actually said it was "a safeguard" for his hearers.

I want to understand God's grace in all its truth and I want to lead others to do the same. It's the power of God unto salvation. Grace is the power that releases fruit-bearing energy in Christians and in Churches.

Grace IS the Gospel.

October 10

The Spirit of Legalism

The term 'legalism' is thrown around a lot in the Church today but I am not sure most people really know what it means. A simple definition of legalism is: *Trying to attain or maintain rightness with God (righteousness) through human effort.*

Most Christians I know will say 'amen' to us not being able to attain righteousness through even our best efforts. However, it is the second term 'maintain' which trips up so many of us and it's in this area that the spirit of legalism gains such a powerful foothold in individuals and then entire churches.

Beginning in grace and then moving on in the power of the flesh is exactly what the Galatian believers were guilty of and the entire letter to the Galatians was written to expose and counter this evil in this midst of God's people. Paul had seen these people set free by the power of God's amazing grace. They had 'attained' their salvation through grace alone. But now, so soon after being set free by God's empowering presence, they had moved on to 'please' and 'serve' God in their own strength and by adhering once again to rules, laws and requirements – forgetting that every single requirement of God was already met by Christ and given to us as a free gift! Not only is our salvation a gift of God's grace – the victorious Christian life is also a gift of God's grace.

Outside of Christ, we cannot please God or bless God or do anything right before God. In Christ, we are already pleasing to God because of the finished work of Christ. When we truly get that – then, and only then, will grace have its effect in us and like Paul, we will gladly work our butts off for God – not to please Him or obey Him or because we are required to – but because we have no choice - it will be the empowering presence of God within us (grace) which compels us to serve and minister – joyfully and without obligation!

October 11

Repentance

Romans 2:4b *"… the kindness of God leads you to repentance."*

Does that Bible reference ring any bells? I would suggest that for most Christians the answer would be no. Unlike John 3:16 or Romans 8:28 or John 1:1 … this obscure verse in Romans 2 is not quoted much at all. Is that because it is not important? Or is it because it grates against too much of the preaching we have all heard so often?

Growing up in the Church I can't say I ever remember God's kindness being talked about in a sermon where repentance was the central thrust. God's wrath, God's judgement, God's holiness all featured prominently – but God's kindness did not seem to fit with the message of repentance I was hearing. Sadly, I believe that is still the case in parts of the Church.

I remember when the truth of this verse impacted me for the first time. It was over thirty years ago but I remember it like it was yesterday. It was like God turned on a light and the full message of the Gospel of God's amazing grace was finally seen, heard, felt and lived! It was an amazing time and God gave me many songs that year and one of them encapsulates the truth of what Paul wrote to the Romans all those years ago. Here are just some of the words:

Your kindness led me to repentance; Your grace has captured my heart; Your overwhelming forgiveness has given my life a new start.

My freedom's secured with the life of Your Son; my ransom is paid and my victory won; my pardon is signed with the blood of the Lamb; so now in Your grace I can stand.

I cannot repay You for what You have done; my rebellion and sin are exchanged for Your Son; I can't understand the reason why You loved me enough to die, but you loved me enough to die!

October 12

Heaven on Earth

Jesus came to release heaven on earth and He has called us to join Him in that mission. That is why in the model prayer He gave us (Matthew 6:10) Jesus told us to pray and declare, *"Your Kingdom come, Your will be done on earth as it is in heaven."*

This is our assignment on earth – and all of heaven is backing this prayer and waiting for its fulfilment. So, we should be compelled to pray and declare, *"Your Kingdom come…"* and then help make that happen. This should not be an optional task if we are a true disciple of Christ wanting to embrace the mission of Christ. This assignment is at the absolute centre of who we are in Christ. It's at the absolute centre of why God has left us on this planet – because God has wonderful plans for this place.

Tragically however, too much of the Church's theology and focus in my lifetime has been wrapped up in the dysfunction of this world and its ultimate end. Many Christians actually get this strange, perverted sense of encouragement when disaster happens. There is a weird sense of affirmation that comes on some people in a crisis or when a tragic event occurs because they believe 'the end is near.' The end of what? Are we disciples of Christ or not? There is no end to His Kingdom and our purpose is to advance His Kingdom!

Everything we do every day of our lives either contributes to that outcome or it takes us and others away from that goal. Our assignment is to release the reality of God's perfect kingdom of light and life and liberty into the brokenness, dysfunction and darkness of this kingdom. Every moment of every day we walk this earth, that is our assignment.

Our DESTINY is to dwell in heaven alone forever.

Our ASSIGNMENT is to bring heaven to earth first.

October 13

Not Ashamed!

The entire foundation of our Christian life and the foundation of the Church – is GRACE. Literally speaking, grace means a free gift. The name of that free gift is Jesus Christ. Jesus lived His life perfectly for us as one of us, completely obeying the law of God and now His performance is credited to us.

God's free gift to us is not only the life, but also the death of Jesus Christ. Our sins are punishable by death and that punishment was endured by Jesus when He died on the cross. That is also a gift given to us – His death is also credited to us. It's as if we suffered the punishment for our sins. Jesus' resurrection is also a gift to us. In Him we have risen above the power and penalty of sin. In Christ we have conquered death. Then after His resurrection, the Lord Jesus poured out His Holy Spirit Who made all this real to us.

The free gift of God's grace is that Jesus lived a life pleasing to God and He now empowers us to live a life pleasing to God after Him, or more accurately, in Him. Another way of saying it, is that Jesus lived His life for us, and now He lives His life through us by the power of His Spirit – and all of this is free. The great Baptist Preacher Charles Spurgeon put it best: *'You stand before God as if you were Christ, because Christ stood before God as if He were you.'*

Romans 1:16-17 *"I am not ashamed of the Gospel, because it* is the power of *God for the salvation of everyone who believes: first for the Jew, then for the Gentile. For in the Gospel a righteousness from God is revealed, a righteousness that is by faith from first to last, just as it is written: The righteous will live by faith."*

Religion says the righteous will live by keeping the law. Paul says very clearly the righteous are not only saved by grace, through faith, but that is also how they must live each day.

October 14

Knowing God

How do we know God? How do we comprehend Him? How do we relate to God? How are all those wonderful stories about God in the Bible converted today into His life-changing supernatural presence in our life? How do we experience divine things? How do we know Jesus is alive and real today? How do we know we have eternal life? I believe the Lord would have us face those questions honestly today.

The things of God can never be known by our physical senses, they are revealed by His Holy Spirit. We can never know God fully with our minds – never! The Bible does talk about our mind being renewed and our mind has a vitally important role to play in living the Christian life. However, our mind is not all that needs to be engaged if we are to have an intimate relationship with God.

It's not that difficult to understand why this may be the case. Our spirit is the agency by which we embrace spiritual things – and the human spirit has died – it is dead because of sin and must be made alive before we can even begin to comprehend spiritual things. Therefore, when I say that we are not able to apprehend God through our intellect, I'm not saying anything new or profound. It just makes sense.

When musical instruments are played, we don't hear them with our eyes, do we? When there is a beautiful sunset – we don't enjoy it with our ears. God gave us ears to hear and eyes to see, and it would be ridiculous to confuse the two. It's just as ridiculous to try and relate to and experience a spiritual, infinite God with our fallen, finite minds.

If we don't experience God as a person – we really don't experience Him at all – and only the Holy Spirit can reveal the person of God to our spirit. Only then will be truly know God.

October 15

The Pit

A man fell into a pit and couldn't get himself out.

A subjective person came along and said, *"I feel for you down there."*

An objective person walked by and said, *"It's logical that someone would fall down there."*

A Pharisee said, *"Only bad people fall into pits."*

A mathematician calculated how he fell into the pit.

A news reporter wanted the exclusive story on the pit.

A tax office man asked if he was paying taxes on the pit.

A self-pitying person said, *"You haven't seen anything until you've seen my pit."*

A fire-and-brimstone preacher said, *"You deserve your pit."*

A Christian Scientist observed, *"The pit is just in your mind."*

A psychologist noted, *"Your mother and father are to blame for your being in that pit."*

A self-esteem therapist said, *"Believe in yourself and you can get out of that pit."*

An optimist said, *"Things could be worse."*

A pessimist said, *"Things will get worse."*

Jesus, seeing the man, immediately took him by the hand and lifted him out of the pit.

October 16

How Devoted are we?

Acts 2:42 *"And they devoted themselves to the Apostles' teaching."*

What was the teaching of the Apostles to which the early Church disciples devoted themselves? Perhaps the best definition given to us is found in the opening verses of I John.

1 John 1:1-4 *"That which was from the beginning, which we have heard, which we have seen with our eyes, which we looked upon and have touched with our hands, concerning the word of life-the life was made manifest, and we have seen it, and testify to it and proclaim to you the eternal life, which was with the Father and was made manifest to us-that which we have seen and heard we proclaim also to you, so that you too may have fellowship with us; and indeed our fellowship is with the Father and with His Son Jesus Christ. And we are writing these things so that your joy may be complete!"*

Does it get any more beautiful than that? Just picture John, along with Peter and the other Apostles, saying this to the newly baptized Church in Jerusalem the morning following Pentecost?

What an introduction to their new journey! What an awe-inspiring vision and insight into the meaning, the way, and the goal of the Christian life! This Christ Who existed from the beginning, Whose fellowship we experience in practical, tangible ways; this Christ Who is eternal life, Who was with the Father and was made manifest to us, this Christ we proclaim to you!

We proclaim Him so that you too may have fellowship with us, for our fellowship is with the Father and the Son! Enter into this fellowship of the Godhead and your joy, like ours, will also be complete!

This is the good news! This is the gospel. How devoted are you to this life-changing truth?

October 17

Facing Your Red Sea

There are many stories preserved for us in the Old Testament which serve as powerful analogies and examples for our experiences in life today. One of the most incredible narratives for me is when God set the captives free from slavery in Egypt and they began their journey towards the promised land.

It could have been a journey of only 8-10 days. However, it took over 40 years and God's people faced many obstacles and made many mistakes along the way. The first, and perhaps the greatest obstacle, was the Red Sea. With the army of Pharaoh's in hot pursuit, the journey was about to be all over before it really began. There was no way past the raging torrent before them. The barrier was just too great - unless God intervened. We know what happened, don't we? But how easily we forget this story when we face our 'Red Sea.'

We also face many challenges in our journey to our 'promised land' and we are meant to draw strength from the many accounts we have been given of God's people finding a breakthrough and trusting God to clear a path. Sadly, we are more likely to be frozen in fear or immobilised by apathy as we sit on the very edge of all that God has promised and all for which we have lived and hoped and struggled and cried and laboured. Perhaps you are at such a place right now?

Do you have the faith to cross that sea? Do you believe God has led you this far and will get you across that sea of doubt and fear and unrealised expectations? Are you ready to trust Him to bring you into the land He promised you? Or will you turn back like many wanted to at that first Red Sea?

Romans 8:31-32 *"If God is for us, who can be against us? He who did not spare his own Son, but gave him up for us all – how will he not also, along with him, graciously give us all things?"*

October 18

Victorious Christian Prayer

All sincere Christians desire a dynamic and fruitful prayer life. Yet so many find themselves defeated when it comes to their communication with God. If the average follower of Christ was asked how much time he or she spends in prayer, they would most probably be too embarrassed to answer. Yet prayer holds the key to developing intimacy with God and consistency and fruitfulness in our walk with Him.

We desperately want to be victorious in our praying but we must first understand the essentials of what prayer is and what prayer is not. Prayer is not a religious obligation. It is not a formal ritual. It is not seeking God as though He's some kind of celestial Santa Claus.

In its purest form, prayer is intimate communication with our God. It is how people who know God get to know God better. It's a loving and listening relationship with the God Who created, saved us and is transforming us each day.

This understanding of prayer will change our perspective on prayer. Without it, prayer becomes a useless drudgery and a tiresome duty rather than a powerful adventure and victory. The latter is what God desires for each of us.

We could meet the Prime Minister, be in partnership with the richest people in the world and yet none of those experiences would compare to the utter thrill and excitement of coming into the presence of the Lord of all creation.

There is no greater joy than having intimate, meaningful conversations with the One Who is above all, sees all and knows all. Think of it – the God Who hung the earth in space; the God Who put the stars in the sky – this same God desires to commune with us – heart to heart. Wow! Nothing can match that and that is what God desires for us all.

October 19

The Greatest Threat to the Church

I really do love the Church. I have devoted the bulk of my life to helping Jesus build His Church. I love the way the New Testament talks about the Church in terms of us being a family, a community, an inter-dependent group of disciples whose primary focus is on loving God and serving others. I also love the fact that God has made me (and every disciple) accountable for the health of the Church on earth.

Having now been in a Church leadership position of one kind or another for over 45 years, I have come to the conclusion that one of the greatest ideological threats to the Church in the western, developed world is not atheism, communism or even false doctrines promoted by those who want to discard Biblical truth and faith. The much greater threat to the Church is the worldview of consumerism.

In this worldview, self is lord. This worldview sees life in terms of shopping: life should present me with the greatest number of goods and services for the least amount of personal expense. Life is directed by my desire to possess and acquire goods and services based on my personal choice. Life is one big shopping mall. The basic assumption is: *"If I can have everything I want, and avoid that which I don't want, then I will be happy."* This worldview has invaded the Christian mind. It afflicts every denomination from the most conservative to the most liberal. It is the worldview which prompts us to ask, *"What is this Church providing for me and my family?"* rather than asking, *"What can I do to make MY Church better?"*

This form of Christianity is idolatrous and unbiblical. It is an insidious, largely invisible cancer which is attacking the heart of the Church right now across the western world. Is your Christian walk about having your needs met or giving yourself away in service to Jesus Christ? Your answer will reveal if you are part of the solution or part of the problem!

October 20

The Light of the World

Matthew 5:14-16 *"You are the light of the world. A town built on a hill cannot be hidden. Neither do people light a lamp and put it under a bowl. Instead they put it on its stand, and it gives light to everyone in the house. In the same way, let your light shine before others, that they may see your good deeds and glorify your Father in heaven."*

With those words Christ set forth an evangelistic standard for His disciples, and all who would follow their legacy of faith.

The Lord had previously called believers to function as salt in this corrupt and decaying world, preserving it from fully succumbing to the ruin of its sin (Matthew 5:13).

But Christ also called His followers to shine the light of His Word into a world dominated by spiritual blindness.

The purpose of letting our light shine and reveal our good works is not to bring attention or praise to ourselves but to God.

Our intent should be that, in all that we are and in all that we do, others may see God in order that they may *"glorify [our] Father who is in heaven."*

Our good works are meant to magnify God's grace and power. This is the supreme calling of life: glorifying God. Everything we do is to cause others to give praise to the God Who is the source of all that is good.

Put simply, the way we live ought to prompt others to glorify God. He is the source of all light in our lives, and the pattern of our lives ought to always point people back to Him.

October 21

Becoming like Christ

Christians should earnestly desire to grow. If we are not becoming more like Christ every day, we are defying what Scripture plainly teaches about the Christian walk:

Romans 8:29 *"For those whom [God] foreknew, He also predestined to become conformed to the image of His Son."*

Christian growth involves transformation from our old way of life into a new and upward Christlike trajectory of change - increasing strength and effectiveness as servants of Christ. That's exactly what Paul describes here:

Romans 12:2 *"Do not be conformed to this world, but be transformed by the renewing of your mind."*

And yet, as every Christian well knows, the old mind is still there with all its habits of self-preoccupation, cravings for sensation, vain imaginations, and its appetite for what is cheap and gross. The old mind is the culprit that keeps us going back to the spiritual junk food. The old mind is the subtle enemy that keeps us feeding only on milk when we should be digesting solid meat. The old mind is what keeps us from being fully transformed and fully committed to Christ and His mission.

In 1 Peter 1:23-2:3, the great apostle compares God's Word to two things that are vital for life and growth: an imperishable seed and the milk of the Word. As Christ taught in His parable of the Sower, God's Word is like a seed that brings about the new birth. Just as a seed contains the power and energy of life, so too does God's Word.

Our goal is to become fully mature and Christlike through feeding on the spiritual 'meat' God has prepared for us.

October 22

Our Battle with Religion

Religion is our feeble attempt to establish and maintain a relationship with God through every means possible other than that which He ordained, provides and empowers. Christianity is not and never has been a religion. At the heart of the Christian faith there is relationship – our restored relationship with God, secured by the life, death and resurrection of Jesus; our ongoing daily walk with God in Christ, as guided by His Holy Spirit; and our repaired relationships with each other as we are united by the Holy Spirit through our shared belief in Jesus Christ.

> Jesus and Jesus alone is the gospel.
> Jesus and Jesus alone is our justification.
> Jesus and Jesus alone is our salvation.
> Jesus and Jesus alone is the author and finisher of our faith.

Jesus Himself made it crystal clear when He said, *"Very truly I tell you, whoever hears my word and believes him who sent me has eternal life and will not be judged but has crossed over from death to life."* (John 5:24) We fully experience the freedom we have in Christ when we look to Christ alone, not just for our salvation, but for our ongoing walk in the Christian life, depending on Him in all things. Our response is love and gratitude for all He has done for us. God is enough and He wants us to live freely in His love and grace, free from the power and penalty of sin, free from all guilt and shame and free from all religious expectation and rule-keeping.

It is for freedom that Christ has set us free (Galatians 5:1) and He has promised to be with us every step of the way through His guiding Spirit. When we truly decide to give the Church back to God and give the ministry back to all the people, not just the elite few, then maybe we will see what Jesus saw - a Church which will bless, rather than break, the heart of our Heavenly Father.

October 23

God is our Shield

Psalm 3:3 *"But you, Lord, are a shield around me, my glory, the One who lifts my head high."*

'Shield' also has means guard, safeguard, shelter, or screen. God shields us from damage, keeps us out of harm's way, stands up for us when we are accused, provides for us when we are in need, and screens everything that comes our way. Before anything can affect us, it must first pass by God.

The terrifying sensation of a rock hitting our windscreen has happened to many of us. We were shielded from harm by the toughened glass. We are also protected by our houses from the elements, but there is no refuge and no defender like God.

Deuteronomy 33:27 *"The eternal God is your refuge, and beneath are the everlasting arms."*

This verse has been a beautiful consolation to me many times over the years. There may be moments in your life when you feel like a truck load of bricks has been dumped on you. Whilst God is never the author of pain and disaster, He is also never caught unawares. He will meet us in our deepest pain.

Tragically, the trauma of losing a child or grandchild can be a sentence of death for some. Many never recover. But as we lie at the bottom of that dark, agonisingly cold valley, we have a choice to trust God to be our shield – to protect us from dying inside through grief and loss – or we can try and rely on our own depleted resources. The latter will never work. Only God will get us on our feet and lead us out of that valley.

Psalm 84:11 *"For the Lord God is a sun and shield; the Lord bestows favour and honour; no good thing does he withhold from those whose walk is blameless."*

October 24

The Gift of Discernment

Francis Frangipane once wrote these powerful words:

"We will never possess mature, ongoing discernment until we crucify our instincts to judge. Realistically, for most of us, this may take an extended, focused season of uprooting old thought-systems, attitudes that were not planted in faith and love for people. In truth, if we will appropriate the discernment born in the "mind of Christ," we must first find the heart of Christ (1 Corinthians 2:16). The heart and love of Jesus is summed up in His own words: "I did not come to judge the world, but to save the world." (John 12:47). Yet even when the Lord does judge us, it is to save and deliver us."

The ability to see the unseen is what we call discernment. Perceiving the spiritual world is a blessing from the Spirit. Its goal is to reveal the essence of what is concealed. However, there are many who believe they are hearing from the Lord regarding one issue or another. Only God knows if they are in some things. However, a lot of people call it discernment while really they are just judging others.

Jesus told us not to condemn. He sends us into the world as co-redeemers, not as judges of man. We have been sent to save individuals, not to condemn them. The critical carnal mind constantly sees a reflection of itself in others. It thinks it is seeing others while actually seeing itself. Jesus calls those who pass judgement on others while committing the same sin themselves: *hypocrites.*

You will only build a foundation for the gift of discernment if you crucify your inclination to judge and embrace Christ's redemptive heart. Your heart will be ready to accept divine dreams, visions, and revelations. You won't be tarnished by prejudice. Rather you will be filled with Christ's wisdom and Christ's heart. Then the gift of discernment will be yours.

October 25

Jesus: The Bread of Life

We regularly consume bread. Only during certain seasons are some fruits accessible. Only during holidays are certain drinks produced. Bread is always available. The Bible says that Jesus is *the bread of life* and so He ought to be brought to our table every time as we allow Him to feed our souls every day, not just during particular months or on special occasions.

Many requirements are satisfied by bread. So too with Jesus He has food for the famous and the lonely. He has assistance for the physically ill and the emotionally ill. He can aid you if your eyesight is clear or if your eyesight is blurry. Every need can be met by Jesus. Can you see why Jesus called himself the *Bread of Life?*

Jesus grew up as a *"small plant before the Lord"* (Isaiah 53:2). One of thousands in Israel. Indistinguishable from the person down the street. Had you seen Him as a boy, you wouldn't have thought he was the Son of God. He was just a boy – like a staff of wheat in the wheat field.

But He was destroyed, just like wheat. He was pummelled and pounded like chaff. *"He was wounded for the wrong we did; he was crushed for the evil we did."* (Isaiah 53:5). And He made it through the flames like bread. On the cross He passed though the fire of God's wrath, not because of His sin, but because of ours. Jesus experienced each part of the process of making bread: the growing, the pounding, the firing. And just as each is necessary for bread, each was also necessary for Christ to become *the bread of life.*

The next part of the process, the distribution, Christ leaves with us. We are the distributors. We can't force people to eat the bread, but we can make sure they have access to it.

John 6:35 *Jesus said to them,"I am the bread of life."*

October 26

Hope

2 Corinthians 3:12 *"Therefore, since we have such a hope, we are very bold."*

The hope Paul describes in 2 Corinthians is the unchanging truth of the gospel. The death of Jesus atoned for our sins and His righteousness became ours.

Think about this amazing reality for believers: God forgives our sins. He remembers them no more! God clothes us with righteousness. That's a powerful hope.

Hope … that changes our thinking

Hope … that makes us bold.

Hope … in Jesus' redeeming sacrifice makes us boldly live with unveiled faces (2 Corinthians 3:13,18). We don't hide who we were, because the change Jesus makes in our lives brings glory to God.

Hope … in Jesus, our righteousness, makes us boldly say no to sin and yes to godly lives through the Holy Spirit's power.

Hope … in Christ's sufficiency (2 Cor. 3:5-6) makes us boldly proclaim the gospel. God uses every believer, regardless of age, education or ability, to share the good news of life in the Holy Spirit.

Hope … in God's gift of eternal life through Jesus moves us to boldly live joyful lives, standing firm in the truth, in the midst of trouble and hardship (2 Cor. 4:7-12).

October 27

Psalm 103

Psalm 103:1-5 *"Bless the Lord, O my soul; all my inmost being, praise His holy name. Praise the Lord, O my soul and forget not all His benefits – who forgives all your sins and heals all your diseases, who redeems your life from the pit and crowns you with love and compassion, who satisfies your desires with good things so that your youth is renewed like the eagle's."*

I'm in awe of the picture that these words create as I pause to reflect on this lovely passage from God's word. We now have all the things that God's mercy delivers. We experience a lot of stress and anxiety because of things we believe we ought to do or should have done but haven't. Here, God informs us that everything is forgiven, including our sins of omission - the things we have neglected to do. The slate is clean.

We can bring Jesus all the things that harm our bodies and souls. A large portion of what we let erode our minds and steal our peace also erodes our bodies. He encourages us to release our thoughts and feelings to Him, which in turn promotes the wellbeing of both our bodies and minds. He draws us towards the Light again. He rescues our lives and delivers us from the pit of evil. He pulls us to Himself so that He can purge, heal, and deliver us.

He also serves as a reminder of the things that He renews and replenishes in our lives. He has crowned us with His unfailing affection and compassion. He is loyal, and we are embraced by His faithfulness. He will give us the ability to push back against the condemnation, the shoulds and oughts of life and embrace His empowering presence – His grace.

What a lovely word image of God's intervention in our lives - first rescuing and redeeming us, then giving us the fresh motivation and energy to fly like the eagle!

October 28

Do Not Worry

Worry comes naturally to us but as Christians we are aware that they we should not worry. So how do we become worry-free? The fact is, the majority of our worries either don't materialise or are resolved, and we shouldn't worry about the things we can't control anyhow.

We must entrust the only One Who is able to handle all the situations we are powerless to change. Only God can do all that He can once we have exhausted our options. Trust God and put your trust in His control and timing. God always takes His time, and His timing is always optimal. The Devil is constantly rushing.

Worrying only makes things worse and, at worst, has little effect other than to make our lives more stressful. Health problems, stress in daily life, strained relationships, and loss of confidence in God can all be brought on by worry. Worry has no positive effect at all.

Can you picture one of your children approaching you and expressing concern about whether the family will be able to afford groceries this month or whether the energy bill will be paid? No child naturally checks their parent's bank account to see if there's enough money in there to get by, but that's what we tend to do when we worry about finances or health issues or anything else that we have no control over.

All of our wants are met by the merciful God who created us. What makes us believe that our perfect heavenly Father won't provide for His own children and in a much better way than our worldly fathers and mothers did for us? Who is more abundant than God?

Matthew 7:11 *"If you then, who are evil, know how to give good gifts to your children, how much more will your Father who is in heaven give good things to those who ask him."*

October 29

When Trouble Comes

Everyone experiences difficulties; it's only a matter of time. So, what do Christians do when they have difficulties? *"Man is born to trouble as the sparks fly upward."* (Job 5:7). What do we do with all these "sparks" in our life, just as worries enter our lives one after another like sparks fly upward continually from a fire? We are thrust into problems as soon as we are born, and for some people, even before they are born!

Why does God allow suffering for His children? Why would anyone choose to stay in a troubled world? How many people do you think would ever consider God if everything in the world went according to plan and everyone was content?

Wealth turns us away from God while difficulties seem to pull us towards Him. That's because wealth is a person's own god; it gives them present support in the here and now as well as future stability. They have never experienced living pay day to pay day. The destitute, the broken and the shattered have nowhere else to turn.

With no other options, many of these oppressed people turn to God. God has been waiting for just that to happen! Because God cannot restore something that is initially not broken, He wanted things to come to an end on their own. Those who are full of themselves cannot be filled by God.

When our vehicle starts to have problems, we look under the hood. So when troubles comes, it doesn't hurt to look under our own 'hood' and see why we are passing through a storm in life. God could prevent them from happening to us, so why doesn't He? I believe it's because He knows these storms are for our own good, and no matter how bad it gets, God will bring good out of it (Romans 8:28).

October 30

Let's Connect

The Bible seems to support the idea that the Christian faith is a deeply relational thing. The list of 'one anothers' is long and includes things like: love one another; be of the same mind towards one another; admonish one another; serve one another; bear one another's burdens; be kind to one another, forbear with one another; comfort one another; confess one's faults to one another, and many more. These reciprocal obligations are challenging to carry out in the digital age.

I worry that the digital generation are slowly losing the face-to-face interaction that is so important for creating and sustaining meaningful and fulfilling connections, to their own detriment. A recent article in the journal Christianity Today makes mention of the rising suicide rate among young Japanese who, as a result of spending absurd amounts of time on technology, had become socially alienated. According to the report, *"They have lost some of what it means to be human."*

We live in a very different world today. Very few people have a home landline now. Almost everyone has a mobile phone. E-mails or text messages or social media are the favoured methods of communication, which are rarely fulfilling. We seem to be losing the desire to speak with people, hear their voices, feel the nuances of their emotions.

I often wonder if Christ's earthly mission had commenced in these 'enlightened' technology driven times, how would Jesus train His disciples and connect with the people He came to save? Instagram? Facebook? Perhaps He would have used those platforms, but how would He have really connected with the hearts of people with whom He served? I am pretty sure that being together, face to face would be the preferred option for Jesus, regardless of which generation He faced. We would do well to adopt the same priority.

October 31

Waiting

One of David's secrets to being a man after God's own heart was waiting on Him. David entered and took a seat before the Lord (2 Samuel 7:18). God was his assurance, and he put his complete trust in Him for all his needs, including direction and instruction (Psalm 25:5), assistance and protection (Psalm 33:20), victory over adversaries and justification (Psalm 37:7,9,34; 52:9), deliverance from trouble and destruction (Psalm 40:1, 59:9), His refuge from betrayal and oppression (Psalm 62:1,5), for His forgiving love (Psalm 130:5-6), and much, much more.

Waiting for God to respond to our prayers is the greatest test of our faith. Waiting puts to the test our reliance on Him as our dependable authority. Waiting is submitting to God's better plan, not necessarily a withdrawal from all effort. By waiting on God, we bring every aspect of our lives under his control and guidance. Running ahead of God will result in chaos, tiredness, and failure.

While we wait, we discover who God is. God is constantly demonstrating His perfection and His capacity to control every aspect of life. He has split-second timing. He is all-knowing, all-aware, and all-caring. He provides evidence of His constant presence. He assures us of His actual dominance over the invisible enemy. We are given the power to focus by His Holy Spirit. We seek evidence, but faith is the substance - not the proof - of what is hoped for and the conviction of what is unseen (Hebrews 11:1).

As we wait, we shall be strengthened to understand the entire scope of His purpose and be encouraged in the grace of waiting as we humble ourselves in the presence of other Christians, open up to receive from the body of Christ, and humble ourselves.

November 1

All Things Work for Good

Romans 8:28 *"And we know that in all things God works for the good of those who love him, who have been called according to his purpose."*

There are so many things we just don't understand. We have no idea whether the economy will suffer or if our team will succeed. We have no idea what our partner is thinking or how our children will develop. Our health could take a turn for the worse without warning.

There are so many uncertainties in life. However, Paul says that there are four things about which we can be absolutely confident at all times.

1. God works. He is engaged in secret activities both above and within any conflict. He hasn't abandoned ship or left us. He works nonstop and never gets tired.

2. God works for our good. Not just for our convenience, enjoyment, or amusement, but rather for our highest good. What else would we expect from the Ultimate Good?

3. God works for the good of those who love Him. See the advantages of loving God! If you make His story your story, it will have a guaranteed happy ending. He incorporates a salvation theme throughout our biography since He is the author of our salvation.

4. God works in all things. The Greek word here is *panta*. Which is also the root of words like *pandemic, panoramic* and *panacea*. It means all-inclusive. God doesn't work through a select few things; God is at work in ALL things.

Your life is not a random assortment of unrelated short stories. Your life is a well created story which is controlled by a good God Who is always working for your ultimate good.

November 2

God's Goal

In a world where everything is bleak and gloomy; when there never seems to be enough; in the midst of messages telling us that we fall short; in a time when we are more focused on how we may acquire the latest smart phone than how we can help the underprivileged; and even in a Church that is battling, quarrelling, and suffering from 'friendly fire' ... God is working among all of this. All of creation is being drawn towards redemption by a stream of hope that constantly runs beneath the surface.

A powerful prayer Jesus uttered soon before His crucifixion neatly sums up the whole purpose of creation:

John 17:19-21 *"For them I sanctify myself, that they too may be truly sanctified. My prayer is not for them alone. I pray also for those who will believe in me through their message, that all of them may be one, Father, just as you are in me and I am in you. May they also be in us so that the world may believe that you have sent me."*

Jesus pleaded for His followers to be as unified as He and the Father. The Trinity's loving unity should be reflected in the Church's loving unity. As stated in "*As you are in me and I am in you, may they also be in us,*" the loving unity of the Church is to actually partake in the loving unity of the Trinity.

The world sees and understands that Jesus Christ is sent from the Father when we display this loving oneness. Because they experience the love of the triune God in us, the world is made aware of the existence of God.

This prayer articulated God's heart for the entire created order as well as for the Church. The reality is that Jesus calls us to be one in the Father and Son, so that the world might believe in Him and embrace His kingdom.

November 3

Taking the Long Way

One of my favourite expressions is: *"God rarely takes us in a straight line."* That statement is not only born from personal experience and observation, it also has a biblical basis.

In Exodus 13, the children of Israel are being led out of Egypt Technically, they are actually being expelled because of the terror of the deaths of the firstborn during the Passover.

Exodus 13:17 *"God did not lead them on the road through Philistine country, though that was shorter. For God said, 'If they face war, they might change their minds and return to Egypt.'"*

Sometimes, when God is taking a long time to get around to what we think the destination should be, we start to question ourselves. Did we hear God correctly? What are we doing wrong? We also question God's actions or inaction. Why is He taking so long to answer? Does He really care?

When we are weak or desperate, we strongly desire relief, and we think the sooner the better. So, when God takes His time, we may even think that He is working against us. The reality is He is working *for* us. As His redeemed children, He is always working for us, whether we can perceive it or not.

He knows His children, what strength we have, and what strength we need. He knows whether or not we can face the temptation ahead of us, or if we need to be led down another path, one that takes us around the trial we would not be strong enough to deal with successfully.

So, when He is leading us the long way, instead of grumbling about the slow pace or diverted route, we should be grateful that He is faithfully, patiently leading us the best way and in His perfect time. He knows what's ahead of us; we don't.

November 4

Confession

1 John 1:9 *"If we confess our sins, he is faithful and just and will forgive us our sins and purify us from all unrighteousness."*

The word 'confession' means, 'agreeing with God.' When we confess our sins, we don't do it to tell God what we've done. He already knows. In confession we say, *"Yes God, I agree that this was wrong"* and then we can turn the other way in repentance. But it's really important we understand the two sides of confession.

So often in confession a child of God lists all their sins and then sits there in quiet guilt. The trouble is most of us don't hear God's reply to us at that point of confession. He says, *"We agree about what you've done. But now can we agree about who you are?"*

There in that private moment the Holy Spirit will bring to mind verses that speak of God's love for you. He will remind you how you are fearfully and wonderfully made, how you are chosen and precious and planned. You need to just sit there quietly until you can agree with God about that too. You need to sit there and rest in God's truth.

It is so easy to see our own flaws and shortcomings, but when God sees us, He doesn't focus on what we've done wrong (love keeps no record of wrongs) - He sees who we are. There are two sides to confession. Agree with God about what you have done and repent, but don't miss the other side. Agree with God about who you are: loved and wanted and precious and forgiven and worth dying for.

In that moment of vulnerability which should always come with confession, *let God love you!* Then move into the world forgiven, empowered and ready to fulfill Christ's mission.

November 5

Be Still and Know

Psalm 46:10-11 *"Be still and know that I am God; I will be exalted among the nations, I will be exalted in the earth! The Lord of hosts is with us; The God of Jacob is our refuge."*

BE ...

God, I say 'yes' to You. I choose to allow Your way to shape me and Your will to direct me in what is best. I surrender instead of resist, I yield instead of fight, I believe instead of doubt.

STILL ...

Father, may Your rest abide and Your peace abound within me. Quieten anxiety that troubles my thoughts and unsettles my emotions. I bring my soul under the control of the Holy Spirit; I stand steady upon the unmovable foundations of Your kingdom; I receive the sufficiency of Your grace and the encouragement of Your promises as You calm my soul.

AND KNOW ...

Lord, thank you that Your word is sure, unchanging, and indisputable. Your word is true. I am certain. You have saved me from guessing, wondering, wishing, or pretending. I know! I believe!

I AM GOD ...

You are Who You say You are. You do what You say You will do. There is no other! You are the highest, the greatest, the best. You have no weakness, no lack and no equal. You are my God, and my Heavenly Father. I find comfort in Your nearness, security in Your voice, courage in Your strength, hope in Your promises. You are enough. More than enough! You are with me. You are my refuge. I am safe in Your care.

November 6

Kindness

Are you kind? When was the last time you did something kind for someone in your family - got a blanket, cleaned off the table, prepared the coffee – without being asked? Think about your school or workplace or Church. Which person is the most overlooked or avoided? A shy student? A grumpy employee? Maybe he doesn't speak the language. Maybe she doesn't fit in. Are you kind to them?

Kind hearts are quietly kind. They let that car cut into traffic and the young mum with three kids move up in the checkout line. They pick up the neighbour's rubbish bin that rolled into the street. They are especially kind at Church and understand that perhaps the neediest person they'll meet all week is the one standing in the foyer or sitting in the row behind them in worship on Sunday.

Ephesians 4:32 *"Be kind to one another, tender-hearted, forgiving one another, even as God in Christ forgave you."*

Jesus said we should love our enemies, do good to those who hate us and bless those who curse us. If we love only the people who love us, what praise should we get?

Kindness at home. Kindness in public. Kindness at Church and kindness with your enemies. Pretty well covers everyone, don't you think? Almost. Someone else needs your kindness. Who could that be? You. Since God is so kind to you, can't you be a little kinder to yourself? He knows everything about you, yet He doesn't hold back His kindness toward you. Why don't you be kind to yourself? He forgives your faults. Why don't you do the same? He thinks tomorrow is worth living. Why don't you agree?

Be kind to yourself. God thinks you're worth His kindness. And He's a good judge of character.

November 7

We Have the Mind of Christ

As Christians, we spend too much time battling with issues which really mean very little in the final analysis. This can consume much of our time throughout our whole life. The fact is, God has so much more for us. He seeks to conform our thought-life to the actual thought-life of Christ.

Indeed, the Holy Spirit comes, not just to give us goose bumps and chills, but to restructure our attitudes and perceptions until we are thinking the thoughts of Jesus. Consider Paul's remarkable insight here:

1 Corinthians 2:14-16 *"But a natural man does not accept the things of the Spirit of God, for they are foolishness to him; and he cannot understand them, because they are spiritually appraised. But he who is spiritual appraises all things, yet he himself is appraised by no one. For who has known the mind of the Lord, that he will instruct Him? But we have the mind of Christ."*

This revelation is stunning: we have the mind of Christ. God wants us to have Christ's actual discernment.

Or consider again what Paul wrote to the Galatians here:

Galatians 4:19 *"My children, with whom I am again in labour until Christ is formed in you."*

Critics will call the revelation of Jesus Christ in us a heresy, as though all we were supposed to have was the name, but not the nature of Jesus Christ. Without this, there is no gospel!

God's goal is not only to see us saved and go to Heaven, but for Christ to be functionally formed and living through us on earth. We are not just to have a dead religion which talks a lot about what Jesus did 2,000 years ago; we are called to possess the very substance of who Jesus is today!

November 8

Overcoming the Flesh

Every human is created with a desperate, insatiable, non-negotiable need to experience life at its best and though most aren't aware of it, we all hunger to be loved unconditionally. This means we are starving to experience profound worth, significance and security. We feel fully alive to the extent that we have this; desperate and empty to the extent that we don't.

God created us with this craving for life at its best as the means of inviting us into the dance of His own eternal triune love, and the only way we experience this life is by accepting His invitation, submitting to Christ's Lordship, and then by participating in this eternal dance. The Kingdom of God is this eternal dance *"on earth as it is in heaven."*

When we're not getting life from our relationship with God, we inevitably try to get it from our environment. We become addicted to idols, which are anything we use to derive our ultimate worth, significance and security other than God. In modern western culture, the most popular idols are things like power, sex, wealth and accomplishments. Life in this fallen world is a veritable feeding frenzy on idols of one sort or another. Idolatrous living is always accompanied by anxiety, strife and other *"works of the flesh"* (Galatians 5).

It's also why 'the flesh' (our fallen, sinful nature) is the source of all conflict and violence in the world. Whether we're talking about celebrity gossip, political fighting or wars between nations, the root of all hostility is idolatry. People are desperately trying to get life from something other than God.

But to the extent that Christ is our life, we no longer need these things to feel fully alive. When we lose these things, we may feel a sense of loss, but this loss will not change our core identity or our sense of being fully alive. That's because true life is found only in the eternal Son of God, Jesus Christ.

November 9

The Fullness of Life

We must always be aware of the fact that there is a constant lure toward idolatry in our demon-oppressed world. It is profoundly easy to get all of one's life from Christ and to be completely free of idols one day but become gripped by idol cravings the next. It's also really easy not to notice this!

This is why getting life from Christ is a daily choice. The call to get life from Christ and revolt against the idolatry of the flesh isn't something we can do once and be done with it. It is a practice that we must, with God's help, strive daily to make a permanent characteristic of our life. We all need to have regular times where we experience that intimate, life-giving communion with Christ and cultivate a moment-by-moment surrendered awareness of God's life-giving presence.

If you find that your sense of being fully alive increases or diminishes based on how well you perform, it's a likely sign that the idolatrous atmosphere of our oppressed world has made inroads in your life. If you discover that what others think about you is beginning to matter too much, or if you discern that your worth, significance and security are beginning to be associated with what you own, it's a likely indication that you're once again becoming conformed to the pattern of this world (Romans 12:2).

When you see this happening, it won't help to beat yourself up. Nor will it help to resolve to work harder at not caring so much about how you perform, or about what others think, or about what you own. In fact, as long as you're hungry for life, this will become just one more idol. Even if you're successful, you'll start to feed off of your success in getting free from idols - which, of course, is just another idol.

Everything we are called to do as Kingdom people must flow out of the fullness of life we have in Christ. It's that simple!

November 10

Unanswered Prayers

Prayer is powerful and effective, but it's not magic. There is no automatic guarantee that what we are praying for is going to come to pass, even when we are praying with faith and in accordance with God's will.

Prayer is a form of co-labouring with God to change the world in a Kingdom direction, but at all times, God is sovereign.

I believe this is why prayer sometimes must be engaged in with persistence. It's not that we are begging God to do what He doesn't want to do. It's that prayer comes up against obstacles that require prolonged work to overcome.

Labouring in the spiritual realm is no different than labouring on a physical level. Light rocks can be moved quickly, but heavier ones require more persistence. So too, some prayer may produce immediate results, for there's little resistance. But some other prayer may face a lot of resistance and require more work. It's all part of our faith journey.

So, let me say it again: prayer is powerful and effective, but it's not magic. It's rather co-labouring with God on a spiritual level to manifest His will *"on earth as it is in heaven."*

All prayer, in essence, is encompassed in the three words which Jesus gave us to pray, *"Your Kingdom Come."* Regardless of the issue, every prayer is effectively calling for God to make real on earth what is already a reality in heaven.

On divine authority, we can trust that our prayer always moves the world closer to the Kingdom of God. But it is not an automatic guarantee that it will accomplish what we are praying for, even when we pray with strong faith and pray in accordance with God's will.

November 11

Our Unexpected God

Jesus came, in part, to finally reveal the absolute truth about God. He is the way and the truth and the life (John 14:6). The word "truth" means "uncovered" and what we find once God is uncovered is that He is completely different than what we fallen humans generally expect God to be.

Definitions of what God is like actually fall short of what we see in Jesus.

God is one, and yet we discover that His oneness is the oneness of eternal perfect love between three distinct Persons.

God is holy, but His holiness is His utterly unique love that leads Him to become sin on our behalf (2 Corinthians 5:21).

God is righteous, but His righteousness is the justice of His love that leads Him to become a cursed criminal for us on Calvary (1 Corinthians 1:18).

God is unfathomably glorious, but His glory is the radiance of a perfect love that leads Him to become one who was despised, humiliated and forsaken out of love for us.

God is immutable, but His immutability reveals to us all the unchangeableness of His eternal love that led Him to change radically and take on our humanity, sin and condemnation.

This is what God is like! He really is this beautiful and loving! God is different than you could ever expect because none of us could ever dream of God being as good as God is. This is the reason Paul prayed that we would be able *"to grasp how wide and long and high and deep is the love of Christ, and to know this love that surpasses knowledge - that you may be filled to the measure of all the fullness of God."* (Ephesians 3:18-29)

November 12

Be the Change

Ghandi once said, *"Be the change you want to see in the world."* It's a profoundly 'kingdom' kind of teaching. It seems to me, however, that too few people adopt Ghandi's philosophy.

It's far easier to focus our attention on how others should be changing. It's far easier to spend our energy assigning blame for the problems of society to others. It's far easier to try to control the behaviour of others by gaining power over them.

This keeps the focus off us and helps us feel righteous and wise. If you think about it, all political conflict is premised on the assumption that we who espouse a particular ideal are more moral or wiser than those who disagree with us.

While everyone is free to assess social problems and work toward political solutions as they see fit, this is not Jesus' way of transforming the world. He never commented on the hot political issues of his day.

Jesus' way of transforming the world is not by assuming a position of moral or intellectual superiority, assigning blame for society's woes on others. Rather, we are called to assume a position of humility and focus our energy on the log in our own eye rather than the dust particle in a neighbour's eye (Matthew 7:1-3).

From a New Testament perspective, the primary job of Kingdom people is to simply **be the change** we want to see in the world. More specifically, we are called to simply be the Kingdom we know is coming.

We are called to manifest the future in the present; the Kingdom of God in the midst of the kingdom of the world; God's will *"on earth as it is in heaven."*

November 13

The Cross: Above All

The way to know what a person really believes is not to ask them but to watch them. Christians frequently say, *"It's all about Jesus,"* but our actions betray us. Judging by the amount of time, energy and emotion that many put into fighting a multitude of battles, ranging from the defence of the inerrancy of the Bible to war against moral issues, one easily gets the impression that Christianity is about a lot of different, equally important, things. This unfortunately sends the message to the broader culture that becoming a follower of Jesus requires a person to embrace all of this.

However is we strip away all the clutter, what is left is simply the cross, where God reveals His true character and invites us to be transformed into His likeness through the power of His love. We trust that our fallen and self-oriented character will be transformed into God's character. That is the kingdom of God, pure and simple.

The significance of the cross is reflected in the fact that the sign of our covenant relationship with Christ is communion. When we look to the cross, we see the heavenly bridegroom wooing us, as His prospective spouse, by opening up His heart and revealing His true character. On the cross we see the heavenly bridegroom demonstrating His perfect love for His prospective bride - all of humanity - even while we have assumed the posture of an enemy toward him (Romans 5:10).

Everything we are to trust God for is found in the cross. We are not involved in a contract that would require us, or even allow us, to comb the Bible to latch onto this or that particular passage as an insurance policy that God will come through for us. We are rather in a covenant in which it is not particular things we trust God for; our trust is rather in God Himself and we trust God to be Who He reveals Himself to be on the cross.

November 14

Overcoming Fear

2 Chronicles 20:3-4 *"And Jehoshaphat feared, and set himself to seek the LORD, and proclaimed a fast throughout all Judah. So Judah gathered together to ask help from the LORD; and from all the cities of Judah they came to seek the LORD."*

Have you ever been in a situation where your circumstances appear absolutely hopeless? Where you felt immobilized and overwhelmed by the challenges surrounding you, with no way out or even a temporary respite in sight? Perhaps under the accumulated weight of it all, you feel as if your entire life is spiralling out of control and falling apart.

That is exactly what happened to King Jehoshaphat and the small tribe of Judah when they were besieged on all fronts by three powerful and blood-thirsty armies rapidly advancing toward Jerusalem. With their enemies mercilessly bent on annihilating them and all the inhabitants of Jerusalem, they were facing a forlorn and hopeless situation, and it looked as though they were bound for a very tragic end.

When Jehoshaphat was informed that a great multitude was coming against him, his first reaction was fear! I don't know about you, but this gives me hope. I'm so glad that the Bible gives us an authentic portrait of who Jehoshaphat was. But what set Jehoshaphat apart was that even when he was fearful, the first thing he did was to *"set himself to seek the Lord"* (2 Chronicles 20:3) and we know the outcome, don't we?

That is something you and I need to learn to do whenever we are fearful. Instead of spiralling deeper into the abyss of self-defeat, know that when you are feeling overwhelmed by your circumstances, that is the time you need to set yourself to seek the Lord. His perfect love for you will cast out all fear and give you all that you need to face whatever is coming.

November 15

Called to Wait

I don't know anyone who particularly likes to wait. Waiting in line, waiting for a delivery, waiting for a repair person to arrive, waiting on our children and spouse. Waiting can be tedious. Waiting can be hard. Especially when we're waiting on God. When we wait on God, we don't know His timing, what the future will look like, or if our days will go the way we want them to. We don't get to see the full picture of our lives like God does. And yet, He tells us to wait and trust Him.

It's not easy because waiting feels like a waste of time. There's a sense of loneliness as we watch others move ahead and we're stuck behind … just waiting. But we are not left alone. As we wait, God promises to be with us.

Isaiah 7:14 *"Therefore the Lord himself will give you a sign: The virgin will conceive and give birth to a son and will call him Immanuel." (Which means God with us.)*

His very name is *God with us*. It's Who He is. God promised us a Saviour and He kept His promise. While we wait and let God work, He does not walk away and He does not leave us. Instead, He draws us close to Him and helps us wait. He makes hope possible when we see no reason for hope. He fills our hearts with a joy that we can't explain and won't find anywhere else. He renews our strength and energy when we have nothing left inside of us. He gives us the ability to see His blessings in the midst of difficulties, and He brings peace to our lives where peace doesn't make sense.

Romans 15:13 *"May the God of hope fill you with all joy and peace as you trust in him, so that you may overflow with hope by the power of the Holy Spirit."*

That's God - helping us wait on Him.

November 16

Faith vs. Fear

When the Israelites first approached the borders of Canaan, Moses sent scouts ahead into the Promised Land to assess the situation. Ten of the scouts came back with reports that focused on the giants in the land, men so big and powerful the scouts feared they could not be defeated.

However, two of the scouts focused on the promise from God that he would hand the land over to the Israelites. One of those scouts, Caleb, silenced the others when he said:

Numbers 13:30 *"... We should go up and take possession of the land, for we can certainly do it."*

Caleb trusted God instead of submitting to his own fear. The opposite of fear is faith, the belief that Jesus is capable of handling anything we may face in life.

But operating out of faith means we must rely on Jesus, remaining dependent on Him to see us through any issue. He brings us to a choice: Will we trust God or will we trust our own fears? We reach that level of trust by knowing the Father and understanding His character. We know the Father by following Jesus.

John 14:9–10 *(Jesus said) "To see me is to see the Father ... Don't you believe that I am in the Father and the Father is in me? The words that I speak to you aren't mere words. I don't just make them up on my own. The Father who resides in me crafts each word into a divine act." (The Message).*

Your fear simply reveals a place where you aren't yet trusting Jesus. So, don't stay stuck in your fear, and don't receive condemnation for your lack of faith. Jesus wants to move you past that into a place where your fears are replaced by faith. Follow Him and learn to trust.

November 17

Rest on Every Side

Psalm 23:1 *"The LORD is my shepherd; I shall not want."*

A well-known picture of God as our Shepherd and healer is articulated in the beautiful 23rd Psalm. It was written by David, a shepherd who saw the Lord as his Shepherd. Take a moment and read the psalm for yourself in your Bible. When you can see the Lord as your Shepherd, you will not lack. Whatever needs you have, you will not lack because your Good Shepherd always provides.

Whatever problems you are faced with, stay close to the Shepherd and allow Him to provide for you. And did you notice the first thing the Shepherd does? The psalmist wrote, *"He makes me to lie down in green pastures."* (Psalm 23:2)

When you allow Him to be your Good Shepherd, He will bring you to green pastures and make you lie down. You can rest, for He will provide for you. He will lead you beside still waters where you can drink and be refreshed. The Hebrew word for 'still' is *manuka*, which means 'rest.' He wants you to rest in the victory He has already won at the cross.

It is not by coincidence that many of Jesus' healing miracles took place on the Sabbath. God told His people to observe the Sabbath as a day of rest (Exodus 20:8–11). When we rest, God still works. I don't know about you, but I can't afford not to have God working every day in my life!

Let me explain that this 'rest' is not inactivity; it is Spirit-directed activity where you allow the Holy Spirit to lead you in what to do, and you do it without worrying because you know that God is in control.

When you place yourself in that position of trust, then God will give you *"rest on every side"* (1 Kings 5:4)

November 18

God's Relentless Pursuit

Christianity is not about our disciplined pursuit of God. It is about God's relentless pursuit of us.

John 4:4–7 *"But He had to go through Samaria. So He came to a city of Samaria which is called Sychar...Now Jacob's well was there. Jesus therefore, being wearied from His journey, sat thus by the well. It was about the sixth hour. A woman of Samaria came to draw water. Jesus said to her, "Give Me a drink."*

I encourage you to read the remarkable story of the Samaritan woman in John 4. Considered a woman with a shady past, she was gossiped about in her village and probably shunned for being a home wrecker, a "stealer of husbands." Hers is not a fictional story. She was a real person, just like you and me. Her problems and pain, like many of ours, were real and hounded her every day, until she encountered a real Saviour!

Despite the custom of the Jews of that day to avoid contact with the Samaritans, John says that Jesus *"had to go through Samaria."* Why? Because He was in pursuit of one woman - this Samaritan at the well. We know from John that this ostracized woman had a life-transforming conversation with Jesus at the well. But make no mistake - it wasn't this woman who sought out Jesus to talk to Him. It was the Saviour who pursued the one whom others shunned.

Do you know that He is still doing that today? Do you have a past you are ashamed of? Are you struggling to overcome something that you know is destroying you? Do you feel all alone and that no one understands the pain you are going through? Talk to Him as the woman at the well did. Taste and touch His grace and compassion for you as she did. And like her, discover Jesus' forgiveness, freedom, and strength so you can walk into a bright new future.

November 19

Listen to Jesus

John 10:3-4 *"To him the doorkeeper opens, and the sheep hear his voice; and he calls his own sheep by name and leads them out. And when he brings out his own sheep, he goes before them; and the sheep follow him, for they know his voice."*

Why does our heavenly Father want us to listen only the Lord Jesus? Why focus on Jesus and grow in the knowledge of His grace? Because neither the law nor the prophets hold the answer to our deepest cry for intimacy and peace with God, and the enjoyment of His presence and power in every area of our lives.

If you look at Scripture, you will see that while Moses and Elijah did mighty exploits, both great men of God still missed the mark. Moses failed and Elijah became discouraged, but the Scriptures tell us that our Lord Jesus, the altogether lovely One, *"will not fail nor be discouraged."* Whereas Moses was impatient, our Lord Jesus is patient with us, especially when we make mistakes and fail. And whereas Moses failed to bring God's people into the promised land, our Lord Jesus finished the work His Father sent Him to do and has ushered us into all of God's blessings and promises.

Elijah became discouraged, Jesus was never discouraged, in spite of people's repeated rejection of Him. He is our rock and our fortress when we are feeling discouraged. All the greatest men and women of God in the Old Testament put together cannot compare with our beautiful Lord Jesus Christ! This is God's beloved Son and today He says to you, *"Arise. Stand in My righteousness and be lifted up from defeat."* In the same way that our Lord Jesus could touch a man with leprosy and make him whole, He can touch any area of deformity, weakness, or shame in your life and totally transform it into wholeness and strength by His grace.

November 20

Change Your Mind

2 Peter 3:9 *"The Lord is not slack concerning His promise, as some count slackness, but is longsuffering toward us, not willing that any should perish but that all should come to repentance."*

The word *repentance* in the New Testament is the Greek word *metanoia*, which simply means 'a change of mind.' *Meta* means change and *noia* refers to the mind. There are religious people who have this idea that repentance means grovelling in the dirt and condemning themselves until they feel they have sufficiently earned God's forgiveness. My question is, how condemned and sorrowful do you need to be before you have genuinely "repented" and after you have repented, should you fail again in the same area, does it mean that you did not really repent completely the first time?

I don't doubt the sincerity of people who think this was about repentance, however, you can be sincere in your intent but sincerely wrong in reality. It is possible to beat your breast sorrowfully, put on sackcloth and ashes, cry your eyes out, and remain unchanged. Sorrow doesn't equal transformation.

True repentance comes from knowing that God has already forgiven you. If you stop condemning yourself and walk in His righteous identity, you will then experience new levels of victory over sin. When wrong thoughts come into your head, the repentance or change of mind that you need is to know that those thoughts don't belong to you. Repentance is not about beating yourself up over those thoughts. Just give those thoughts no room to flourish by ignoring them and continue to be established and secure in your identity in Christ.

Fill your mind with His thoughts, His living Word, His peace, His joy and His love. The fruit of that will always be genuine repentance.

November 21

This is our God

How we see God is important because a faulty perception of God can result in a lifetime of fear and bondage.

Too many people have a wrong impression of God because for many generations people have portrayed Him as hard, angry, unfeeling and condemning; a hard taskmaster who is just waiting for us to trip up so He can pounce on us!

These portrayals of God cause many sincere people to have an unhealthy fear of God. And when they believe that God is against them and out to punish them, they find it impossible to break out of their sins, addictions, anxieties or fears.

If you've been shown a God of judgment and anger all your life, let the Scriptures reveal to you God's true nature:

Psalm 86:15 *"But you, Lord, are a compassionate and gracious God, slow to anger, abounding in love and faithfulness"*

Daniel 9:9 *"The Lord our God is merciful and forgiving."*

Psalm 25:6 *"O LORD, Your tender mercies and Your loving-kindnesses . . . they are from of old."*

1 John 4:8 *"God is love."*

This is our God! Our God is love! He is gracious, slow to anger and patient. He is full of forgiveness, loving-kindness, and tender mercies. If you want to further understand the true nature of God, just look at Jesus and listen to His words here:

John 14:9–10 *"He who has seen Me has seen the Father ... The words that I speak to you I do not speak on My own authority; but the Father who dwells in Me does the works."*

November 22

Right Place – Right Time

Psalm 91:1 *"Whoever dwells in the shelter of the Most High will rest in the shadow of the Almighty."*

Ecclesiastes 9:11 *"I have seen something else under the sun: The race is not to the swift or the battle to the strong, nor does food come to the wise or wealth to the brilliant or favour to the learned; but time and chance happen to them all."*

I believe that the prayer of protection in Psalm 91 marks the times we are living in and gives us a crystal-clear reason why we don't have to live in fear.

In Ecclesiastes 9, King Solomon tells us that the winner of the race is not necessarily always the fastest one, and the person who wins the battle isn't necessarily always the strongest. He points out that men of understanding are not the only ones who gain riches and men of skill do not always experience favour.

Solomon then goes on to talk about those who are *"like fish taken in a cruel net"* or *"birds caught in a snare."* (he's saying this of the "sons of men" and not the "sons of God." As believers, we are the sons and daughters of God.)

There are therefore two categories of people - those who are blessed because they find themselves in the right place at the right time, and those who are caught off guard in an evil time and find themselves in the wrong place at the wrong time.

As a son or daughter of God, you can rest assured today that the blessing of being placed in the right place at the right time is yours all because of our Lord Jesus! Despite the dangerous times we live in, you can expect Him to always protect you and deliver you from every snare of the enemy.

November 23

Hold Fast

Hosea 2:15 *"I will return her vineyards to her and transform the Valley of Trouble into a gateway of hope."*

Maybe you are going through a difficult valley. Maybe you are disappointed with God because you have lost a loved one or because you have been battling that medical condition. I want to encourage you not to ask, *"Why?"* Asking why will only lead to a downward spiral into depression.

The fact is, in this fallen world, we don't have all the answers. But what I do know is this: God is a good God. He loves us, and He is never the cause any pain we go through. Our faith in Him is not based on our experiences; it is based on the unchanging, eternal Word of God.

Even when things don't go the way you want, don't remain in your disappointment. The devil wants you to get angry with God and to give up on His promises.

Keep believing that God is for you, not against you. Even if the enemy has destroyed something in your life, or the days of your youth have been stolen from you, keep believing that God can redeem what you have lost . (Joel 2:25, Job 33:25).

Hebrews 10:23 *"Let us hold fast the confession of our hope without wavering, for He who promised is faithful."*

Keep on looking to the Lord for your breakthrough, and if you find that you are too tired to believe anymore, I pray that this promise will carry you through:

Isaiah 40:31 *"But those who wait on the Lord shall renew their strength; they shall mount up with wings like eagles, they shall run and not be weary, they shall walk and not faint."*

November 24

Faith Awakening

Romans 10:17 *"So faith comes from hearing, and hearing by the word of Christ."*

Have you ever felt like you needed more faith? Have you ever thought to yourself that if you just had more faith, you would see your financial breakthrough or healing? I have good news for you today: faith is not a struggle. The Scriptures show us that the exercise of faith and the works of the law are complete opposites (Gal. 3:2, 5).

The more people become self-conscious and the more they look at their self-efforts to receive from the Lord, the weaker their faith actually becomes.

Once we stop pointing out what is wrong with people and start telling them what is right with them because of Jesus, faith will be imparted, and they will begin to experience an explosion of God's empowering presence like never before.

When believers know that they have already been made righteous by the blood of Jesus, everything changes in their mind, their heart, their attitude and their lives. When people begin to see more of Jesus; when they become more and more conscious of Jesus having been crucified on their behalf, the barriers to faith just melt away!

Why? Because the more they see what Jesus has done for them; the more they see what Jesus has qualified them for; the more faith springs up within them and the presence and power of Jesus Christ explodes within them. Hallelujah!

You don't have to wish that you had more faith for whatever miracle you are asking God for right now. You don't have to try to conjure up more faith. The more of Jesus you embrace and welcome, the more that faith will rise in your heart.

November 25

Say 'Yes!' to Jesus

2 Corinthians 3:14,18 *"But their minds were made dull, for to this day the same veil remains when the old covenant is read. It has not been removed, because only in Christ is it taken away ... And we all, who with unveiled faces contemplate the Lord's glory, are being transformed into his image with ever-increasing glory, which comes from the Lord, who is the Spirit."*

Are you consumed with the person of Jesus? I hope you are. The Apostle Paul was.

1 Corinthians 1:30 *"You are in Christ Jesus, who has become for us wisdom from God - that is, our righteousness, holiness and redemption."*

Jesus Himself is your wisdom, your righteousness, and also your holiness! The Greek word used here for *holiness* is *hagiasmos* - the same Greek word used for *sanctification*. Our holiness or sanctification is found in the person of Jesus. So, whenever you have an unclean thought, or a stirring in you, or a temptation to sin, stop and look at Jesus and the cross. See and experience His love, forgiveness and grace afresh. Jesus is your victory over every temptation, every addiction, every bondage and every attack!

Some people believe that all you have to do is say 'no' to temptation. But your willpower is really no match for sin. The reality is, the more you try to say 'no' by your own efforts, the worse it becomes. In the midst of all your struggles and temptation, say YES to Jesus. Say, *"Lord Jesus, I thank You that You are my righteousness, my holiness, and my redemption."*

Turn every temptation into an opportunity to look to and praise Jesus! As you behold Jesus, may you grow from glory to glory and shine as a testament to all of His goodness!

November 26

Fearless

Psalm 91:5–6 *"You shall not be afraid of the terror by night, nor of the arrow that flies by day, nor of the pestilence that walks in darkness, nor of the destruction that lays waste at noonday."*

I love how Psalm 91 reminds us that we have round-the-clock protection. Whether it's at night or in the day. Whether it's in darkness or at noonday. Whether we are faced with a terror or confronted by arrows. Whether pestilences threaten or destruction looms, we do not fear because our God, who watches over us, neither slumbers nor sleeps (Psalm 121).

The reality is the world we live in seems to be engulfed in negative news and fear. We often hear reports of senseless terrorist attacks on innocent civilians, horrific accidents claiming multiple victims. I know that many can't help but dread that the same tragedies could befall them. But I want you to know that in the midst of all that is happening in the world, you can be fearless, and this comes from knowing the Lord as the God of peace.

Romans chapter 15 ends with the apostle Paul saying, *"Now the God of peace be with you all"* (Rom. 15:33). Paul was speaking over the people for God to manifest Himself as the God of peace in their lives. In other words, even though God is always with us, we may not always experience Him as the God of peace. Do you know what happens when God does manifest Himself as the God of peace in your life?

Romans 16:20 *"And the God of peace will crush Satan under your feet shortly. The grace of our Lord Jesus Christ be with you. Amen."*

The God of peace will crush every fear, every worry and every anxiety because grace - the empowering presence of God - is the only thing against which the devil has no defence.

November 27

To God be the Glory

Ancient Babylon was a spectacular kingdom that included one of the Seven Wonders of the Ancient World, the Hanging Gardens of Babylon. Babylon's ruler, King Nebuchadnezzar, was surveying the city one day from his balcony and this is what he said:

Daniel 4:30 *"Look at this great city of Babylon! By my own mighty power, I have built this beautiful city as my royal residence to display my majestic splendour"*

While those words were still in the king's mouth, a voice came from Heaven:

Daniel 4:31-32 *"O King Nebuchadnezzar, this message is for you! You are no longer ruler of this kingdom. You will be driven from human society ... Seven periods of time will pass while you live this way, until you learn that the Most High rules over the kingdoms of the world and gives them to anyone he chooses."*

Nebuchadnezzar took personal credit for what God gave him the ability to do. We can work hard, save, and invest wisely. We can have the ability to buy our own food and clothes and make payments on a car or house. Rather than congratulate ourselves on what a good job we are doing, let's realize that God has given us everything we have.

Deuteronomy 8:18 *"Remember the Lord your God. He is the one who gives you power to be successful."*

James 1:17 *"Whatever is good and perfect is a gift coming down to us from God our Father, who created all the lights in the heavens."*

If God has blessed you in your life in any way, give all the glory to God. Everything you have and everything you are, is all a blessing from Him.

November 28

Facing Trials

Romans 5:3 *"We can rejoice, too, when we run into problems and trials, for we know that they help us develop endurance."*

Children are so cute when they're babies. They're so helpless and dependent. But as they get older, they learn certain skills. They learn to feed themselves and dress themselves. They learn to take care of themselves. They can't be babies forever. In the same way, we don't want to be baby Christians our entire lives. We want to grow up and mature.

I love the way J. B. Philips words some of the very familiar passages in the book of James. For example:

James 1:2–4 *"When all kinds of trials and temptations crowd into your lives my brothers, don't resent them as intruders, but welcome them as friends! Realise that they come to test your faith and to produce in you the quality of endurance. But let the process go on until that endurance is fully developed, and you will find you have become men of mature character with the right sort of independence."*

God allows hardship and trials in our lives so that we'll grow up spiritually. A teacher, for instance, might say to the class, *"I'm going to test you today. It's a pop quiz. So, close your textbooks and take out a sheet of paper."* When I was in school, I was never excited when the teacher announced a pop quiz because I wasn't prepared. I hadn't learned the material.

God may bring pop quizzes into our lives as well. He tests us to see if we have learned the material. We are so quick to tell others how to live. We are so quick to tell others to have faith and to pray about things. But often when trials and hardships come into our lives, we panic. Don't resist those times. One day you will look back on them as vital intersections in your faith journey.

November 29

God's Best Work

Ephesian 2:10 (Amp) *"For we are God's [own] handiwork (His workmanship), recreated in Christ Jesus, [born anew] that we may do those good works which God predestined (planned beforehand) for us [taking paths which He prepared ahead of time], that we should walk in them [living the good life which He prearranged and made ready for us to live]."*

A traveller visiting a logging area in Northwest America was interested in seeing how the logs that would be used for furniture were chosen. As the logs came down the river, the logger would suddenly reach out and hook one, pull it up, and then set it down. He would sometimes wait for a few minutes before grabbing another. There didn't seem to be any rhyme or reason to his choices. After a while, the visitor said to him, *"I don't understand what you're doing."*

The logger explained: *"These logs may all look alike to you, but I can recognize that a few of them are quite different. The ones that I let pass came from trees that grew in a valley. They were always protected from the storms. The grain is rather coarse. The logs that I pulled aside are from high up on the mountain, where they were beaten by strong winds from the time they were quite small. That toughens the trees and gives them a fine grain. We save these logs for our best projects."*

It was through trying and testing that the logs were prepared for choice work. The same could be said of us as Christians. When we look back over our journey with God, we will see that it was the tough times that God used most to shape us into who we are today.

Could it be that God's best work in us happens on our worst days? Next time you are facing the trials which invariably will come your way, remember God is doing His best work!

November 30

Looking for Jesus

Like it or not, you and I are the only 'Jesus' people around us will ever see and they couldn't care less about our spiritual gifts; our power ministry; our knowledge of the grace of God; our anointed worship; our spiritual discernment; our biblical leadership structure and all the other wonderful changes that may have taken place to renew us and revive us and re-focus us. Those things are all important but they are for us, the Church. What about the ones who are yet to bask in God's glory? What about those outside the Church who have no choice but to look at you and me and make a judgement about God based on what they see in us (or don't see)?

They don't care how gifted we are; they don't care how long we've been a Christian or how knowledgeable we are; they don't care about our training or equipping; they don't care that we got a word from the Lord for someone last Sunday; they don't really care about anything that happens inside the Church; they don't care that we worship a God of power, if that same God has not changed us so radically that they see it with their own eyes and hear it with their own ears and are gripped by the reality of who we now are in Christ.

Those who need the Gospel are also not impressed by our evangelism programs. They simply need to see transformed lives. They need some concrete evidence that God is real and that He can completely change their life too. They don't want to hear us talk about How powerful God is when we just act like everyone else when they see us. Our attitudes, our character and our transformed life will say so much more than any spiritualised witnessing they may hear from us.

Whether they know it or not, those looking in from the outside are saying one thing: *Show me Jesus!* That's Who they are really looking for. That's Who they really need to see.

December 1

Feasting on God's Presence

Picture a flock of sheep in a green pasture. What do they normally do there? They eat. When a sheep lies down in a green pasture it can only mean one thing: it's full. In fact, it's so full that it has no more desire to eat and lies down. When David starts Psalm 23 with, *"The LORD is my shepherd; I shall not want. He makes me lie down in green pastures. ..."* he's saying that he's so full that even in the presence of what others would call food, he doesn't feel compelled to eat. His soul is full from feasting on the presence of the Shepherd.

This is not just a David-thing. In the wilderness wandering, God fed the children of Israel with manna, a small cracker-like substance that magically appeared on the ground each morning. And they could only gather enough for one day because it went bad overnight. The Israelites couldn't keep any of it in the freezer for later!

And yet, through this strange bread, God met all their needs while they were in the wilderness. Manna was not supposed to replace food for them for all time; it was just supposed to keep them alive and fed and healthy in the wilderness. Manna represented God's presence in a time of emptiness.

Later, in John 6, we read where Jesus fed the 5,000 with just five loaves and two fish, and He explained that the manna the children of Israel ate in the wilderness was a foreshadowing of His presence with people through the Spirit. He said, *"My flesh is the bread that came down from heaven."* And when we feast on Him, we can be full - even in the wilderness, when our bellies feel empty.

So, in our time of wilderness wandering, when we're in a place that lacks normal bread, we can feast on a better kind of bread - the satisfying bread of God's promises and presence.

December 2

People Just Like Us

1 Corinthians 16:17–18 *"I am delighted to have Stephanas, Fortunatus, and Achaicus present, because these men have made up for your absence. For they have refreshed my spirit and yours. Therefore, recognize such people."*

Here's what we learn from this obscure passage: In every age, God builds His Church through ordinary people. Stephanas, Fortunatus, and Achaicus don't have any books of the Bible named after them, and if Paul hadn't mentioned them here, we would have never heard of them. They faithfully gave, prayed, opened up their houses for hospitality, and spoke early words of refreshment to each other.

But they were flawed people, too. The Corinthians were not a neat, tidy bunch. They were fighting, arguing, and strutting around like idiots - far from any 'super Christian' notions we might have of them. If they had social media, we would be disgusted by what we saw. Yet they transformed the world!

Think about it. Somehow a group of disorganized, rag-tag, blue collar, backwoods people transformed an empire. Rome was a place of incredible power: The ruins that have survived 2,000 years point to this incredible civilization. And, yet, in less than 300 years, the whole empire had, by and large, turned its back on its heritage and converted to Christianity.

The birth of the Church is absolutely miraculous and utterly inexplicable apart from the power of the Spirit. And the people our God used were ordinary people like Stephanas, Fortunatus, and Achaicus - who believed Jesus was real and took Him at His word.

If God used them, He can certainly use you too!

December 3

What a Friend we Have in Jesus

Friendship is inspired by Jesus. Throughout one of the most obvious examples of friendship in the Bible, that of Jonathan and David, the parallels are clear.

Jonathan served his friend David, even at great personal cost to himself, just as Jesus did when He took your place at the cross. When David was in need, Jonathan walked 30 miles to warn him. Jesus, of course, came much farther than that. He crossed the gap between heaven and earth, eternity and time, deity and humanity. Jonathan gave up his right to the palace to put David in it; Jesus purchased your place in the Palace of God at the cost of His own blood.

Jonathan was not the rightful heir to the throne; Jesus was, and He gave it up for you anyway. Jesus laid aside His royal robe and took off the belt of His rights and the sword of His judgment and gave them all to you, even though He was the rightful heir. And when you turned your back on Him and betrayed him, He refused to walk away from you, even when He had every right to. What a friend! Jesus' friendship enables you to be this kind of friend, too. Crawford Loritts says,

How can you be this kind of friend? You must be overwhelmed with the friendship of Jesus Christ. Jesus gave his own life, his own sword, his own robe so that you could be saved. And in doing so, he transformed you.

But what about when your friends disappoint you? When you feel the need for a friend but they just let you down? Every earthly friend disappoints - even the good ones. And that's where you can lean on Jesus not as your example of a friend, but as your actual friend. As with all things in the Christian life, healthy friendships start with Jesus.

December 4

Jesus is Enough

A global pandemic, the worst cost of living crisis in decades, world conflict and wars … it's a challenging time to be alive. For many people, this is the first time in their lives they have been forced to take life literally one day at a time - not by choice but because it's all they can handle.

The fact is, we can't fully plan for the future because we don't know what the future will look like. We're truly living day to day. But living day to day is not liberating for everyone. It can be very frustrating. We like the control of having a plan. We like knowing what to expect tomorrow and next week and hopefully next year … and we certainly don't like glancing at the calendar and thinking, *"Who knows what's coming?"*

When we listen to the teaching of Jesus though, we find that He seems to speak directly to our context. Jesus offers very few guarantees about our future. He promises to be with us (Matthew 28:20). He promises to sanctify us (Philippians 1:6). Beyond that, we aren't given very much detail.

Instead of a plan for tomorrow, we are given a promise for today: Ask God and He will provide us with *"our daily bread"* (Matthew 6:11). In other words, God will provide today whatever we need for today. Don't worry about tomorrow!

What God teaches us during uncertain times is a truth we should cling to every day of our lives - that He gives strength for today and bright hope for tomorrow. We may want more detail than that but usually Jesus won't give it.

In Christ, we can look to the future, see Jesus is already there, and say, *"That is enough."*

Never forget that truth: *Jesus is enough!*

December 5

Pasture Time

If I asked you what you did today, what would you say? Perhaps you would say, *"Not much"* or *"Same old, same old"* or *"Nothing important."* Believe it or not, God is using your faithfulness to build character in and through you. It's not wasted time. It's pasture time. When God wants to prepare someone, He often sends them to the pasture, not the palace.

Where did King David learn to shepherd God's people? Not by going straight to the top. David learned to tend God's sheep by tending literal sheep in the pasture. It may have looked like menial work to everyone else, but God was shaping David for future service.

I've seen this pattern so often: When God chooses someone, He sends them through a time of monotonous faithfulness in which they have to show whether they'll be faithful in small things. The big things come later - the small faithfulness is God's first assignment.

I first discerned the call of God to full time ministry when I was 14 years old, as I rose from the waters of baptism. I knew that day where my life was headed. Little did I know that God had 'pasture' plans for me. I was 30 years old before I finally entered Bible college and saw that first conviction become a reality. Everything I did in those 16 years shaped me and prepared me for what God had called me to be.

So be faithful and intentional in your pasture time. God was cultivating David's heart through long periods of reflection, silence, solitude and prayer. David placed a very high priority on his relationship with God, not despising the small things of each day. Don't despise your pasture time. God is there. God is working - not just on your future, but even more importantly, He is working on you – today, and every day.

December 6

Seek God First

In 1 Samuel 28, King Saul's fear and insecurity are exposed as he faces the Philistine army. He had already lost the assurance of God's protection, and he was scared of everything - the future, going bankrupt, losing his status, what others thought of him. But what he didn't know was that these feelings of fear and jealousy were key indicators that he was out of fellowship with God. In his lack of communion with God, Saul was met with silence. Time and time again, he tried to hear from the Lord, but time and time again, the Lord didn't answer him. God had shut out Saul from His direction.

In his attempts to save himself, Saul visits a medium (fortune teller) and supposedly has an encounter with the deceased Samuel, who asks why Saul has disturbed him. Saul explains his distress. Samuel's reply was not what Saul wanted to hear. *"Tomorrow you and your sons will be joining me here in the land of the dead."* (1 Samuel 28:19)

Saul was so desperate to know what God wanted him to do that he missed God Himself completely. He wasn't interested in knowing God personally, he only wanted God's protection from the Philistines to preserve his own life. So, he resorted to tactics he knew to be sinful, because seeking God's help and power had replaced seeking God Himself.

The truth is that God never promises that following Him will keep us from failing. Rather, He tells us that in all things - success or failure - He will sustain us and be enough for us, and He will use our lives to bring glory to him.

In reality, the more we seek God Himself, the more we will discern His will in the context of our loving relationship with Him. Knowing God's will is the natural outcome of knowing God. So always seek God Himself first.

December 7

The Power of Praise

Praise is adoration of God for who He is: His person, His character, His name. It is loving God because He is God.

The Bible gives lots more exhortations for praise than prayer, because God is altogether lovely, holy, and always worthy of our worship.

There are so many reasons to praise God. Here are just a few:

Praise is where God lives. (Psalm 22:3)

Praise provides access into His presence. (Psalm 100)

We are created for praise. (Ephesians 1:12, Isaiah 43:21)

We are saved to praise. (Psalm 106:47)

God delights in it. (Psalm 149:1, 4)

God inspires it. (Psalm 40:3)

God is due it. (Psalm 29)

God commands it in the Scriptures. (Psalm 34:1, 3)

Jesus modelled it by example. (Matthew 6:9)

Praise stirs up faith. (Romans 4:20-21)

Whilst it is encouraging to examine the power of praise, let's never forget this one thing: we praise God because He is worthy of our praise - that is an end in itself. What God might do in response to our praise is entirely His call, by His grace.

True praise is not transactional - we don't praise God in order to secure something from Him. We praise God because He is God and because He is always worthy of our praise.

December 8

In Christ Alone

There is a huge difference between declaring that Jesus is the Christ, the Son of the Living God; believing in Christ, the Son of the Living God and allowing that truth to transform your life. Even Satan believes that Jesus is the Messiah, but Satan most certainly has not allowed that truth to renew his mind and transform his heart.

That's the difference between religion and the Christian faith. Religion is external, superficial, and powerless. The Christian faith is internal, life-changing and powerful. There are many millions of people who have adopted or inherited a religion which has been built around the historical Jesus and His teaching, but they are yet to actually meet the present, living, reigning, life-changing Jesus.

They may have made some kind of proclamation about Christ at some point in their life, but they are yet to experience true transformation in Christ.

Christianity is not about reading a book and deciding you want to follow the rules contained therein. That's not Christianity, that's life-destroying legalism. That's religion and God hates religion!

We can't declare that Jesus is Lord and then decide how Jesus will interact in our life. If Jesus is Lord, then Jesus gets to decide what our life will look like under His Lordship and that could be radically different to what we want or expect.

My hope is not in my ability to follow Him. My hope is not in my service or Church commitment. My hope is only in Jesus Christ, Who died for sinners. It really is that simple.

Where does your hope lie?

December 9

Living Hope

I want to draw your attention to four verses in Peter's first letter. Allow the Spirit of God to really drive these words and their meaning deep into your heart:

1 Peter 1:3 *"Praise be to the God and Father of our Lord Jesus Christ! In his great mercy he has given us new birth into a living hope through the resurrection of Jesus Christ from the dead..."*

Resonate with the words "living hope" Jesus gave you a new abundant life in Him. Be blessed as your life in Him unfolds daily, one step of faithfulness at a time.

1 Peter 1:4 *"... into an inheritance that can never perish, spoil or fade, kept in heaven for you ..."*

You are an heir to a rich inheritance, all the riches of Christ Jesus. His purposes for you are in His keeping power. They can never die, or spoil, or fade away without fulfilling His heart for you. You are right in the middle of God's plan.

1 Peter 1:5 *"... who through faith are shielded by God's power until the coming of the salvation that is ready to be revealed in the last time."*

God surrounds you with His favour like a shield. You are shielded by His power, so that in every dark thing you've experienced, you can live large and strong. God is a lot bigger than your circumstances.

1 Peter 1:6 *"In this you greatly rejoice, though now for a little while you may have had to suffer grief in all kinds of trials."*

As Jesus is revealed in you, you can rejoice no matter what comes your way. The display of His glory comes through your wounds. In Christ you can rejoice even in your suffering and trials.

December 10

Abiding in Christ

The presence of God is the mark of divine authority, and this is the backbone of our assignment to disciple the nations. This is not an optional extra. This is the heart and soul of how you and I were designed. We were designed and then assigned by God to be on this planet as citizens of another world.

As a citizen of that world, I am to look for the one or two others with whom I can meet and come into a place of agreement, so that the manifest presence of God will settle upon our gathering together. That's what Jesus promised.

Then in that position, we touch heaven and change earth; we take what is real in God's kingdom and make it real in this kingdom; we make decisions that actually shape the course of human history. That's why Jesus could say what He did:

John 15:7 *"If you remain in me and my words remain in you, ask whatever you wish, and it will be done for you."*

So, you see any lack of answers to prayer is not a problem on God's part. The lack of answers to prayer is a problem on our end and it's often connected to our ability and willingness to truly abide in Christ.

The felt presence of God is one of the keys to answered prayer and living apart from that; doing our best to mimic God's will; doing our best to pray for things that we think ought to happen - just won't work. It's not that our prayers are wrong necessarily, it's not that what we've requested is against His will, we are just missing the strength of abiding in Christ.

'Abiding in Christ' should not just be a theological term we preach about, write about and pray about, it should be a lived reality for the people of God everywhere!

December 11

Forgive

I do not write this lightly; I've lived it and learned (slowly at times) that the way we forgive people who have deeply hurt us is nowhere close to the forgiveness with which God forgives us. As I have repeatedly read the story of Joseph's reconciliation with his brothers (Genesis 37-50), I have been moved each time by the deep compassion and mercy he extended to them. He taught us a valuable and beautiful lesson on forgiveness.

We don't know how long it took him to reach that level of forgiveness after his brothers plotted to murder him, tossed him into a pit, and then sold him into slavery. Personally, I doubt it was early on because the hurt was so fresh and deep at that time. Maybe it was a work God accomplished in his heart through a slow and gradual process over the many years he was falsely imprisoned.

Maybe it was when he was released from prison and saw the enormous responsibility and position God had placed him in. Maybe his heart was opened then to a deeper understanding of God's ways, as He learned God's assignment for him was to save the people from famine. Whenever it was that the healing work of forgiveness took place in Joseph's heart, I am thankful that he obediently humbled himself and allowed God to bring this about in him.

I have seen many people resist God's work of forgiveness in their lives, and the result is always bitterness. When others have deeply hurt and betrayed us, may we find it in our hearts to forgive as God forgives, as God taught Joseph to forgive, and as Stephen forgave those who stoned him (Acts 6 and 7). Stephen's story is compelling beyond words. With his dying breath, he forgave those who were taking his life – just like Jesus did on the cross. Only God can birth this in our hearts.

December 12

God's Masterpiece

Proverbs 8:30-31 *"Then I was the craftsman at his side. I was filled with delight day after day, rejoicing always in his presence, rejoicing in his whole world and delighting in mankind."*

Ephesians 2:10 *"For we are God's masterpiece ..."*

God delights in how He made you. You are His masterpiece. You are His song to be sung in a key of music that is unique to you; in a rhythm, a harmony and an orchestration that God rejoices to sing inside of you. The music of heaven graces your life as others see and hear and touch who you are, so that they receive from Him the awesome display of His delight in you.

Appreciate the delightful work of God's hands that you are. God designed what you do to be built on the foundation of who you are in Him.

Ecclesiastes 3:11 *"He has made everything beautiful in its time. He has also set eternity in the hearts of men; yet they cannot fathom what God has done from beginning to end."*

You are not a tool designed to function to do good works because the world needs them done. God has given you the authority and compassion to be a part of meeting needs, but higher than that, you are beautiful and complete.

You are a worshiper who sings back to Him the songs of heaven. You are brave with holy boldness, kept by the One Who stands strong in you. You are a warrior who fights the right battles because you listen to your Commander.

You have wise and gracious words that come from the wellspring of a righteous heart. You are fine-looking as you reflect the image of Jesus. You possess the signature that the Lord is with you. Rejoice in who you are: God's masterpiece.

December 13

Triumph Through Trials

James 1:2-4 *"Consider it pure joy, my brothers and sisters, whenever you face trials of many kinds, because you know that the testing of your faith produces perseverance. Let perseverance finish its work so that you may be mature and complete, not lacking anything."*

Our faith will be tested; this is just a fact of life. How we deal with these times is what is most important. Often when trials come our way, or things don't go our way; we quickly pray to God for the trial to end or pray for the circumstance to go our way instead. Not that there is anything wrong in praying this way. However, if we only pray this way and fail to find God at work, we could be missing out on His blessing.

James 1:5-6 *"If you need wisdom, ask our generous God, and he will give it to you. He will not rebuke you for asking. But when you ask him, be sure that your faith is in God alone. Do not waver, for a person with divided loyalty is as unsettled as a wave of the sea that is blown and tossed by the wind."*

Sometimes we are led into trials or difficult circumstances in order so that we may grow. It is not that God has forsaken us, or that He is not with us; in fact, it is quite the opposite. His promise to us is that He is forever faithful, and that He is always there with us. When we truly believe this, we can allow ourselves to see these trials differently.

Take a moment to step back from your trial. Step outside of it and ask God to give you a new perspective - His perspective. When we see things how God sees things, we grow, and we are continually transformed by His Grace. This dysfunctional, broken world can throw all manner of trials our way and some of them are really hard to endure. However, God has promised to always be there to teach us and bring us through.

December 14

Dealing with Doubt

When my children were young, they liked to ask questions. After asking a question and receiving an answer they would invariably ask, *"why?"* We should encourage children to ask questions - it's a part of the learning process. When it comes to God, however, we are often afraid to ask questions when we have concerns or doubts. It's as if asking a question of God equates to a lack of faith. That's nonsense.

Doubt and unbelief are very different. The word *doubt* comes from the Latin word *dubium,* which means *to hesitate.* Unbelief is a wholesale rejection of an idea or principle. Plenty of men and women in the Bible hesitated and had doubts: Abraham (Genesis 16), David (Psalm 13), Thomas (John 20). Doubt is not a sin - it's just the result of being human. As long as we are breathing, we will be subject to doubt. But it doesn't have to be faith-shattering and it doesn't have to lead to unbelief.

If you're struggling with doubt, there are some things you can do which are very helpful. First of all, share your doubts with a trusted friend. Don't keep them hidden. You might feel shame because you have doubts but finding out that other people might share those doubts can be empowering.

Also, look for God at work in you and around you. If you watch the evening news it seems like God is not working at all. However, look for stories of hope and redemption.

You can also ask for help. Don't be afraid to pray an honest prayer to God and ask for help. Ask God to reveal Himself to you more clearly and to help you with your doubt. In Mark 9 Jesus meets a man who has a demon-possessed son. The man is lacking in faith but soon realizes his error and says plainly, *"Lord, I believe ... help me in my unbelief!"* What a great prayer for us to pray whenever the doubts creep in.

December 15

When God Seems Far Away

I believe one of the greatest challenges facing Christians today is that many people feel far away from God. Maybe this is not a surprise to you because you've felt this way too. If so, don't worry, it's normal. Sometimes I feel far from God also.

I read recently about a lady who shared with her Pastor that after following Jesus for 35 years she suddenly felt like He was far away. *"It's like I'm on a boat and Jesus is on the shore,"* she said. *"As the boat drifts from the shore, Jesus gets farther away until I can barely see him or hear him. No matter how hard I paddle the boat, I can't get closer to him."* She buried her head in her hands and said, *"How do I return to God?"* The Pastor had a surprising response. He said, *"You can't return to Him because you're not far from Him at all. It only feels that way."*

If you ever feel like you are far away from God, remember this: don't trust your feelings! It's easy to feel like you are far away from God. Maybe it has been a long time since you read your Bible, or perhaps you haven't fellowshipped with a Church family in a few months. When that happens, you probably feel disconnected from God. But remember that feelings are not facts - they are just feelings. Feelings can be manipulated easily and feelings are heavily influenced by our surroundings and how we are being treated by others. What is more important than feelings are facts. Like this one:

Hebrews 13:5 *"I will never leave you or forsake you."*

Jesus also promised His disciples that He would always be with them (Matthew 28:20). So, if you feel like you are far from God, and you're wondering what you can do to draw closer to Him, remember this: God is already there! He hasn't gone anywhere! Just thank Him for His abiding presence and trust Him to guide you.

December 16

Discipleship

True discipleship is a divine romance; it's a sacred dance; it's a journey of surrender; it's a daily journey to the cross. It's about us embracing the most privileged opportunity we have been given which is to die to ourselves and trust God for our resurrection and reward. God says, *"Humble yourself under My mighty hand and I will exalt you in due time."*

I don't ever want to get to a place where the resurrection and reward God gives me turns me away from seeking first the Kingdom to God and His righteousness. In simple terms that means that nothing should be held closer to my heart than God Himself.

Over my many years in ministry I have probably come across a thousand books, sermons or videos on discipleship. One author or teacher will give us twelve steps to discipleship, another only has six steps. In fact, there has been so much teaching on discipleship that the whole concept has become overwhelming for many people in the Church. That's sad.

When you drill down through all the waffle, all the legalistic mumbo jumbo and requirements, the confusing theological language about discipleship, you find one simple reality: *relationship.* It's all about our relationship with God.

The source of all those wonderful qualities of a good disciple which we are exhorted by well-meaning preachers to achieve through hard work and discipline, is our relationship with God. We will never align ourselves with God by our hard work, diligence and human effort.

We only align ourselves with God by spending time with Him and getting to know Him personally. Our greatest need is God Himself. Our greatest desire should be God Himself. The rest will flow.

December 17

The Weed of Unbelief

I found myself reflecting on the Parable of the Sower again this past week. As you know, the seed in this parable is the word of God and the soils represent the condition of people's hearts. The most important truth to come from this story is that the productiveness or the fruitfulness of a word that God spoke does not validate whether it was from God or not.

In this parable we are presented with four different kinds of soil. Three of these soils were no good but the seed was still authentic - it just didn't bear fruit. The seed is never the problem. The fault is never in what God says – the fruitfulness is determined by the soil. So, God's word is not validated by what we do with it. God is not on trial by what I do - I am.

Matthew 13:22 *"The seed falling among the thorns refers to someone who hears the word, but the worries of this life and the deceitfulness of wealth choke the word, making it unfruitful."*

If you are a gardener, you will know that if you stop caring for your garden, it will not be long before the weeds are up to your knees and the good plants are not even be visible. We will always have weeds, so here's the challenge we face.

God's word comes to us – this good seed which we receive into the soil of our heart. But we have this other word; and this other idea; and we have this disappointment; or that criticism; or this complaint; or this doubt or fear. We've got all these other seeds that are vying for the same nutrients in our soil. They all want to germinate and take root in our heart.

Now without doubt, the most serious weed of all is unbelief. There may be faith in your garden but unbelief is there as well. The weed of unbelief will overpower the good plants every time. We must remove those weeds by believing what God has said and acting on that belief – every day.

December 18

The Key Ingredient

What was the key ingredient to the success of the early Church? What was the secret of those first disciples' success in establishing a Church which grew at a phenomenal rate each year for more than two generations? Did they just follow a plan and tick off the tasks each day? Did they simply decide one day that they would devote themselves to the Apostle's teaching, share rich fellowship every day, share meals with each other in their homes and worship together every day? Were these things simply on their 'to do' list or part of some strategic plan and the rest just happened? Absolutely not.

So, what was it that allowed our forebears to get it so right for so long and have such an incredible impact on the world around them? Well, the correct question is not 'what' … but 'Who' made all this possible. This 'Who' is mentioned in almost every chapter in the book of Acts and multiple times in many chapters. Of course, I am speaking about God, the Holy Spirit. Everything about the early Church which made it powerful, effective, real, world-changing and dynamic – was initiated and empowered by the Holy Spirit.

This should not surprise us, because the One Who birthed this miracle of the Church, Jesus Christ, operated exactly the same way! Long before the book of Acts and the birth of the Church, Jesus modelled this Spirit-led lifestyle to His first disciples. Everything Jesus said and did during His earthly ministry was under direction and anointing of the Holy Spirit.

This is why Jesus told the disciples to wait until the Holy Spirit came upon them too. Without the Spirit, we are aimless and dangerous; we are ineffective; we are powerless; we are disconnected from heaven and the power of God. All we have is religion and a man-made institution which is completely powerless to change the world.

December 19

Pressing On

The Apostle Paul amazes and humbles me as I read his words in the third chapter of his letter to the Philippians. His earnest desire was to press forward and become all that a disciple of Jesus can become in this life. He had no desire to be average or mediocre. He detested the very notion!

Paul humbly, but intensely breathed his greatest desire, with passion and longing in words like: "*That I may gain Christ."* ... "*That I may be found in Him."* ... "*That I may know Him.*"

His Christian faith was an ongoing, exciting journey with God, as he testified many times: "*I follow after; I press on toward the mark... I have not obtained.... I am striving to lay hold of that for which Christ laid hold of me.*"

An alarming number of people who identify as Christians across the world today are complete strangers to the desire, longing and the Spirit which drove Paul forward each day.

Many are content to believe that this is as good as it gets and that we should just be thankful and cultivate what we already have. Why are so many Christians deaf to the clear appeals in the Scriptures concerning spiritual desire, progression and longing in our walk with God?

Why are we so quick to accept the view that we have arrived at some spiritual plateau and that we just need to maintain what we have in Christ? Some days it feels like the Church is in a holding pattern just waiting to land in heaven - going round and round in circles waiting for their home-coming.

Have we forgotten that Jesus brought heaven here over 2,000 years ago and commissioned us to tell the world that the kingdom of heaven is here?!

December 20

The Grace of God

For many years now, people have been asking me why I place such a heavy emphasis on grace in my preaching. I emphasise the grace of God in my preaching and in the style of ministry that unfolds under my leadership, because that's what Jesus and Paul did - so basically, I'm just following their lead. They both emphasised the grace, goodness and love of God and the fact that God has taken the initiative in our direction.

God has spoken to us, called us, forgiven us, redeemed us and transformed us. He did all this unconditionally, by His grace, before we were even born! Then we showed up and had our eyes and ears opened by God the Holy Spirit and we believed into that reality and participated in His grace. That is the good news! That is the gospel!

Another reason why I emphasis grace is because it releases joy in people. If you want to sum up Paul's personal ministry, it was to increase the joy of his followers (Philippians 1:25-26).

We only have one life to live, and I would like to live that life with as much joy as possible and so would you, I'm sure. I'd also like those who are part of the Church to be happy and to experience the inexpressible and glorious joy of the Lord.

So, I will preach grace in order that your joy may increase and that will make Church a joyful place to be, and people outside the Church will once again be attracted to us.

Jesus came to demolish the strongholds of religion each day as He preached, lived, and demonstrated God's amazing grace. I've been called by God to do the same.

I want people to bear the rich fruit they were created and called to produce, by God's grace, for God's glory, in the power of God's Spirit!

December 21

God is my Refuge

There is a place of immunity for the believer, a spiritual fortress in Christ that shelters us from the attacks of the devil. For those who abide in this stronghold of God, the onslaught of the wicked one does not touch them. Here, in this secret dwelling with the Almighty, we are hidden from the effects of the accuser's tongue; we are sheltered from the assignment of the destroyer.

The dictionary defines immunity as *"freedom or exemption, as from a penalty, burden, duty or evil."* This is how the living God wants His children to walk: in freedom from the penalties and burdens of sin, delivered from the duties of legalistic religion, protected and triumphant over the assault of the evil one.

Survey the landscape of the Bible and you will find hundreds of examples of God's loving protection. Every time the Lord pleaded with sinful Israel to return to Him, it was to urge them back under His protection. Each time they responded, they were secured again within the shelter of God.

Deuteronomy 32:10 *"He shielded them and cared for them, guarding them as the apple of his eye."*

God is not only our Creator; He is also our Father. As such, it is inconceivable that He would leave His precious children unprotected. In Matthew 6:8, Jesus says our Father knows our needs before we ask Him. If we, even in our fallen condition, seek to provide for our children, how much more does God in His perfection seek to shelter and care for His children!

The more we possess the true knowledge of God, the more accessible His provisions for us become. God has prepared an abiding place for us where all that we need concerning life and godliness is already ours in Christ (Ephesians 1:3).

December 22

Taking Every Thought Captive

Today's thoughts are tomorrow's actions.
Today's jealousy is tomorrow's temper tantrum.
Today's bigotry is tomorrow's hate crime.
Today's anger is tomorrow's abuse.
Today's lust is tomorrow's adultery.
Today's greed is tomorrow's embezzlement.
Today's guilt is tomorrow's fear.

Is it truth like the above which prompted the Apostle Paul to write, *"We capture every thought and make it give up and obey Christ."* (2 Corinthians 10:5).

Do you hear some battlefield jargon in that passage *"capture every thought"* – make it give up and obey Christ! We are the soldiers and those thoughts are the enemies.

Do you remember the thoughts that came to Jesus, courtesy of the mouth of Peter? Jesus had just prophesied His own death, burial, and resurrection, but Peter couldn't bear the thought of it. *'Peter took Jesus aside and told him not to talk like that.'* (Matthew 16:22-23) *Jesus said to Peter, "Get away from me, Satan! You are not helping me! You don't care about the things of God, but only about the things people think are important."*

What if you did that? What if you took every thought captive? What if you took the counsel of Solomon:

Proverbs 4:23 *"Be careful what you think, because your thoughts run your life."*

Don't become a victim of your thoughts. You have a vote. You have a voice. Change those thoughts, and you change the person. If today's thoughts are tomorrow's actions, then why not fill your mind with thoughts of God's love?

December 23

True Peace

Psalm 29:1 *"The Lord will give strength to His people; the Lord will bless His people with peace."*

All you have to do is switch on the television any night of the week and tune into any news bulletin and you will see that we are living in the midst of a world full of turmoil. Most of the news is bad news. If that news was all we had to gauge our world by, we would stay in a constant state of depression.

Our age is characterised by the absence of peace and the presence of turmoil. We could probably name another fifty countries with internal strife, turmoil and civil war going on right now. This world is truly broken!

Why do we live in such turmoil? One succinct answer is that we are ourselves in turmoil. This observable outward conflict is merely the evidence of the inward turmoil that men and women have in this world. The wars and strife going on in our world are simply a depiction of the inner turmoil going on within the souls of men and women. A lack of peace in the nations simply reflects a lack of peace in people's hearts.

Just look at the worldly quest for peace. Peace movements are nothing new. There have always been those who cry "peace!" Many do so today. There are demonstrations and protests for peace. And it seems to me that any person who has a respect for life should want peace. Yet we do not have peace. Why? Perhaps the answer lies in the nature of the peace we are pursuing. It is apparent that there are many in this world frantically involved in a quest for peace, but is the peace that is being sought true peace? Jesus gave us the answer:

John 14:27 *"Peace I leave with you; My peace I give to you; not as the world gives, do I give to you."*

December 24

Selflessness

Selflessness is our story. This is who we are. Children of the One True God. Triune, mysterious, mighty, and sovereign.

The pages of Scripture were divinely penned for us to find, read, digest, and embrace. God encourages, admonishes, and guides us through the relevance of an ancient text that has become the most widely read book in the whole world.

The story of the incarnation is much more than a cute manger scene. It is the story of the power of God coming to earth to save His children.

So, let's aim to make it about who Jesus is, and Whose we are. If all we do each day is sit and spend time in prayer with Him, it will prove to be enough. Because the more time we spend with the One Who is the way, the truth, and the life, the more we recognize Whose we are.

Day by day, let's become selfless. More of Jesus - less of us.

Let that be our daily commitment, and the wonder will surely follow. We will never get to the end of the mystery that is our God. He is breathtakingly compassionate in His love for us, not wanting even one to perish.

Bring on the wonder, and let the love of Jesus, the sweet babe born to Mary under the breathtakingly bright star to the tune of a choir of angels, flow through us with power and majesty every day of the year – not just at the designated time.

We find our peace in Christ, alone. Not in other people, not in ourselves, not in anything this broken world might offer us. He is our all in all. The more selfless we become, the greater His reality in our lives.

December 25

Peace, Hope, Love and Joy

Political and social unrest dominate the news and economic distress grips this entire world. People are easily overcome by a sense of hopelessness and fear. As we embrace Christmas again, it seems appropriate to refocus our attention on the reason we celebrate at all.

Christ entered history in times like ours: the Mediterranean world was under the occupation of the brutal Roman Empire. Corruption and abuse abounded. Taxes were too high, the common man oppressed, the ruling powers capricious and often malevolent.

Citizens were disillusioned; the nation of Israel had lost sight of their calling, having lost sight of the God Who had called them. The effects of wide-spread paganism were superstition, devaluation of life, and a lack of natural affection.

On this Christmas Day, I want to invite you to see beyond the distress of this unsettled world as you consider the words He spoke through His prophets and apostles, offering peace, hope, love and joy in Christ for all who trust Him.

I pray these words will bless you and bring you closer to the Saviour Who came, lived, loved, died, rose again and is here with us right now:

Isaiah 7:14 *"Therefore the Lord himself will give you a sign: The virgin will conceive and give birth to a son, and will call him Immanuel."*

Isaiah 9:6-7 *"For to us a child is born, to us a son is given, and the government will be on his shoulders. And he will be called Wonderful Counsellor, Mighty God, Everlasting Father, Prince of Peace. Of the greatness of his government and peace there will be no end."*

December 26

Thinking Like a Servant

To think like a servant is one of the key aspects of serving God. If it wasn't so unattainable, this might be fine. It seems like we are all built to simply think about ourselves.

Because it goes against human nature so much, giving preference to others is one of the true marks of a Christian. Because of this, God is the source of the desire, and the Holy Spirit is the agent of action. Paul said of Timothy:

Philippians 2:20-21 *"I have no one else like Timothy, who genuinely cares for your welfare. All the others care only for themselves and not for what matters to Jesus Christ."*

The key to embedding a servant mindset in your thoughts is concealed in these verses. It all begins with Jesus. He becomes the centre of your attention as you fall in love with Him. As you do this, you learn more about Him and get to know Him like you would a friend. Eventually, you start to understand that what matters to Him, also matters to you.

Additionally, this is not merely a matter of familiarity. There is also a supernatural component at play in this situation. The Holy Spirit in you is connected to what matters to Jesus, and the Spirit responds to the cry of truth from deep within you.

Other people mattered deeply to Jesus. He could tell when they were in anguish and hurting. The Bible says that He was a man of sorrows and acquainted with grief. If not from the suffering of those around Him, then where did that anguish and grief come from? He was actually bearing their sorrow. He sympathised with their anguish.

When other people matter to us like they do to Jesus, then we might be thinking like a servant!

December 27

Foolish Pride

You may have heard the true story of the Army officer who had just been promoted to Colonel. He was feeling pretty good about himself and kept catching himself looking in the mirror saying, *"I'm a Colonel now,"* and saluting himself.

As this Colonel is getting his new office arranged, he hears a knock at the door and says, *"Who is it?"*

The guy answers, *"It's Private Andrews."*

The Colonel thinks, *"Oh, I'll impress this kid,"* so he picks up his phone and starts speaking loudly. *"Yes, Mr. President, I know, Mr. President, I understand, Mr. President. Yes, I'll get right on it, Mr. President. Thank you."*

Then he says, "OK, come in, Private."

When the young man enters, the Colonel says, *"I'm sorry I had you wait, I just had to finish up an important conversation with the President. What can I do for you, son?"*

The private sheepishly answers, *"I'm sorry, sir, I was just sent over by the communications department ... to hook up your phone."*

Pride makes us look foolish. Pride is the root sin behind so many other sins and spiritual dysfunctions. Pride was at the heart of Adam and Eve's rebellion. No wonder C.S. Lewis called pride the granddaddy of all sins. That's also why the Apostle Paul gave us this warning:

Romans 12:3 *"For by the grace given to me, I tell everyone among you not to think of himself more highly than he should think. Instead, think sensibly, as God has distributed a measure of faith to each one."*

December 28

Embrace Suffering

Many Christians believe that if we live like we are supposed to, we can avoid, or at least minimize suffering. A related assumption is that life will, one way or another, inevitably turn out positive. This is the vague optimism that comes through in clichés like, *"Every cloud has a silver lining,"* or *"It's always darkest before the dawn."*

The Bible offers a different perspective. Rather than assuring God's children that life will be free from suffering, Scripture actually *promises* suffering will be a reality for us all.

The question for believers is not whether we will endure pain, that's guaranteed; the question is *how* we will endure pain? Will we bring God our aching hearts in these moments or try to cope on our own?

If you are walking with someone who is going through pain, don't try to explain everything. You may be trying to explain what can't be explained. Just sit with them. Weep with them as they weep and pray along with the Spirit for them.

If you are in a season of pain, bring your pain to God. Bring it to others. Are you having a hard time seeing what 'good' could come from your suffering? Be honest about that.

But whatever you do, take your honest laments to the One Who understands them. If you are a child of God, He is doing something in your life. That includes your moments of pain.

We might love to know the 'why' behind our suffering, but God may only reveal that in eternity. For now, what you've got to hold on to is the character of God. When you can't see God's hand, remember this: you can always trust God's heart.

December 28

The Pursuit of God

Psalm 27:4 *"One thing I ask of the LORD, this is what I seek: that I may dwell in the house of the LORD all the days of my life, to gaze upon the beauty of the LORD and to seek him in his temple."*

All of us are seekers. Within all of us there are those things which we desire. We all have goals; we all have dreams. And we are all hopeful that those dreams may one day come true.

What is it you seek? Are the things which you seek worth seeking? Some of the things we seek may not be what the Lord desires for us. Some of those things may even hurt us were we to acquire them. So, we must be careful to evaluate what we seek in light of their true worth.

We must also ask ourselves the question of why we seek those things. The fact is that all of us are involved in the living of life. But in that process, we find that things don't always go smoothly.

The road of life has many a bump, many a pothole, and as we weave our way around the hairpin curves and over the steep hills, we find that some things which we thought were important no longer seem so. We come to understand that there is more to life than meets the eye.

All of us struggle and have problems. Everywhere people are hurting and are in need, and what the world around us holds forth to meet those needs are really only shallow substitutes for the real thing.

It is the real thing for which we are to seek. That should be our priority today. We must seek that which will make life worth living and that can only be found in the heart of God.

December 30

The Church Reborn?

When we read the New Testament and gain an accurate understanding of what the Church really is and learn about the plan and purpose of God in establishing the Church, then we should regard the Church as the most significant, the most powerful and the most influential reality in the world.

From God's perspective, the Church is not peripheral to the world; the world is peripheral to the Church.

The Church which we discover and encounter in the New Testament is not only established by the omnipotent Creator of the universe, but it's also empowered by Him on a daily basis through His Spirit, to be the light in a dark world.

The Church was created to have a global impact - to touch every heart and life on this planet. That is the Church we are introduced to in the New Testament, but look around today, and you will realise that the modern Church barely resembles the New Testament Church.

For all intents and purposes, the Church we see in the New Testament fell asleep at some point between Acts chapter 2 and today. We may still be the same Church theologically speaking, for there's only one, but our presence and influence in society is at such a low ebb that it could be argued the Church is asleep on the job!

The Church will only awaken from its slumber and impact this nation when you and I get a firm grasp on what the Church really is at its core and what God's plan and purpose is for His people. Go back and read the Gospels and the Book of Acts and then read them again, and again, and again … until your mind is saturated with the reality of the Church as it was when the Holy Spirit birthed it long ago.

December 31

Keep Walking

Psalm 23:4 *"Yea, though I walk through the valley of the shadow of death, I will fear no evil; For You are with me; Your rod and Your staff, they comfort me."*

On many occasions throughout our lives, we find ourselves in a valley not of our choosing. They can be the most difficult places to navigate. What do you do when you're in the valleys of life? How do you get through them?

We've all been there at one time or another; and if not, hold on, because you will. This fallen world in which we live is a passing shadow described by David as *the valley of the shadow of death*. Beyond his description, David gives us insight into how we can get through these valleys.

First and foremost, keep walking! **If God brought you to it, God will bring you through it.** However, you have to keep walking. You will never get through it if you stop in the middle of the valley. Don't quit. God isn't done yet. This valley is not His destination for you. Keep walking and before you know it, you will get to the other side of that struggle.

Whether your valley was caused by circumstances beyond your control or your own failure, just keep walking and never forget this saying: *If you're not dead, you're not done!*

If you are currently experiencing a dark valley in your life, take comfort in the counsel of God's Word and keep walking. The valley is only temporary. It's just a shadow. The Eternal, Everlasting, Unfailing, Almighty God is with you!

The best news of all: tomorrow is new day and a new year! God's mercies are new every morning and a fresh blessing is waiting for you as you embrace the new chapter before you.

www.ingramcontent.com/pod-product-compliance
Lightning Source LLC
Chambersburg PA
CBHW062030290426
44109CB00026B/2585